# Theory Essentials for Today's Musician

*Theory Essentials for Today's Musician* offers a review of music theory that speaks directly and engagingly to modern students. Rooted in the tested pedagogy of *Theory for Today's Musician*, the authors have distilled and reorganized the concepts from the thirty-three chapters of their original textbook into twenty-one succinct, modular chapters that move from the core elements of harmony to further topics in form and 20th-century music. A broad coverage of topics and musical styles—including examples drawn from popular music—is organized into four key parts:

- Basic tools
- Chromatic harmony
- Form and analysis
- The 20th century and beyond

*Theory Essentials* features clear and jargon-free (yet rigorous) explanations appropriate for students at all levels, ensuring comprehension of concepts that are often confusing or obscure. An accompanying workbook provides corresponding exercises, while a companion website presents streaming audio examples. This concise and reorganized all-in-one package—which can be covered in a single semester for a graduate review, or serve as the backbone for a brief undergraduate survey—provides a comprehensive, flexible foundation in the vital concepts needed to analyze music.

**Ralph Turek** is a theorist, composer, author, jazz pianist, Professor Emeritus at The University of Akron, and a veteran of thirty-five years of teaching in the music theory classroom. He is the co-author of *Theory for Today's Musician*.

**Daniel McCarthy** is a familiar name in contemporary American music. As a composer, he has received distinguished faculty research/creativity awards at Indiana State University and The University of Akron, where he is Chair of the Composition and Theory Section in the School of Music. He is the co-author of *Theory for Today's Musician*.

# Theory Essentials for Today's Musician

## Ralph Turek and Daniel McCarthy

Routledge
Taylor & Francis Group
NEW YORK AND LONDON

First published 2018
by Routledge
711 Third Avenue, New York, NY 10017

and by Routledge
2 Park Square, Milton Park, Abingdon, Oxon, OX14 4RN

*Routledge is an imprint of the Taylor & Francis Group, an informa business*

© 2018 Taylor & Francis

The right of Ralph Turek and Daniel McCarthy to be identified as authors of this work has been asserted by them in accordance with sections 77 and 78 of the Copyright, Designs and Patents Act 1988.

All rights reserved. No part of this book may be reprinted or reproduced or utilised in any form or by any electronic, mechanical, or other means, now known or hereafter invented, including photocopying and recording, or in any information storage or retrieval system, without permission in writing from the publishers.

*Trademark notice*: Product or corporate names may be trademarks or registered trademarks, and are used only for identification and explanation without intent to infringe.

*Library of Congress Cataloging-in-Publication Data*
Names: Turek, Ralph, author. | McCarthy, Daniel William, 1955- author.
Title: Theory essentials for today's musician / Ralph Turek, Daniel McCarthy.
Description: New York ; London : Routledge, 2017. | Includes index.
Identifiers: LCCN 2017015820 (print) | LCCN 2017020208 (ebook) | ISBN 9781315201122 (ebook) | ISBN 9781138708815 (hardback) | ISBN 9781138708822 (pbk.)
Subjects: LCSH: Music theory.
Classification: LCC MT7 (ebook) | LCC MT7 .T904 2017 (print) | DDC 781—dc23
LC record available at https://lccn.loc.gov/2017015820

ISBN: 978-1-138-70881-5 (hbk)
ISBN: 978-1-138-70882-2 (pbk)
ISBN: 978-1-315-20112-2 (ebk)
ISBN: 978-1-138-09875-6 (pack)

Typeset in Galliard & Swiss 721
by Florence Production Ltd, Stoodleigh, Devon, UK.

Musical notation image used in the text design
© Brailescu Cristian/Shutterstock.com

Visit the companion website:
www.routledge.com/cw/turekessentials

Printed and bound in the United States of America by Sheridan

# Contents

*Detailed Contents* vii
*To the Instructor* xiii

## PART ONE
## BASIC TOOLS 1

1 Elements of Diatonic Harmony 3
2 Cadences and Harmonic Rhythm 19
3 The Outer-Voice Framework/Embellishing Tones 31
4 Part Writing and Chorale Analysis I 45
5 Part Writing and Chorale Analysis II 63
6 Part Writing and Chorale Analysis III 77

## PART TWO
## CHROMATIC HARMONY 91

7 Secondary Function 93
8 Modulation I 107
9 Mixing Modes 121
10 Altered Predominants and Dominants 137
11 Modulation II 155
12 Harmonic Extensions and Chromatic Techniques 175

## PART THREE
## FORM AND ANALYSIS — 191

13  Melodic Form — 193
14  Contrapuntal Forms — 207
15  Small Forms — 231
16  Sonata Form — 249
17  Rondo — 263

## PART FOUR
## THE TWENTIETH CENTURY AND BEYOND — 271

18  Syntax and Vocabulary — 273
19  New Tonal Methods — 289
20  Non-Serial Atonality — 301
21  Serial Atonality — 319

*Appendix A*   Intervals, Modes and Key — 355
*Appendix B*   Selected Rhythm Topics — 339
*Appendix C*   Basic Harmonic Structures — 347
*Appendix D*   Part-Writing Guidelines — 351

*Glossary* — 353
*Credits* — 371
*Index* — 373
*Track Listing* — 379

# Detailed Contents

*To the Instructor*     xiii

## PART ONE
## BASIC TOOLS

**1 Elements of Diatonic Harmony**     3
    Lead Sheet Notation     3
       *Lead-Sheet Chord Symbols; Expanded Symbols*
    Figured Bass Notation     5
       *Realizing a Figured Bass*
    The Diatonic Chords     8
       *Diatonic Triads in Major Keys; Roman Numeral Symbols; The Primary Triads; Diatonic Triads in Minor Keys; Showing Inversion; The Diatonic Seventh Chords*
    Functional Tonality     13
       *Chord Function; The Circle of Fifths; Harmonic Motion*
    The Ground Bass     16
       *The Common Practice Period*

**2 Cadences and Harmonic Rhythm**     19
    Cadences     19
       *Cadence defined; Cadences and Style; Standard Cadences; Cadential Variants*
    Harmonic Rhythm     27
       *Harmonic Rhythm Defined; Harmonic Rhythm and Meter*

## DETAILED CONTENTS

**3 The Outer-Voice Framework/Embellishing Tones**   31
   Melodic Principles   31
      *Voice Ranges; Motion between Voices*
   Creating an Outer-Voice Framework   33
      *1:1 Counterpoint*
   Embellishing Tones   36
      *Step-Step Combinations; Step-Leap Combinations; Step-"Rep" Combinations*

**4 Part Writing and Chorale Analysis I**   45
   The Four-Voice Texture   45
   Review of Melodic Principles   46
   Voicing Chords   47
      *Spacing; Doubling*
   Connecting Chords   50
      *Consecutive Perfect Fifths and Octaves; Voice Crossing and Overlap; Common Tones*
   The Chorale   54
   Root-Position Triads   54
      *Guidelines for Connecting Root-Position Triads; The Short Rule of Chord Connection*
   Part Writing Suspensions in Root Position   59
      *Doubling in Suspensions; Suspensions in Bach's Chorales*

**5 Part Writing and Chorale Analysis II**   63
   First Inversion   63
      *Inversion and Bass Line; Doubling; Chord Connection; Harmonic Weight; Suspensions*
   Second Inversion   69
      *Doubling; The Cadential Six-Four Chord; The Passing Six-Four Template; The Pedal Six-Four Chord; The Arpeggiated Six-Four Chord*

**6 Part Writing and Chorale Analysis III**   77
   Dominant-Functioning Seventh Chords   77
      *The $V^7$: Common Practice; The Unresolved Leading Tone; The Unresolved Seventh; Delayed Resolution; The Leading Tone Seventh Chord*
   Non-Dominant Seventh Chords   84
      *Function, Resolution, Frequency, Inversion, Incomplete Chords, Altered Forms; Seventh Chords and Chain Suspensions; The $I^7$*
   Voice Leading Summary   89

## PART TWO
# CHROMATIC HARMONY 91

**7 Secondary Function** — 93
  Secondary Dominants — 93
  *Tonicization; The Tonicizing Tritone*
  Secondary Leading Tone Chords — 98
  *The Secondary Leading Tone Triad*
  Voice Leading — 100
  *Basic Principles; Secondary Function and Chromatic Lines; Harmonic Sequence and Secondary Function*

**8 Modulation I** — 107
  Modulation Defined — 107
  Modulation by Common Chord — 107
  *Pivot Chord Defined; Crossing the Tonal Border; Multiple Common Chords*
  Chromatic Modulation — 112
  *Chromatic Modulation Defined; The Rule of Chromatics; Multiple Accidentals; Modulation or Tonicization?*

**9 Mixing Modes** — 121
  Vocabulary and Syntax — 121
  Change of Mode — 121
  *Change of Mode Defined; Keys Related through Mode Mixture; Enharmonic Change of Mode*
  Modal Borrowing — 125
  *Modal Borrowing Defined; Common Borrowed Harmonies; Voice Leading*
  Chromatic-Third Relationships — 129
  *Diatonic versus Chromatic Third Relationship; The Common Chromatic-Third Relationships; Chromatic Thirds, Mode Mixture, and Tonicization; Voice Leading*

**10 Altered Predominants and Dominants** — 137
  The Neapolitan Sixth Chord — 137
  *Neapolitan Sixth Chord Defined; The Harmonic Nature of the Neapolitan; Insertions before V*
  Augmented Sixth Chords — 143
  *The Augmented Sixth Interval; Types of Augmented Sixth Chord; Constructing an Augmented Sixth Chord; Voice Leading; The Neapolitan and Augmented Sixth Chords*
  Altered Dominants — 151
  *Altered Dominants Defined; The Raised Fifth; The Lowered Fifth; Altered Secondary Dominants*

## 11 Modulation II — 155

"In Search of Harmonic Logic" — 155
Recognizing the Signals — 155
    *Chromatic Pitches; Clue Chords; Cadences; Thinking Through a Modulation*
The Tonal Border — 158
    *Chromatic Modulations*
Enharmonic Function — 165
    *The Enharmonic German Sixth Chord; The Enharmonic Diminished Seventh Chord*

## 12 Harmonic Extensions and Chromatic Techniques — 175

Climbing the Overtone Series — 175
The Dominant Ninth Chord — 175
    *Types of Dominant Ninth Chord; Secondary Dominant Ninth Chords; Inverted Ninth Chords*
Other Ninth Chords — 182
Eleventh Chords — 182
Thirteenth Chords — 182
Linear Chromaticism — 186
Harmonic Sequence — 188

## PART THREE
# FORM AND ANALYSIS — 191

## 13 Melodic Form — 193

Within the Phrase: Motive and Sequence — 193
The Phrase — 194
    *Phrase Length; Phrases and Cadences; The Musical Sentence; Phrase Relationships*
Combining and Extending Phrases — 198
    *The Period; Parallel Period; Contrasting Period; Phrase Group; Double Period; Cadential Elision; Cadential Extension*

## 14 Contrapuntal Forms — 207

J. S. Bach's Chorale Harmonizations — 207
Bach's Two-Part Inventions — 208
    *The Bach Inventions (Profile); Motive and Countermotive; The Devices of Counterpoint*
Analysis of Invention No. 6 — 210
    *Invertible Counterpoint; Sequence; Fragmentation; Tonality; Implied Harmony; Invention Analysis Checklist*

| | | |
|---|---|---:|
| | The Fugue | 218 |
| | *Fugue Defined; Subject and Answer; Real and Tonal Answers; The Exposition; Subsequent Entries and Episodes; The Final Statement—The Closing Section; Link, Counterexposition, and Coda* | |
| | Analysis: Bach Fugue No. 16 (WTC, Book I) | 226 |
| **15** | **Small Forms** | **231** |
| | Ways of Looking at Form | 231 |
| | *Motivic Analysis; Similarity and Contrast; Musical Processes* | |
| | Statement and Restatement | 236 |
| | The Coda | 240 |
| | Statement and Contrast/Binary Forms | 242 |
| | *Sectional versus Continuous Forms; Symmetric versus Asymmetric Forms* | |
| | Statement-Contrast-Restatement | 244 |
| | *Rounded Binary versus Ternary Form* | |
| **16** | **Sonata Form** | **249** |
| | A Brief History | 249 |
| | *Origins; Establishment, Departure and Return* | |
| | Mozart: *Eine kleine Nachtmusik* (first movement) | 250 |
| | *The Exposition; Primary Tonality and Theme; Transition; Secondary Tonality and Theme; Closing Area; Development; Retransition; Recapitulation; Coda* | |
| | Summary of *Eine kleine Nachtmusik* (first movement) | 261 |
| **17** | **Rondo** | **263** |
| | Perspective | 263 |
| | *Refrain and Episode* | |
| | Beethoven: Piano Sonata op. 13 (second movement) | 264 |
| | *The Rondo Theme; The First Episode; The First Refrain; The Second Episode; The Second Refrain; The Coda; Summary* | |

## PART FOUR
# THE 20TH CENTURY AND BEYOND — 271

| | | |
|---|---|---:|
| **18** | **Syntax and Vocabulary** | **273** |
| | Syntax | 273 |
| | *Debussy's Syntax; Planing; The Non-Functional Mm7 Chord;* | |
| | Modality | 277 |
| | *The Church Modes; Modal Cadences* | |
| | New Melodic and Harmonic Structures | 280 |
| | *Pentatonicism; Quartal and Quintal Harmonies; The Whole Tone Scale; Other Scales* | |

## 19 New Tonal Methods — 289
### New Tonal Ventures — 289
*Quartal Harmonies; Polychords; Polytonality; Bimodality and Dual Modality; Pandiatonicism*
### Stravinsky — 296
*Stravinsky (Profile);* The Rite of Spring
### Bartók — 298
*Bartók (Profile); "Boating" (from* Mikrokosmos Book V*)*

## 20 Non-Serial Atonality — 301
### Perspective — 301
### Atonality: Tools and Terminology — 301
### Unordered Set Analysis — 305
*Normal Order and Set Type*
### Analyzing the Set Type — 308
*Best Normal Order; Prime Form; The Interval Class Vector; The Z Relationship; The Set Class*
### Applications in Analysis — 313
### Hints for Analysis — 316
### Another Way

## 21 Serial Atonality — 319
### Serialism — 319
*Serialism Defined; Basic Tenets*
### The Matrix — 324
*Constructing a Matrix; Indexing a Matrix*
### Finding the Row — 326
### Hexachordal Symmetry — 331

| | | |
|---|---|---|
| *Appendix A* | Intervals, Modes and Key | 355 |
| *Appendix B* | Selected Rhythm Topics | 339 |
| *Appendix C* | Basic Harmonic Structures | 347 |
| *Appendix D* | Part-Writing Guidelines | 351 |

*Glossary* — 353
*Credits* — 371
*Index* — 373
*Track Listing* — 379

# To the Instructor

Whatever their major, graduate students are often required to take at least one analysis course as a part of their degree work. However, not all graduate students are equally prepared to undertake such a course. This recognition has led to an increase in the number of graduate theory review courses being offered or required at colleges and universities. The need for a book that services this course has been noted.

*Theory Essentials for Today's Musician* is a condensed version of *Theory for Today's Musician,* second edition. It has been written specifically as a graduate theory review text, although it may be useful as well for accelerated undergraduate theory courses. To adapt to the accelerated pace of such courses, the number of examples and assignments have been pared, explanations have been abbreviated, and knowledge of the more rudimentary topics has been assumed. Some of the basics have been placed in the appendices rather than presented as chapters. If your students need a refresher on this material, it should be addressed before undertaking Chapter One. The text speaks in a slightly more elevated tone appropriate to a graduate-level study of music theory. Likewise, the exercises chosen for inclusion are those more appropriate to the graduate level.

We've designed the book with maximum flexibility for you, the instructor, in mind. It is sectioned into four large, relatively autonomous units: Basic Tools (Chapters 1–6), Chromatic Harmony (Chapters 7–12), Form and Analysis (Chapters 13–17), and The Twentieth Century and Beyond (Chapters 18–21). Each of these parts can be used on their own, apart from the others, so that you can choose what to cover based on your assessment of the particular needs of your graduate students (whose needs may vary from year to year).

It is likely that you'll cover the early chapters rather quickly and spend more time on the topics from Parts Two, Three and Four. In any case, we invite you to be creative in your use of the book, to amplify and condense as you see fit. We hope your need to *clarify* is minimal.

Ralph Turek and Daniel McCarthy

# Basic Tools

# PART ONE

1  Elements of Diatonic Harmony  3
2  Cadences and Harmonic Rhythm  19
3  The Outer-Voice Framework/Embellishing Tones  31
4  Part Writing and Chorale Analysis I  45
5  Part Writing and Chorale Analysis II  63
6  Part Writing and Chorale Analysis III  77

# CHAPTER ONE

# Elements of Diatonic Harmony

As the harmonies of Western music became more varied and complex, abbreviated methods of symbolizing them arose. Two systems of musical shorthand are particularly relevant for the schooled musician: lead sheet notation and figured-bass notation. The former is a common way of notating popular music and jazz, whereas the latter is integral to a working knowledge of Baroque music—the music of Vivaldi, Bach, Handel, and their contemporaries.

> **KEY CONCEPTS IN THIS CHAPTER**
> - lead-sheet notation
> - figured bass
> - the diatonic chords
> - functional tonality

## LEAD-SHEET NOTATION

A **lead sheet** provides a melody (and lyrics if present) on a single staff, with chord symbols above the staff. The chord symbols provide the basis for an improvised accompaniment. Example 1-1 shows the notation in its simplest form.

**EXAMPLE 1-1**  Albert Hammond and Carol Bayer Sager: "When I Need You"

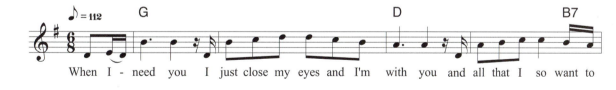

*Note*: Chord changes are placed where they occur in the music. A given chord remains in effect until the next change occurs.

## Lead-Sheet Chord Symbols

Lead-sheet symbols show a chord's root and quality. Example 1-2 shows common ways of expressing this.

### EXAMPLE 1-2  Triads

### EXAMPLE 1-2  Seventh Chords

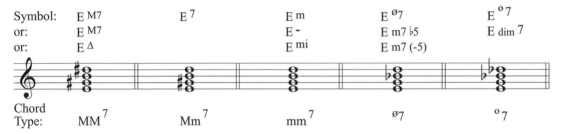

## Expanded Symbols

The bass line often is the second most important melodic element in a song. A more melodic bass can be obtained through inversion and, when necessary, it can rescue a lackluster melody. For these reasons, composers/song writers have found it necessary to indicate inversion when using lead-sheet symbols.

Example 1-3 is a solo piano rendering of Example 1-1. The lead sheet offered an incomplete view of the actual bass line. Yet the bass adds much to the song.

### EXAMPLE 1-3  Albert Hammond and Carol Bayer Sager: "When I Need You" 🔊

Arr. R. T.

ELEMENTS OF DIATONIC HARMONY 5

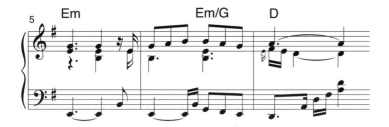

The chord symbols added in mm. 2, 4, and 6 show both the chord (left of the slash) and the bass note *when different from the chord root* (right of the slash) which reflect the bass line more accurately.

## EXAMPLE 1-4

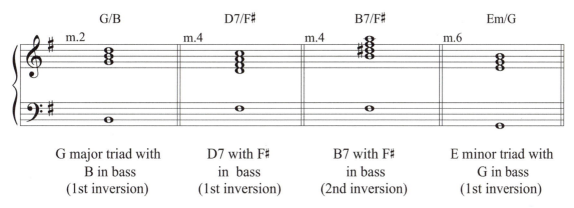

G major triad with B in bass (1st inversion)

D7 with F♯ in bass (1st inversion)

B7 with F♯ in bass (2nd inversion)

E minor triad with G in bass (1st inversion)

## FIGURED BASS NOTATION

During the Baroque era (*ca.*1600–1750), a shorthand system of notation provided the information necessary for the harpsichordist, organist, lutenist, or (mostly in Spain) guitarist to improvise an accompaniment. Similar in concept to today's lead sheet, this system of notation consisted of a bass line with Arabic numerals beneath the staff called **figured bass**, indicating the harmonic structure to be added with the bass. Known as the **continuo**, the bass was played by a string (cello) or woodwind instrument (bassoon) while the harmonies were **realized** (improvised) on a keyboard (or lute, etc.). In Example 1-5, the bottom staff contains the part that the continuo performers would likely have seen. The grand staff above it shows a realization of this figured bass.

# BASIC TOOLS

**EXAMPLE 1-5**  G. F. Handel: "Hallelujah" (from *The Messiah*)

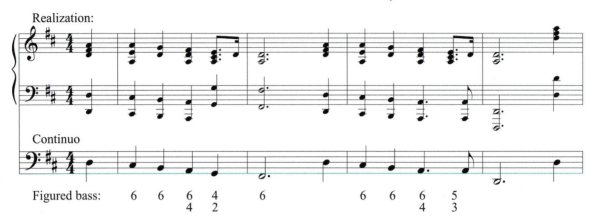

Although the points that follow relate figured bass to chord inversion, it is important to know that composers and performers of the time thought in terms of intervals only—not chord inversion, a concept unknown to all but the last generation of figured-bass composers.

## Realizing a Figured Bass

1. The numbers indicate intervals to be added *in any octave* above—*never below*—the bass notes.

### EXAMPLE 1-6A

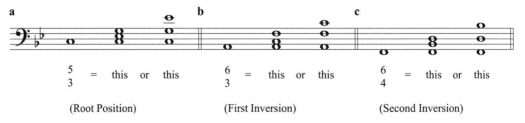

2. The intervals to be added are diatonic—that is, found within the key. Chromatic pitches are never added or subtracted unless the figure so instructs.

3. An accidental alone always refers to the *third above the bass note*.

**EXAMPLE 1-6B**

4. An accidental preceding or following a numeral indicates a chromatic raising or lowering of the pitch to which the numeral refers. Raised pitches are also indicated by a plus sign or by a diagonal stroke through the numeral.

**EXAMPLE 1-6C**

These figures all mean a raised sixth (along with the diatonic third) above B.

**EXAMPLE 1-6D**

These figures all indicate a raised sixth (and diatonic third) above C.

5. The figures for seventh chords are:

**EXAMPLE 1-7**

|  | Root pos. | First inv. | Second inv. | Third inv. |
|---|---|---|---|---|
| Symbol: (abbreviated) | 7 | 6<br>5 | 4<br>3 | 4<br>2 |
| Complete Symbol: | 7<br>5<br>3 | 6<br>5<br>3 | 6<br>4<br>3 | 6<br>4<br>2 |

Like lead-sheet notation, the figured bass evolved. Composers often omitted all but the most essential figures, even forgoing *all* figures where the harmony could be easily deduced. This left much to the interpretative powers of the performers.

# BASIC TOOLS

Although an elegant system, figured bass as a means of improvisation within the continuo remains associated with Baroque music, and it is still a prized skill used by musicians specializing in music from that period. However, the figures themselves eventually found a wider use in tandem with Roman numerals and form the composite chord symbols that have become standard in harmonic analysis today. We'll consider these symbols next. The complete abbreviated list of figured bass symbols for triads and seventh chords is listed below (Example 1-8):

## EXAMPLE 1-8

| 6 | 6 | 7 | 6 | 4 | 4 |
|---|---|---|---|---|---|
|   | 4 |   | 5 | 3 | 2 |

## THE DIATONIC CHORDS

Play or listen to the following arrangement.

EXAMPLE 1-9 "Amazing Grace" (folk hymn) 🔊

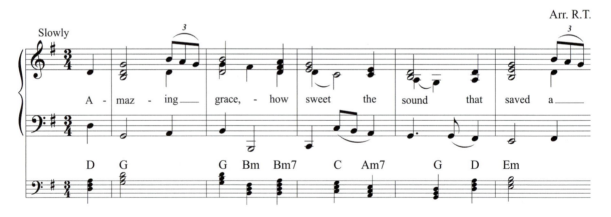

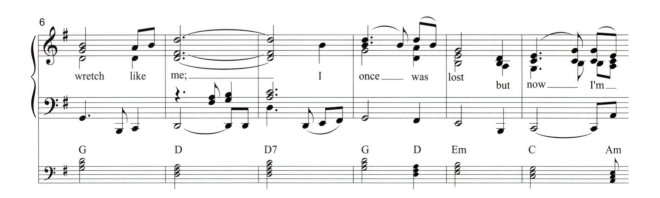

# ELEMENTS OF DIATONIC HARMONY

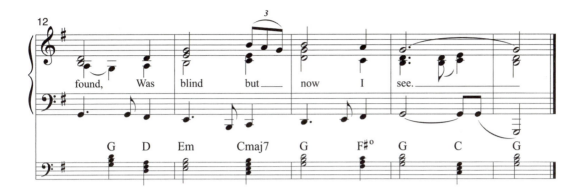

All seven triads in the key of G are used, along with two seventh chords. Clear examples of each chord appear on the added staff at the points where they occur. Some of the chords are inverted and some contain extra tones for added dissonance and variety.

## Diatonic Triads in Major Keys

The seven triads are arranged in Example 1-10a so that their roots form a G major scale. Each triad bears a name, known as its **function**, that reflects the position of its root within the scale and its relationship to tonic. The same names designate the scale degrees, which are indicated by placement of a caret (^) above the degree number (Example 1-10b).

### EXAMPLE 1-10A

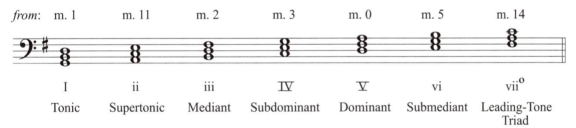

### EXAMPLE 1-10B

$\hat{5}$ Dominant: a fifth above the tonic and a point of instability requiring eventual resolution to the tonic

$\hat{3}$ Mediant: the midpoint between tonic and dominant

$\hat{2}$ Supertonic: "above" the tonic

$\hat{1}$ **Tonic:** **The chord of maximum stability**

$\hat{7}$ Leading tone: "leading" to the tonic by half step

$\hat{6}$ Submediant: the midpoint between tonic and subdominant

$\hat{4}$ Subdominant: a fifth below the tonic

### Roman Numeral Symbols

The Roman numerals in Example 1-10 designate both the scale degree of the chord roots and the quality of the chords. Upper case numerals denote major triads; lower cases denote minor triads. A "+" following an upper case numeral denotes an augmented triad (not diatonic in major) and an "o" following a lower case numeral denotes a diminished triad.

### The Primary Triads

I, IV, and V are sometimes called the **primary triads** because, collectively, they contain all of the pitches present in the scale. Numerous folk songs, hymns, and other traditional melodies are harmonized with only these three chords.

Example 1-11 shows "Amazing Grace" harmonized using only the primary triads.

**EXAMPLE 1-11** "Amazing Grace" (folk hymn)

### Diatonic Triads in Minor Keys

In the minor mode, the variable sixth and seventh scale degrees ($\hat{6}$ and $\hat{7}$) create a larger pool of potential harmonies. Example 1-12a shows the most common triads. They use the pitches of the harmonic minor form *except for the mediant*, which is almost always a major triad (III)—*not augmented* (III+). However, $\hat{6}$ and $\hat{7}$—raised ascending and lowered descending—create a second possibility *for every triad but the tonic*.

## EXAMPLE 1-12A

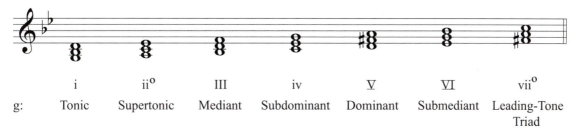

## EXAMPLE 1-12B

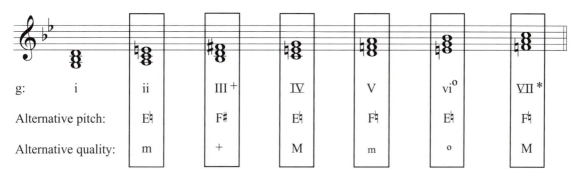

* The **VII** is named **subtonic,** since it is a whole step (rather than a half step) beneath the tonic.

## Showing Inversion

The figured bass symbols, 6 (short for $^6_3$), and $^6_4$, are used with the Roman numerals to show inversion. The absence of a superscript signifies root position.

## EXAMPLE 1-13

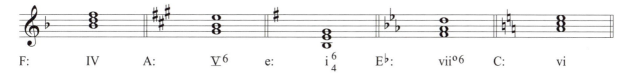

## The Diatonic Seventh Chords

Example 1-14 shows the Roman numeral symbols for the diatonic seventh chords.

### EXAMPLE 1-14A Major

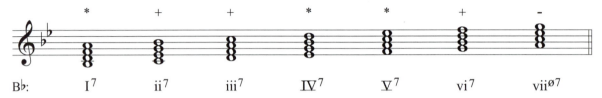

### EXAMPLE 1-14B Minor

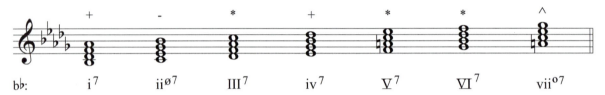

- \*   Major triad with diatonic seventh: $I^7$, $IV^7$, $V^7$, $III^7$, $VI^7$
- \+   Minor triad with diatonic seventh: $ii^7$, $iii^7$, $vi^7$, $i^7$, $iv^7$
- ~   Diminished triad with diatonic seventh: $ii^{ø7}$, $vii^{ø7}$
- ^   Diminished triad with diatonic seventh: $vii^{o7}$

In diatonic seventh chords:

- The basic triad is symbolized as before.
- A superscript 7 indicates a *diatonic* seventh above the chord root.
- The sole exception is the $vii^{ø7}$ in major. The ø distinguishes this chord, called a **half-diminished seventh chord**, from the **fully diminished seventh chord** (see diminished seventh chord) that appears on the leading tone in minor keys.
- As with triads, inversions are shown by adding figured bass superscripts: $^6_5$ for first inversion, $^4_3$ for second inversion and $^4_2$ for third inversion.

### EXAMPLE 1-15

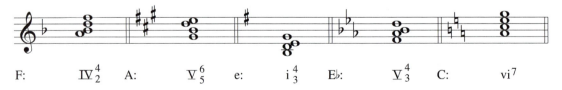

# ELEMENTS OF DIATONIC HARMONY

## FUNCTIONAL TONALITY

### Chord Function

Beyond identifying the chord root and quality, Roman numeral symbols provide insight into a chord's place in the scale *and* its function in the key. This chord is represented by the lead-sheet symbol "Am" (or A- or A$^{mi}$). However, in the key of C it's vi, while in the key of G it's ii, and in the key of F it's iii. The same chord *has a different purpose and different musical effect* in each of these keys.

Although the G major triad (boxed) is voiced identically in both excerpts that follow, in the key of G it suggests finality, whereas in the key of C it creates the expectation that something (probably the tonic) will follow.

**EXAMPLE 1-16A** Stephen Sondheim and Leonard Bernstein: "One Hand, One Heart" (from *West Side Story*)

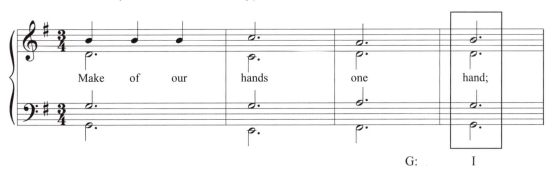

**EXAMPLE 1-16B** Franz Gruber: "Stille Nacht" ("Silent Night")

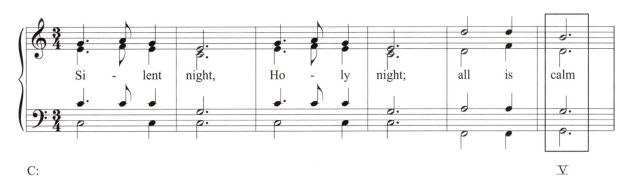

If you like word play, you can think of it this way:

*A key is a chord's context, and its context is key.*

In **functional tonality**, chords vary in status, behavior, and stability. The chord built on the tonic is the chord of maximum stability, the ultimate chord of repose. The vii°, built on the leading tone, is the least stable-sounding. Between these extremes lie the other chords, whose behavior depends on many factors.

## The Circle of Fifths

Observe the forward momentum created by chords whose roots are related by descending fifth.

**EXAMPLE 1-17A**

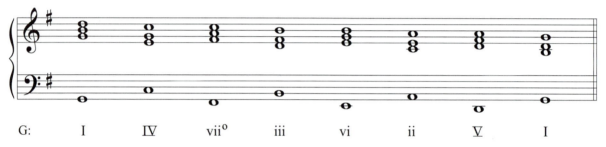

**EXAMPLE 1-17B**

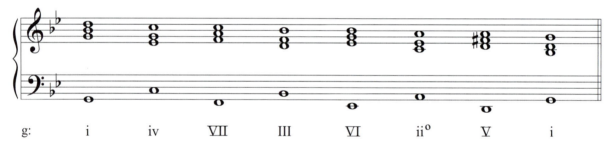

*Notes:*

1. The root movement in both the major and minor modes is downward by fifth (upward by fourth is the same thing).

2. One of the chords in Example 1-17b uses F♯ while the others use F♮. The reason has to do with the variable seventh degree in the minor scale, to be discussed later.

Example 1-18 shows two works separated by time and style that largely travel the same harmonic byway—the circle of fifths.

### EXAMPLE 1-18A  W. A. Mozart: Rondo K. 494

*Note:* The fifth (blackened) has been omitted from each seventh chord, a common practice then and now.

### EXAMPLE 1-18B  Joseph Kosma and Johnny Mercer: "Autumn Leaves" Arr. R.T.

Circle-of-fifths patterns are subject to modification. The IV and ii share common tones and a functional relationship in that they tend most strongly toward the dominant and are thus termed **predominants**. In the same way, vii° and V tend toward the tonic. Reconciling the circle of fifths with common-tone relatedness yields the following paradigm that governs much functional harmonic motion.

## EXAMPLE 1-19

Notice that IV can approach I from either side, as *pre*-dominant because of the common tones it shares with ii, or as *sub*dominant because of its fifth relationship to I. In the former role, it functions as a tonic approach and in the latter role, it often functions as a tonic expansion or elaboration.

## Harmonic Motion

Any two chords that move toward the tonic in the manner of Example 1-19 are said to "progress," and the chord succession is termed a **progression.** Motion in the opposite direction has been termed **retrogression** and repeated chords or functions (as IV-ii or V-vii) **repetitions**. All three types of motion are found in most tonal music.

Some theorists consider IV, ii, vi and iii *all* to be predominant *functions*, and in a general way this is true because the goal of most musical phrases is to arrive at either the tonic or dominant.

## THE GROUND BASS

A **ground bass** is a bass line that repeats over and over throughout a composition. The ground bass was popular in the Baroque era, where it usually took one of three basic forms.

## EXAMPLE 1-20

**Diatonic major**

**Diatonic minor**

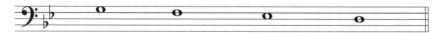

**Chromatic**

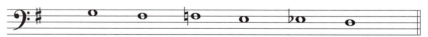

*Note:* The minor pattern outlines the descending melodic minor scale form (identical with the natural minor form).

These bass lines support a variety of harmonic patterns that do not necessarily follow the circle-of-fifths paradigm. Common for the major form are the following, each of which might be continued in several ways:

## EXAMPLE 1-21

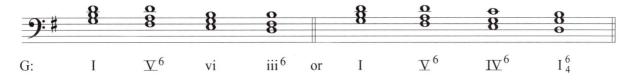

This plan and numerous variants have been used time and again in every musical style period.

George Frideric Handel made extensive use of scalar bass lines.

## EXAMPLE 1-22 G. F. Handel: *Concerto Grosso* op. 6, No. 12 (second movement)

*Note:* The descending scale (B–A–G–F♯–E–D–C♯–B) described by the bass and echoed by the melody in embellished form (starting at m. 96) generates the v⁶—an alternative minor-key harmony).

---

Listen to how dramatically a change in mode from major to minor can affect the sound.

## EXAMPLE 1-23

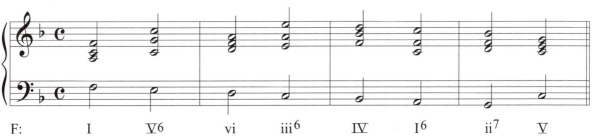

### a Major

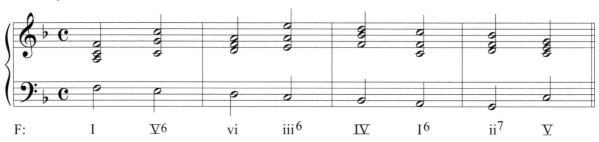

Scalar bass lines generate harmonic successions that run generally counter to the circle of fifths. This underscores the nuance possible in functional tonality. A compelling melodic pattern in the bass or any other voice can provide the logic that makes a retrogressive harmonic pattern more effective.

## The Common Practice Period

Functional tonality is the harmonic language of the **common practice period**—the music composed roughly between 1650 and 1900 (and beyond in some popular and concert-music styles). In functional tonality, the diatonic harmonies of a key exist in a hierarchical relationship. At the top of the harmonic food chain stands the tonic, and most harmonic patterns move toward it. Their conclusions, called cadences, are the topic of Chapter Two.

## SUMMARY OF TERMINOLOGY

- chromatic alteration
- circle of fifths
- common practice period
- continuo
- diatonic
- diminished seventh chord
- dominant

- figured bass
- ground bass
- lead sheet
- leading tone triad
- mediant
- nonchord tone
- predominant

- progression
- realization
- retrogresion
- subdominant
- submediant
- subtonic
- tonic

# CHAPTER TWO

# Cadences and Harmonic Rhythm

## CADENCES

A **cadence** is a point of relative repose. Music is filled with such moments. Cadences may entail a breathing point in the melodic line, an ebb in the harmonic flow, a respite from rhythmic activity, or all of these. They perform a function similar to the artfully timed caesuras in an effective orator's delivery—they group, separate, emphasize, and dramatize ideas.

> **KEY CONCEPTS IN THIS CHAPTER**
> - standard cadences
> - cadential variants
> - harmonic rhythm and meter

The feeling of musical repose created by a cadence is often rhythmic—a longer note value, or a brief silence.

**EXAMPLE 2-1** Mozart: Piano Sonata, K. 332 (first movement)

Perhaps even more often a cadence is harmonic—a two-chord succession that conveys one of two messages:

1. "This is the end of something." (a conclusive cadence)
2. "This pause is only momentary." (an inconclusive cadence)

These messages appear repeatedly in the course of a musical work.

**EXAMPLE 2-2** Mozart: Piano Sonata, K. 332 (first movement) 🔊

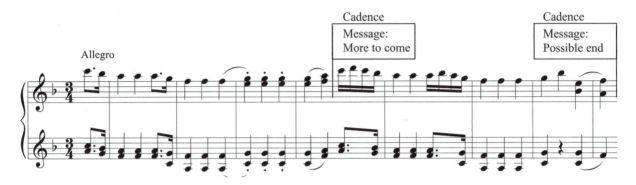

## Cadences and Style

During music's long and evolved history, changing harmonic patterns were favored for cadences, and they are recognizable features of the various styles. Examples follow.

**EXAMPLE 2-3A** Dufay: "Communio" from Missa Sancti Jacobi (1428)

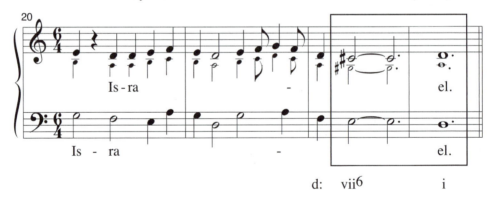

*Note:* The "double leading tone" preceding an open-fifth chord, typical of the Burgundian period (1450–1600), has a distinctive archaic flavor. You'll hear it in scores for films or plays that are set in that historical time frame. Although Roman numerals are used to show the chords' relationship to each other, this music is neither major nor minor in the functional sense.

### EXAMPLE 2-3B "Scarborough Fair" (English folk song)

*Note*: "Scarborough Fair" has a touch of modality to it, as does much English music. This is chiefly due to the lowered seventh scale degree (subtonic).

---

### EXAMPLE 2-3C Jon Hendricks and Bobby Timmons: "Moanin'"

*Note*: This cadence also has a modal quality, owing to the raised sixth scale degree, C sharp.

---

Eventually, cadences became more or less standardized; the cadence-ending chords were usually I or V. Four types were employed.

## Standard Cadences

The **authentic cadence** (AC) is the most common and conclusive. Signature features are melodic movement from leading tone to tonic, often with bass motion from 5 to 1, as in these progressions: in major, V–I, $V^7$–I, or $vii^{o6}$–I; in minor, V–i, $V^7$–i, or $vii^{o6}$–i.

### EXAMPLE 2-4 Schubert: "Standchen"

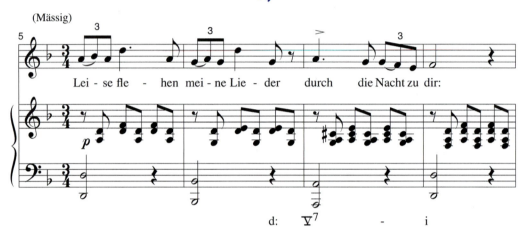

Some authentic cadences sound more conclusive than others. When the melody (usually the highest voice in the texture) ends on the tonic, and the bass leaps from dominant to tonic, the most conclusive of all effects is produced. This is called a **perfect authentic cadence** (PAC).

### EXAMPLE 2-5

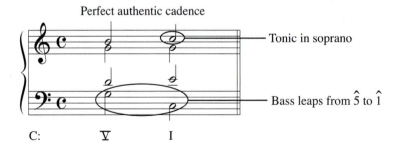

Any authentic cadence lacking *either* the $\hat{5}$–$\hat{1}$ motion at the bottom or the tonic ending on the top is called, logically, an **imperfect authentic cadence** (IAC).

## EXAMPLE 2-6

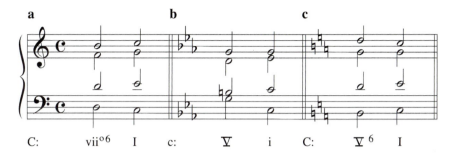

Also conclusive-sounding is the **plagal cadence** (PC) heard in the familiar "Amen" intoned at the end of hymns. The harmonic pattern is IV–I (major) or iv–i (minor). The plagal cadence, appearing less often in the standard repertory than the authentic, is considerably more common in rock and other gospel- and blues-based music, where IV rivals V in importance at cadences.

## EXAMPLE 2-7

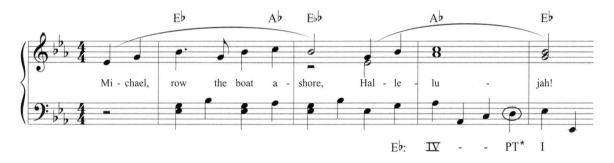

*Note*: *PT= passing tone, to be described in Chapter 3.

---

The **half cadence** sends a message that promises continuation. Because of this, it almost never ends a piece. The half cadence embraces a wider variety of harmonic patterns than the authentic or plagal. In theory, it can end on any chord but I. In practice, this final chord is usually V, but a chromatic chord or almost any diatonic harmony might precede it (?–V). One particular pattern that appears in minor keys only, iv$^6$–V, has acquired a special name, the **Phrygian half cadence.** The cadence is named for the descending half step in the bass, a distinctive feature of the Phrygian mode. Following are examples of half cadences.

**EXAMPLE 2-8A** Beethoven: Piano Sonata op. 26 (first movement)

**EXAMPLE 2-8B** Mendelssohn: Kinderstück, op. 72, No. 1

A **deceptive cadence** is one in which V resolves (deceptively) to anything but the anticipated tonic (V–?). The most common deceptive cadence—V–vi (V–VI in minor keys)—gives an impression of intermediate finality.

**EXAMPLE 2-9** Beethoven: Piano Sonata op. 7 (third movement)

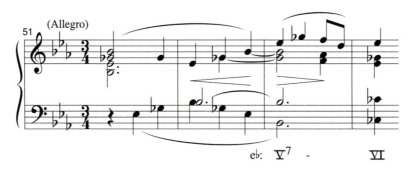

## Cadential Variants

Although other cadences *can* be found in our vast musical repertoire, many can still be viewed as variants of one of these standard types. The addition of a melody note (B♭) subtly changes the chord pattern of the cadence in Example 2-10a, but the effect is still plagal (note that the $\hat{4}$–$\hat{1}$ bass motion is still present). Example **b** shows an inconclusive cadence ending on IV, sometimes called a "plagal half-cadence."

**EXAMPLE 2-10A** Brahms: Waltz op. 39, no. 15

**EXAMPLE 2-10B** Robert Burns: "Auld Lang Syne"

One of Leonard Bernstein's most enduring scores, *West Side Story*, is filled with distinctive harmonic nuances that include some unusual cadences.

**EXAMPLE 2-11** Stephen Sondheim and Leonard Bernstein: "Maria" (from *West Side Story*)

## SUMMARY OF STANDARD CADENCES

(Minor shown in parentheses)

    Authentic (AC):    V–I (V–i) can be perfect (PAC) or imperfect (IAC)
                                vii°–I (vii°–i) imperfect (IAC)

    Plagal (PC):        IV–I (iv–i)

    Half (HC):          IV–V (iv$^6$–V); ii$^6$–V (ii$^{o6}$–V); I–V (i–V); vi–V (VI–V)

    Deceptive (DC):    V–vi (V–VI)

## EXAMPLE 2-12

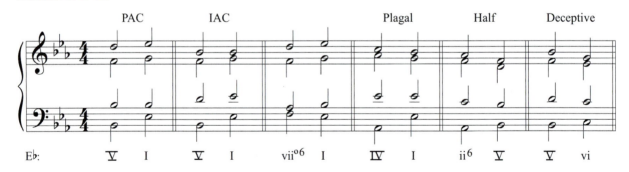

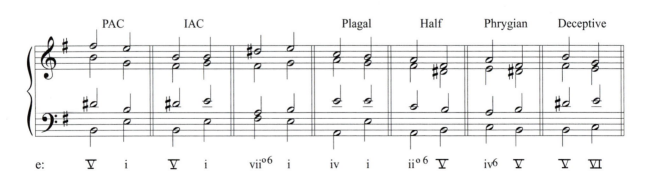

In the standard cadences:

- The final chord is a *root-position triad*.
- The final chord is either a major triad (I, V, or VI) or a minor triad (i or vi).
- The half cadence *always* ends with a major triad (V).

Traditional thinking holds that a pause on other than I, V, or vi is not truly a cadence. Still, a pause is a pause is a pause (to misquote Gertrude Stein). Some theorists use the term "contrapuntal cadence" to describe such musical moments.

## HARMONIC RHYTHM

Harmonic rhythm refers to: (1) the *rate* at which the chords accompanying a melody change; and (2) the rhythmic *patterns* formed by those chord changes. A new harmony can occur as often as every beat or with every melody note or as infrequently as every couple measures or longer. Tempo and harmonic rhythm often display an inverse relationship. *Often*, but not *always*. In Example 2-13, both harmonic rhythm and tempo amble along at a leisurely gait. In compensation, the melody is moderately florid.

**EXAMPLE 2-13** Beethoven: Piano Sonata op. 22 (second movement)

Variables notwithstanding, generalizations can be made:

- Harmonies change more often on strong beats than on weak beats, and more often on *down*beats than on *up*beats.
- The final chord of a cadence is usually metrically stronger than the chord that precedes it.
- The tonic tends to occupy stronger metric positions than the dominant (the half cadence I–V a notable exception).
- The rate of chord change often increases with the approach to a cadence.

Example 2-14 illustrates these four points to a greater or lesser degree.

**EXAMPLE 2-14** Schumann: "Volksliedchen" (No. 9 from *Album for the Young*, op. 68)

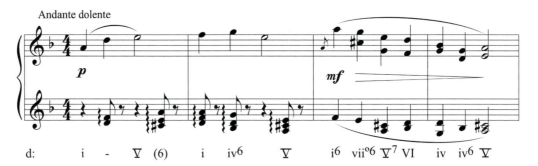

## Harmonic Rhythm and Meter

Patterns of harmonic change define—in fact, in many cases create—meter. Following are typical harmonic rhythms in two common meters. Short works may employ a single pattern whereas longer and more complex music will likely contain more variety.

**EXAMPLE 2-15**

Example 2-16 contains several examples of the harmonic rhythms shown above. The harmonic rhythm is plotted for the first two measures.

### EXAMPLE 2-16  J. S. Bach "Herz und Mund und Tat und Leben" (Chorale from Cantata 147)

A regularly recurring harmonic rhythm produces a sense of meter. An occasional shift in harmonic rhythm and/or melodic accentuation adds interest. The excerpt that follows employs a melody comprising quarter notes exclusively. The harmonic setting lends interest because of its metric ambiguity. Notice the syncopated subdominant chord on beats 2 and 3 of m. 1 and the weak metric position of all the tonic chords except the first, including the weak-beat cadence.

### EXAMPLE 2-17  Chopin: Nocturne op. 37, no. 1

In Example 2-18, the agogic accents (accents by duration) in the melody (>) reinforce harmonic changes on the second beat of each measure to "turn the beat around" at the outset. The common term for this is **metric shift**.

**EXAMPLE 2-18** Chopin: Etude op. 10 no. 3

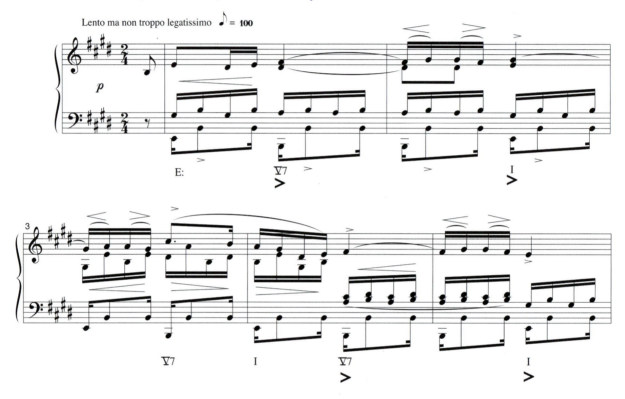

To summarize:

- Harmony and rhythm in combination create the cadences that separate musical ideas.
- The rate and patterns of chord change in a piece comprise its harmonic rhythm.
- Meter is an aspect of rhythm, accent creates meter, and harmonic patterns create accents. Conversely, a metric shift can occur when harmonies consistently change on the measures' weak beats.

## SUMMARY OF TERMINOLOGY

- authentic cadence
- harmonic rhythm
- Phrygian half cadence
- cadence
- imperfect authentic cadence
- plagal cadence
- deceptive cadence
- metric shift
- half cadence
- perfect authentic cadence

# CHAPTER THREE

# The Outer-Voice Framework/Embellishing Tones

**KEY CONCEPTS IN THIS CHAPTER**

- melodic principles
- motion between voices
- creating an outer-voice framework
- embellishing tones

When interesting melodies combine to form attractively voiced harmonies that flow logically, we say the result is "musical." The technique that makes it happen is **voice leading**. Since around 1650, composers have observed voice-leading principles that balance two forces, one horizontal (the melodic force) and the other vertical (the harmonic force). These forces make opposing demands. Perhaps most important in writing for any number of voices is the counterpoint between the highest and lowest. **Counterpoint** and its more general synonym **polyphony** describe the simultaneous sounding of two or more melodic lines displaying independent rhythms and contours. These lines must complement each other in such a way that they form a *coherent combination*.

## MELODIC PRINCIPLES

Counterpoint is only as strong as the individual melodic lines that compose it. The principles that follow apply to every voice in the texture.

1. *Range*: Each voice remains within its range.

### EXAMPLE 3-1

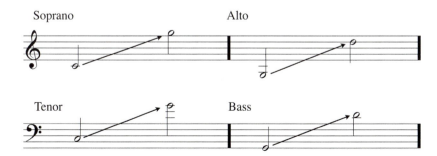

*Note*: The pitch ranges of the tenor and bass replicate the ranges of the soprano and alto an octave lower.

2. *Motion*: Each voice moves primarily by stepwise motion.
3. *Chromatics*: Chromatic intervals such as the augmented second formed by $\hat{6}$ and $\hat{7}$ of the harmonic minor scale are avoided.
4. *Leaps*: Leaps larger than a fifth occur sparingly. Leaps are generally followed by stepwise motion or a pitch repetition.

   Successive leaps in the same direction are avoided except when those pitches arpeggiate the underlying harmony. (The bass has more latitude here because it functions both as a melodic voice and a harmonic foundation.)
5. *Sensitive tones*: **Sensitive tones**, also called "tendency tones," are resolved. These include the leading tone—it resolves upward by a half step; chord sevenths—they resolve stepwise downward; $\hat{6}$ and $\hat{7}$ in minor keys, which form a sensitive duo—they are raised to move upward to the tonic and lowered to move downward to the dominant; and altered tones—they resolve by half step *in the direction of the chromatic inflection* (raised pitches go up, lowered pitches go down).

## EXAMPLE 3-2

   a   =   leading tone (resolves upward)
   b   =   chromatically raised pitch (resolves upward)
   c   =   $\hat{6}$ and $\hat{7}$ (raised in ascent, lowered in descent)

6. *Counterpoint*: A strong counterpoint between the outer voices is accomplished by using contrary and oblique motion where possible. Too much parallel motion—particularly intervals of the same type (thirds in succession, for example)—can undermine counterpoint by creating the impression of a single harmonized line.

## EXAMPLE 3-3 Types of motion between voices

   a   =   **similar motion**: voices move in the same direction but by different intervals
   b   =   **parallel motion**: voices move in the same direction by the *same* interval (avoid too much of this)
   c   =   **contrary motion**: voices move in opposite directions (favor this)
   d   =   **oblique motion**: one voice remains stationary while the other voice moves toward or away from it.

*Note*: In parallel motion, the numerical value of the interval between the two voices is maintained, although its *quality* may change —that is, a major third A/F moving to a minor third B♭/G is still considered parallel motion.

## CREATING AN OUTER-VOICE FRAMEWORK

### 1:1 Counterpoint

The simplest way to create a soprano-bass counterpoint is to start with a single note in one voice against a single note in the other. This is called, variously, **note-against-note counterpoint**, **1:1 species** or **first species**. We'll begin with an existing melody and its harmonic underpinning.

**EXAMPLE 3-4** Jean Paul Égide Martini: "Plaisir d'amour" (Adapted)

We'll first convert the Roman numeral symbols into a bass line.

**EXAMPLE 3-5**

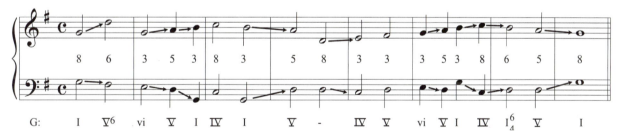

*Notes*:

1. Every note of the melody is supported by a single note in the bass.
2. The bass, a realization of the given chord symbols, supplies the root of each harmony in all but two cases (m. 1 and m. 7).
3. Together, the two voices sound *only consonances* (shown between the staves). This is typical in 1:1 counterpoint.
4. Despite the bass's confinement mostly to chord roots, it has been disposed in a way that maximizes contrary motion against the melody (shown by the arrows).

Example 3-5 is **contrapuntal** in that the soprano and bass display independent contours. But notice the *melodic* shortcomings of the bass—too many leaps, too many Ds, too repetitive sounding, and it combines with the melody to produce a large number of hollow-sounding perfect consonances. These problems are remedied in Example 3-6.

## EXAMPLE 3-6

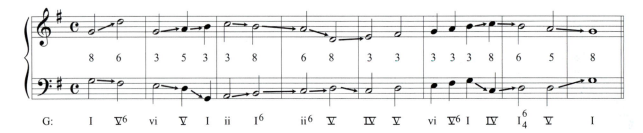

*Notes*:

1. Changes have been made in mm. 3, 4 and 6. The inversions and minor changes in harmony result in a more stepwise bass.

2. The number of perfect consonances has been reduced from 9 to 7, and the number of imperfect consonances has been correspondingly increased, resulting in a fuller-sounding counterpoint.

3. Contrary motion still outnumbers any other single motion (9 occurrences).

Room for improvement remains. The successive thirds in mm. 5 and 6 rob the top line of its melodic independence. Example 3-7 further enhances the counterpoint.

## EXAMPLE 3-7

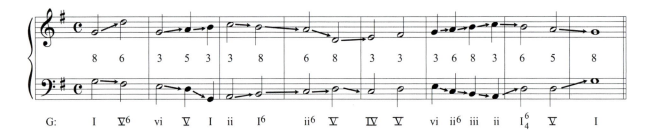

*Note*: The changes in m. 6 reduce the number of consecutive thirds to three, a generally practiced limit for thirds or sixths in succession. A further benefit is the additional contrary motion, especially desirable in approaching the cadence.

Although parallel motion occurs in the foregoing and following examples—even successive parallels such as the thirds in m. 5–6 of Example 3-7—notice the absence of *perfect consonances of the same type* in succession. **Consecutive** (also called parallel) **perfect consonances** (octaves, fifths, fourths, and unisons) have long been avoided.

## EXAMPLE 3-8

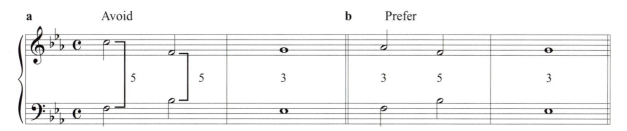

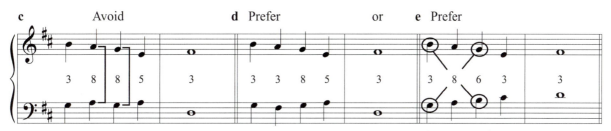

Octave occurs between voice exchange.

*Note*: Eliminating the consecutive octaves in **c** has produced consecutive thirds instead (**d**). Consecutive imperfect consonances do not carry the restriction of perfect consonances. Another solution is offered (**e**) by creating a stepwise ascent from G to the tonic D, resulting in a "voice exchange" between the upper and lower voices.

### FOR PRACTICE

On separate manuscript paper, compose a soprano and bass over the given harmonic framework. Use as much contrary and oblique motion as possible, balance conjunct and disjunct motion, and use as many imperfect consonances as possible for a full sound. Again, take care to avoid consecutive perfect consonances.

## EXAMPLE 3-8A

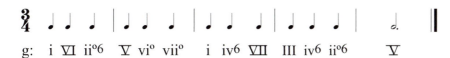

g:  i  VI  ii°6  V  vi°  vii°  i  iv6  VII  III  iv6  ii°6  V

## EMBELLISHING TONES

First species counterpoint lacks rhythmic independence. This is not necessarily a bad thing. In fact, hymns, anthems, folk music and the like involve mostly this species. However, two-voice counterpoint benefits from the rhythmic independence achieved through 2:1 (two notes against one) and 3:1 relationships, and the simplest way to achieve this is to add embellishing tones to one voice or the other.

**Embellishing tones** decorate or connect more important, consonant, or stable pitches. Most embellishing tones exist within a harmonic environment against which they are either consonant or (more frequently) dissonant. When dissonant against the harmony, they are called **nonchord tones**.

Embellishing tones may be distinguished by the way they are approached and left: (1) step-step, (2) step-leap, and (3) step-repetition (step-rep).

### Step-Step Combinations

The root, third, fifth, and seventh of any chord can be connected by **passing tones** (PT), which "pass" stepwise between the adjacent chord members. Similarly, two pitches a whole step apart can be connected by a "chromatic passing tone."

### EXAMPLE 3-9

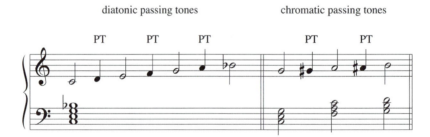

*Passing tones are usually unaccented relative to the following note.* However, they can occur in accented metric positions as well.

**EXAMPLE 3-10** Rossini: *Petite Messe Solonelle* ("Kyrie")

*Note*: Six of the nine PTs in mm. 2–4 are accented relative to the chord tone that follows.

**Neighbor tones** (NT) are pitches that lie a step (or half-step) above or below a consonant tone *and its repetition*. Like passing tones, they can be accented or unaccented. Those that lie above the consonant tone are called upper neighbors; those that lie below are called lower neighbors. All the NTs in Example 3-11 are unaccented.

## EXAMPLE 3-11

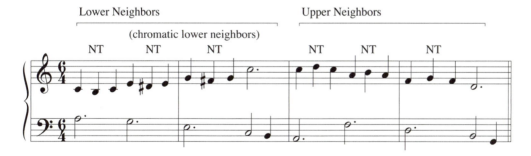

## FOR PRACTICE

Identify the embellishing tones in Example 3-12. The melody begins in the tenor "voice" and moves to the alto.

## EXAMPLE 3-12 Mendelssohn: *Overture to The Hebrides*, op. 26

By creating steps between chord members, passing tones and neighbor tones are responsible for many of the scalar passages in melodies. This is not to suggest that melodies should be viewed merely as filled-in arpeggiations. Although it's often possible to do just that, melody and harmony obey separate laws while influencing and complementing each other.

### Step-Leap Combinations

This group comprises the appoggiatura and escape tone. The more common is the **appoggiatura** (APP), which is approached by leap and resolved by step. In a true appoggiatura, the dissonance is stronger metrically than its resolution. Unaccented appoggiaturas are sometimes called **incomplete neighbors** (IN). The **escape tone** (ET) is the opposite of the appoggiatura in that it is approached by step and left by leap (normally in the opposite direction) and is normally unaccented.

## EXAMPLE 3-13A Mozart: Piano Sonata K. 279 (first movement)

**EXAMPLE 3-13B** Mozart: Piano Sonata K. 283 (first movement)

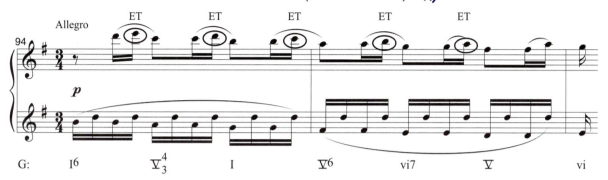

Measure 5 of Example 3-13a contains this pitch pattern: C-D-C-B-C. If the italicized C in the middle of the pattern were removed, a step-leap figure called the **double neighbor** (DN) would result: C-D-B-C. This is, essentially, the upper *and* lower neighbor (or vice versa) of a repeated pitch. The repeated pitch most often occurs at the beginning and end of the figure, as in Example 3-4 (*G-F#-A-G*), creating the precise interval motion of step-leap-step. Notice that the leap must change direction in order to return to the original pitch by step.

**EXAMPLE 3-14** Rodgers and Hammerstein: "Some Enchanted Evening"
(from *South Pacific*, act 1, no. 9)

*F major triad with added 6th

## Step-"Rep" Combinations

In this final category are the anticipation, suspension, and retardation. These embellishing tones differ from the others in that they are temporal displacements of *existing* tones rather than *extra* tones added for decoration. In the **anticipation** (ANT), one voice moves by step to its next tone before the other voices move. It arrives at the next chord early, usually by step. It forms a dissonance against one or more of the existing voices until they, too, move. At that point, the pitch is repeated but is no longer dissonant.

Example 3-15 shows the most common context for the anticipation—an authentic cadence in which the melody arrives at the final tonic prematurely, ahead of the other voices.

**EXAMPLE 3-15** John Francis Wade and J. Reading: "Adeste Fidelis"

The **suspension** and **retardation** result when a pitch is repeated or sustained prior to its stepwise resolution to a more stable tone. In a suspension, that resolution is downward; in a retardation, it's upward. Suspensions (SUS) and retardations (RET) are opposites of the anticipation in that:

- Their pattern is *rep-step* rather than *step-rep*.
- Their arrival at the next chord tone is *late* rather than early.
- The suspended dissonance is metrically stronger than its resolution.

Example 3-16 illustrates the four common suspensions: 9–8, 7–6, 4–3, and 2–3.

## EXAMPLE 3-16  Common Suspensions

*Notes*:

1. The numbers 9–8, 7–6, and 4–3 show the intervals formed *against the bass* by the suspended tone (either a 9, 7, or 4) and its stepwise resolution to a consonance (8, 6, or 3). These designations are used no matter how many octaves separate the suspended voice and bass.

2. The numbers 2–3 (as in m. 2) show the intervals formed by a suspension *in the bass voice* when the suspended tone resolves stepwise downward, dropping away from the upper voice with which it is initially dissonant (in this case, the tenor). The bass suspension is the only one in which the second number is larger than the first (2–3) because its downward resolution *increases* the distance between it and the upper voice.

3. The characteristic pattern (rep-step) of the suspension is marked. In the first two cases (mm. 1–2 and mm. 2–3), the pitch repetition appears as tied notes. In the last (m. 7), the pitch repetition is present within the half-note E♭. The absence of a tie renders this suspension less visually conspicuous. Ties are also absent in **rearticulated suspensions**, as in m. 5, where the repeated E♭ in the alto is sounded again at the point of suspension (beat 2).

Suspensions and retardations comprise three notes: (1) a consonant pitch; (2) its repetition, usually dissonant against a voice that has changed pitch; and (3) its stepwise resolution (downward in a suspension, upward in a retardation) to a pitch once again consonant. These elements are called the **preparation**, **dissonance**,* and **resolution**.

### EXAMPLE 3-17

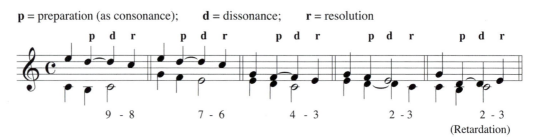

* In certain suspension-like figures such as 6–5, the suspended tone is technically not dissonant.

Example 3-18 contains 9–8 and 7–6 suspensions and an anticipation.

### EXAMPLE 3-18  Beethoven: Piano Sonata op. 27, no. 2 (second movement)

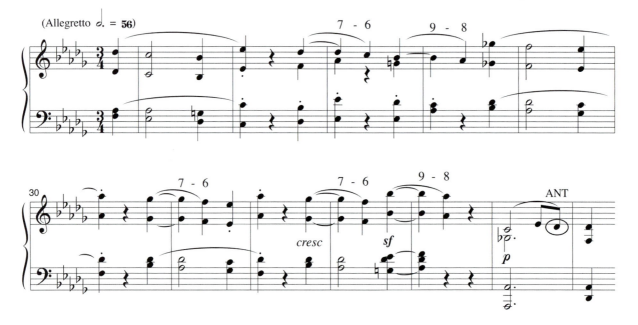

Certain situations require a change in the way that suspensions are designated. For example, a suspension may occur over a bass and/or harmony *that changes at the point of resolution.*

## EXAMPLE 3-19

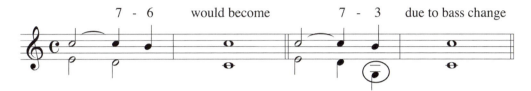

In order to avoid the complication arising from myriad suspension figures such 7–3, 9–6, and so on, it is common to measure both the suspended tone and its resolution against *the point of initial impact.* By this method, the suspension in Example 3-19 remains a 7–6 suspension despite the changing bass.

When simultaneous embellishing tones *of the same type* move *in the same direction in the same rhythm,* they are termed **double passing tones**, **double neighbor tones** (not to be confused with the double neighbor described and shown in Example 3-14), **double suspensions**, and so on. A double retardation at cadences is common in music of the Classical period.

## EXAMPLE 3-20  Mozart: Piano Sonata K. 331 (first movement)

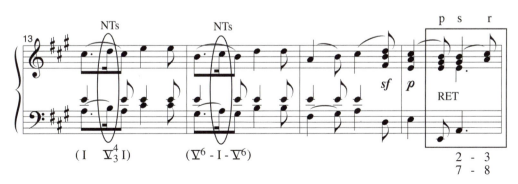

*Note:* The double neighbor tones in m. 13 and m. 14 are embellishing tones but not *nonchord tones*, because they actually change the harmony—to a $V^7$ in m. 13 and to a I in m. 14.

## BASIC TOOLS

> **FOR PRACTICE**
>
> Identify the double passing tones and double neighbor tones—upper and lower, accented and unaccented—in Example 3-21.

**EXAMPLE 3-21** Tchaikovsky: "Arabian Dance" (from *The Nutcracker*)

(Some notes have been omitted to simplify performance at the piano.)

Western music has witnessed the freedom march of dissonance. By the late Baroque era, all the standard embellishing tones were in place. However, in Bach's music, embellishing tones are short and nestled comfortably amid chord tones, whereas in the music of later composers, they are longer and more prominent.

## SUMMARY OF TERMINOLOGY

- counterpoint
- contrary motion
- consecutive octaves
- note-against-note consecutive fifths
- oblique motion
- outer-voice framework
- parallel motion
- polyphony
- sensitive tones
- similar motion
- voice ranges
- 2:1 counterpoint

# CHAPTER FOUR

# Part Writing and Chorale Analysis I

## THE FOUR-VOICE TEXTURE

The four-voice texture has been around so long that it is considered standard. Four voices are necessary for the complete sounding of a seventh chord, and simple triads sound best when the bass is reinforced (doubled). The four-voice texture provides fullness without turbidity, permitting the melodic motion of the individual voices to be heard clearly. Finally, the SATB (Soprano–Alto–Tenor–Bass) format conforms to the ranges of the basic male and female voice types.

**KEY CONCEPTS IN THIS CHAPTER**

- chord voicing (spacing and doubling)
- chord connection principles
- the chorale: analysis of part writing
- part writing suspensions

In much music, the number of musical lines, or "voices," varies. However, we'll start with music for four *fixed* lines, and we'll focus on vocal music for these reasons:

- Voice ranges are narrower and thus more manageable than instrumental ranges.
- Timbral contrast is less pronounced.
- Problems of instrumental transposition do not exist.
- Although most musicians tend to imagine a pitch before playing it, singers must then produce that pitch unaided by keys or valves. This requires that extra care be taken with voice leading in vocal music.

# BASIC TOOLS

## REVIEW OF MELODIC PRINCIPLES

The melodic principles cited in Chapter 3 apply equally to all voices in the texture. They are summarized here:

1. Keep each voice in its proper range.

2. Move each voice primarily by stepwise motion.

3. Avoid writing dissonant (augmented or diminished) melodic intervals.

4. Use leaps larger than a fifth sparingly, and follow them when possible with stepwise motion or a pitch repetition.

5. Resolve the sensitive tones.

6. Create good counterpoint between the outer voices.

Most of these principles can be observed in the following four-voice rendering.

**EXAMPLE 4-1** Stephen Sondheim and Leonard Bernstein: "Somewhere" (from *West Side Story*)

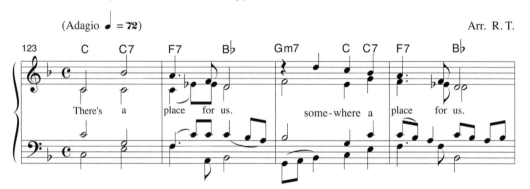

*Notes*:

1. The voices are within their respective ranges. The inner voices, sandwiched between the soprano and bass, necessarily display a more restricted range.

2. Stepwise motion prevails. The largest leaps aside from those in the melody occur in the bass. The leap of a sixth in m. 124 is followed by stepwise motion, as are all the other leaps in the bass.

3. In each seventh chord, the seventh is resolved stepwise downward.

4. A balance of conjunct and disjunct motion is achieved through passing tones and inversion.

5. Most of the motion between the melody and the bass line is contrary or oblique.

# PART WRITING AND CHORALE ANALYSIS I

## FOR PRACTICE

1. In Example 4-1, only the most basic chord symbols are given. Expand the lead-sheet symbols and add symbols as necessary to reflect more accurately the bass line.

2. Compare the ranges of the four voices. Locate each of the seventh chords and identify their inversions.

3. The sevenths might be analyzed as embellishing tones. Identify the types.

## VOICING CHORDS

### Spacing

*The better the blend, the better. Use homogeneous (more or less equidistant) spacing between the upper voices by keeping adjacent pairs (soprano and alto, alto and tenor) within an octave of one another.* Greater distance is acceptable—in fact, often desirable—between the tenor and bass. One reason is that the bass needs the freedom to move about to fulfill its harmonic role in the most melodic way. Another is that chords spaced with a wider interval on the bottom tend to sound "cleaner" than those with a smaller interval on the bottom. The lower the pitches involved, the more pronounced the "muddiness" becomes.

As a general rule: When a bass is below c, place the tenor above e.

### EXAMPLE 4-2A recommended

### EXAMPLE 4-2B not recommended

*Note*:

1. In a, spacing is more or less equal among the upper three voices.
2. In b, the spacing is less uniform. In the first three chords, the distance between alto and tenor is greater than an octave. In the first chord, moreover, the small interval between tenor and bass produces a thick sound. In the fourth chord, the distance between alto and soprano is greater than an octave.

## Doubling

When a three-note chord is distributed among four voices, something must be doubled. Composers' preferences have been consistent:

1. Sensitive (tendency) tones (the leading tone, altered tones, and sevenths) are not doubled.
2. In major and minor triads, the bass is usually doubled, although in first inversion a doubled soprano is slightly favored.
3. Diminished (and augmented) triads usually are placed in first inversion with the bass doubled.

These guidelines can be further distilled into this "short rule for doubling": *The bass of a triad can usually be doubled unless it's a sensitive tone.*

Example 4-3 is an arrangement of "Plaisir d'amour" (from Chapter 3), here presented in its adapted American form by numerous popular artists.

**EXAMPLE 4-3** George Weiss, Hugo Peretti, and Luigi Creatore: "Can't Help Falling in Love"

## PART WRITING AND CHORALE ANALYSIS I

*Notes:*

1. Eleven triads are in root position. The bass (root) is doubled in 8 of these.
2. Three triads are in first inversion. In the first (m. 1) the soprano is doubled. In the second (m. 5), a diminished triad, the bass is doubled. In the last (m. 6), the bass is doubled.
3. Two triads are in second inversion (in m. 2 and m. 7). The bass is doubled.
4. Spacing among the upper three voices is fairly uniform throughout, varying with the melodic contours but never exceeding an octave between any two voices.
5. When the bass drops to c or lower, the interval formed by it and the tenor is never smaller than a fifth.
6. A complete dominant seventh chord appears at m. 5, beat 4. The seventh (C), a sensitive tone, is resolved stepwise downward.

---

Melodic considerations occasionally demand different doubling. When doing so, it's usually better to double scale degrees 1, 4, and 5 than degrees 2, 3, and 6. (Degree 7 is too unstable to be doubled in most situations.) At other times it might be desirable to omit a chord member from a triad. The tone most often omitted is the fifth.

In m. 6 of the preceding example, the E minor triad contains a doubled third instead of a doubled bass (the root).

## EXAMPLE 4-4

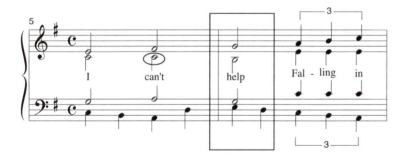

The alto C in m. 5 (circled) becomes the chord seventh on beat 4, a sensitive tone that wants a stepwise downward resolution. The tenor—the only other voice available to double the bass note E in m. 6—would need to leap downward to do it. This would then be followed by another leap. Doubling the third, G, produces a more singable tenor.

## CONNECTING CHORDS

The central mission in part writing is to guide the voices through a harmonic succession by leading them down separate melodic corridors. The corridors tend to be narrow, and they normally neither merge nor cross. Within these confines, each line should be musical and singable and faithful to the melodic tendencies of the pitches while producing harmonies that are spaced and doubled well. Visualize it this way:

### EXAMPLE 4-5

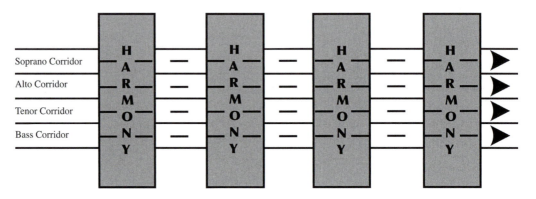

### Consecutive Perfect Fifths and Octaves

In addition, certain principles govern the combined movement of the individual voices. When two voices forming a perfect fifth or a perfect octave (or a perfect unison) move to pitches that form an identical interval, the result—termed consecutive fifths or consecutive octaves—is a practice that was avoided from the fifteenth century onward.*

### EXAMPLE 4-6

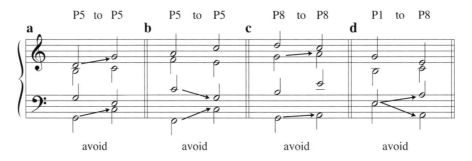

Bach characterized consecutive fifths, octaves, and unisons as the most egregious part-writing error. However, attitudes change with time. Today, even in more traditional settings, we are likely to view the effects of parallels as less adverse than poor doubling, poor spacing, or a poorly contoured line.

---

* Some theorists prefer to use the terms "parallel fifths" and "parallel octaves."

# PART WRITING AND CHORALE ANALYSIS I

## Voice Crossing and Overlap

Voice crossing—a soprano pitch placed lower than the alto pitch, a bass pitch placed higher than the tenor pitch, and so on—and voice overlap—the soprano dipping below an immediately preceding alto pitch, the bass rising above the preceding tenor pitch, and so on—can obscure the melodic action of the individual lines.

### EXAMPLE 4-7

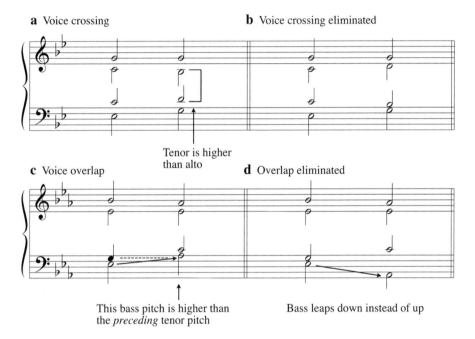

Because their range of motion is restricted at times by the soprano and bass, the alto and tenor are the voices most prone to crossing and overlap. Furthermore, crossing and overlap are less visible in these voices because, in closed-score notation, the alto and tenor occupy separate staves.

Voice crossing and overlap are exceptional practices that are justified for melodic or other reasons. When they occur, their duration is usually brief. Also, the less extreme the crossing or overlap, the less disruptive it is.

### EXAMPLE 4-8 J. S. Bach: "In Dulci Jubilo"

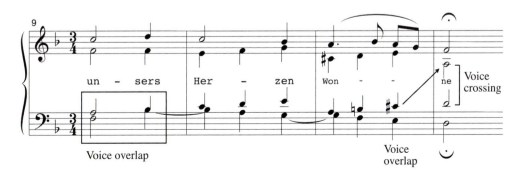

*Notes:*

1. The voice overlap between the tenor and bass in m. 9 could have been avoided by moving the bass down to the lower-octave B♭. But this would have given Bach the unfortunate choice of continuing the ensuing scalar descent into the bass's extreme low register or breaking up the scale by transposing part of it up an octave. Possibly reluctant to do either, he opted for a brief and minimal overlap.

2. The voice overlap and voice crossing in mm. 11–12 permit the tenor to resolve the sensitive tone C♯, and they avoid the "offensive" consecutive octaves that would result if both the alto and bass moved from E in m. 11 to D in m. 12.

## Common Tones

Where common tones are present between two adjacent chords, retaining them in the same voices results in the smoothest voice leading.

### EXAMPLE 4-9

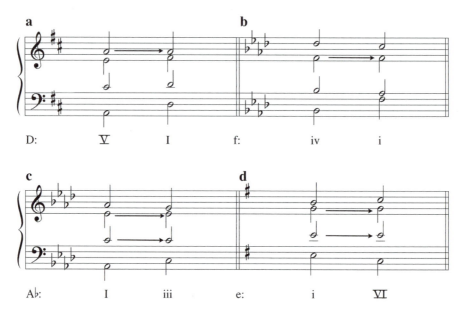

Where no common tones are present between chords, moving the upper voices in contrary motion to the bass minimizes the chances of writing consecutive perfect fifths or octaves.

## EXAMPLE 4-10

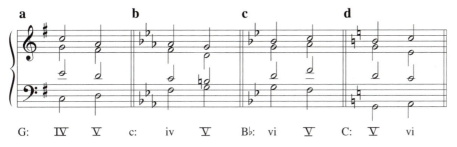

Note:

1. In a, b, and c, the three upper voices move in contrary motion to the bass.
2. In d, the soprano moves parallel to the bass because the melodic force requires that the leading tone resolve to the tonic, producing alternative doubling.

Arrows indicate common tones in Example 4-11.

## EXAMPLE 4-11 John Fawcett and Hans George Naegeli: "Blest be the Tie" 🔊

Note: Where a common tone is present, it has been retained in the same voice in all but one case (m. 11–12), where the composer opted for consecutive unisons between the soprano and alto (m. 12, beats 1–2).

## THE CHORALE

Part writing is most easily observed and practiced through music of limited melodic range that is rhythmically uncomplicated, harmonically compact, and **syllabic**—that is, each syllable of text accorded a pitch of its own—in a word, music that's hymnlike. Fortunately, one of the legacies of J. S. Bach and his contemporaries is a large corpus of harmonized chorales. A chorale is a Lutheran hymn. Chorale melodies were drawn from a number of sources and used for congregational singing in the Protestant worship service during the sixteenth century. Bach and others made four-part arrangements as part of larger sacred compositions called cantatas and Passions.

In their harmonic imagination and in their balance of melodic and harmonic forces, Bach's harmonizations provide a compendium of eighteenth-century harmonic practice. They have remained models of voice leading for succeeding generations of musicians.

## ROOT-POSITION TRIADS

Triads whose roots lie a fifth or fourth apart, as in authentic, plagal, and half cadences, contain a common tone.

### EXAMPLE 4-12

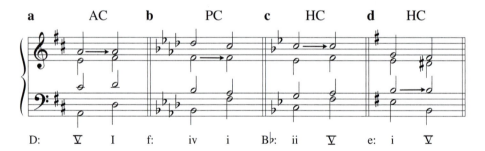

*Notes*:

1. Each root-position chord contains a doubled bass (root).

For melodic or other reasons, the common tone might not be retained. Preferred doubling and spacing is then obtained by moving the upper voices contrary to the bass.

### EXAMPLE 4-13 J. S. Bach: "Herr Christ, der ein'ge Gott's-Sohn"

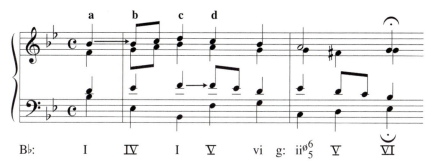

*Notes*:

1. From a to b and from c to d, the common tone between the chords has been retained.
2. From b to c, the common tone has not been retained. (Bach would have had to change the melody to do so.) The upper voices ascend while the bass descends.

---

Chords whose roots are related by the interval of a third or a sixth have two common tones.

### EXAMPLE 4-14

Common tones retained   (minimal feeling of harmonic motion)

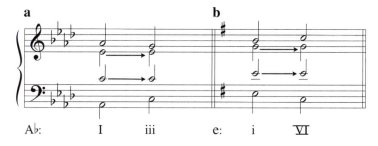

Retaining two common tones minimizes the impact of a chord change. If all four voices move to a new pitch, the soprano usually moves contrary to the bass.

### EXAMPLE 4-15

No common tones retained   (greater feeling of harmonic motion)

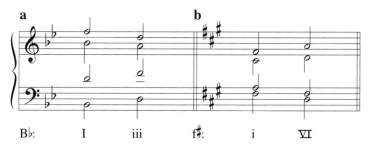

*Note*: Moving all the voices produces leaps in more than one voice at the same time and so should not be overused.

---

Chords with roots a step (or half step) apart, as in the half cadences IV–V or vi–V, have no common tones. In these cases, the three upper voices generally move contrary to the bass.

**EXAMPLE 4-16**

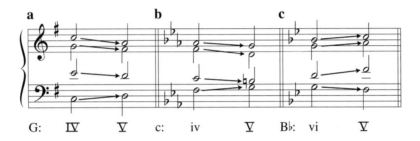

Occasionally, the melody and the bass will move through a second relationship in parallel motion. This situation is especially prone to producing consecutive fifths and/or octaves; you should be diligent about moving the inner voices contrary to the bass.

**EXAMPLE 4-17** J. S. Bach: "Jesu Leiden, Pein und Tod"

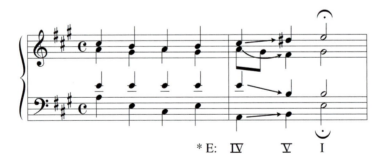

The parallelism between soprano and bass may have been one reason why J. S. Bach more often followed IV with vii°6 than with V.

Root movement by second also occurs in the deceptive cadence. The leading tone in the soprano sounds best when resolved upward to the tonic, but doing so creates parallel motion between the soprano and bass. Typically, then, the inner voices move in the opposite direction.

## EXAMPLE 4-18

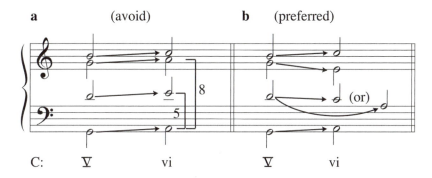

*Notes*:

1. In a, the alto and tenor produce consecutive octaves and fifths against the bass. The consecutive fourths between the alto and tenor are, in themselves, permissible. (Recall that, in two-voice counterpoint, they were considered objectionable.)
2. In b, the tenor has the option of doubling the bass note A (normal doubling) or, as here, doubling the tonic, which is the chord third. This is an acceptable alternative doubling that produces smoother voice leading.

In minor-key deceptive cadences, the leading tone resolves to the tonic even in an inner voice. This is because the leading tone has only two possible ways to go—up to the tonic (preferred) or down to the submediant by way of an augmented second.

## EXAMPLE 4-19

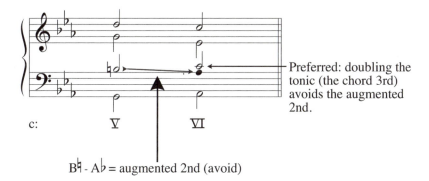

*Note*: Recall that the augmented second was considered an awkward melodic interval. Here, the tenor should ascend to double C—the third of VI. Alternative doubling is preferred to the augmented second.

### FOR PRACTICE

Discuss Bach's part writing of the minor-key deceptive cadence in Example 4-20. Disregard the enclosed chords.

**EXAMPLE 4-20** Bach: "Christ lag in Todesbanden"

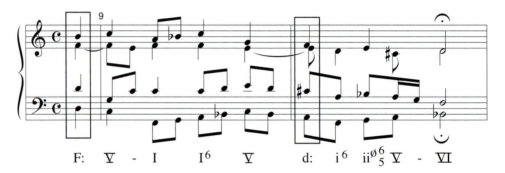

A summary of procedures for connecting root-position triads follows.

## Guidelines for Connecting Root-Position Triads

1. In fifth relationship: Retain the common tone in the same voice; if not retaining the common tone, move the three upper voices contrary to the bass.

2. In third relationship: Retain both common tones, or retain neither while moving the soprano contrary to the bass, taking care to avoid large leaps or voice overlap.

3. In second relationship: Move the soprano and, if possible, the other voices contrary to the bass. But in the deceptive cadence: resolve the leading tone when it appears in the soprano, and in minor keys, resolve the leading tone in all cases.

You can see a theme here: the soprano and bass should move in contrary or oblique motion as often as possible. In fact, a concise guideline for connecting chords begins with the following recommendation.

## The Short Rule of Chord Connection

Move the soprano and bass in contrary or oblique motion, favor steps over leaps, avoid awkward melodic intervals, and retain common tones between chords where possible.

In Example 4-21, numbers on the music correspond to the numbered procedures listed in the foregoing summary.

# PART WRITING AND CHORALE ANALYSIS I

**EXAMPLE 4-21** J. S. Bach: "Ermuntre dich, mein schwacher Geist"

\* This harmony will be studied in Chapter 7

*Notes*:

1. A 4–3 suspension occurs in the soprano in m. 3. Recall from Chapter 3 that a suspension is a temporal displacement of the chord tone to which it resolves (see p. 40). Here, it merely delays by a beat its motion opposing the bass.

2. A triad with tripled root and omitted fifth appears in m. 4. Here Bach yielded to the melodic force rather than the harmonic by resolving the alto's leading tone upward to the tonic G instead of moving it downward to the chord fifth D to obtain a complete triad.

## PART WRITING SUSPENSIONS IN ROOT POSITION

*Note*: You might wish to review the discussion of suspensions in Chapter 3 (pp. 40–43) at this point.

Measure 3 from Example 4-21 is reprinted next. A 4–3 suspension appears in the soprano. The only note that changes from beat 2 to 3 is the suspended tone, which resolves stepwise downward. (The octave leap in the bass doesn't count as a change.) In b the suspension has been removed.

## EXAMPLE 4-22

*Notes*:

1. The two chords are in second relationship. Accordingly, the upper voices move contrary to the bass.
2. Both triads are in root position with the bass doubled.

## Doubling in Suspensions

The doubling in a chord containing a suspension is normally the same as it would be in the absence of the suspension.

Since both the 4–3 and 9–8 suspensions occur over root-position triads, the bass (root) should be doubled. In the 4–3 suspension, the resolution is the chord third. This means that one of the remaining two voices must double the bass, and the other must supply the chord fifth, as in Example 4-22. In the 9–8 suspension, the resolution tone doubles the bass. The remaining voices must supply the third and fifth of the chord.

Example 4-23 shows 9–8 suspensions added to authentic and deceptive cadences.

## EXAMPLE 4-23

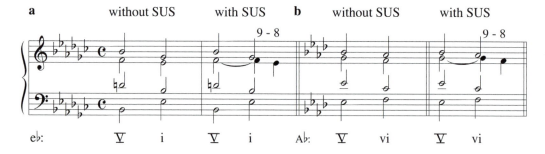

*Note*: The suspensions are shown in the chord symbols themselves. The doubling in the resolution chord, a root-position triad, is the same with or without the suspension.

Most of Bach's chorale harmonizations contain suspensions—one to four on average. Although they can be found in all voices, the alto is the preferred voice, followed by the tenor.

### EXAMPLE 4-24A J. S. Bach: "Jesu, Jesu, du bist mein"

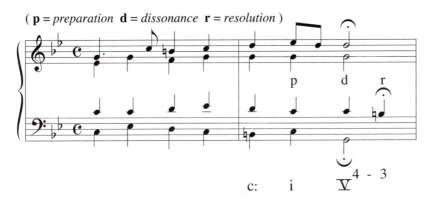

### EXAMPLE 4-24B J. S. Bach: "Du grosser Schmerzensmann"

*Notes:*

1. a contains an anticipation in the soprano (m. 2) in addition to the 4–3 suspension in the tenor.

2. In both a and b, doubling is normal (a doubled bass) at the points where the suspensions resolve.

3. When a 4–3 or 9–8 suspension occurs over two triads whose roots are fifth-related, the common tone can usually be retained in the same voice, as shown in a, where the alto retains its G on beat 3.

---

Both 4–3 and 9–8 suspensions are possible between root-position triads a fifth or a second apart. The most common harmonic settings are:

| 4–3 suspension | | 9–8 suspension | |
|---|---|---|---|
| p | d—r | p | d—r |
| I | V | V | I |
| IV | I | I | IV |
| V | vi | V | vi |
| IV | V | IV | V |

p = preparation   d = suspension dissonance   r = resolution

The 9–8 and 4–3 are the most common suspensions. They are also the only ones that resolve over root-position triads. You can think of the relatively rare 2–3 retardation as an upward-resolving suspension:

### EXAMPLE 4-25

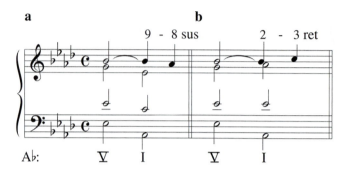

*Note*: The voice leading must change in b in order to preserve a doubled bass when the suspended tone resolves upward to the chord third instead of downward to the chord root.

Because the 7–6 suspension and the 2–3 suspension (not 2–3 retardation) resolve over first-inversion triads, we'll consider them in Chapter 5.

Root-position triads are the foot soldiers of four-part harmony. Central to most cadences, they shoulder the harmonic weight in phrase interiors as well, outnumbering both first-inversion and second-inversion triads. They support 9–8 and 4–3 suspensions.

Much about the treatment of root-position triads applies to triads in inversion as well. This makes the handling of root-position triads arguably the most important part-writing skill.

## SUMMARY OF TERMINOLOGY

- chorale
- consecutive perfect consonances
- contrary motion
- counterpoint
- fifth relationship
- homogeneous spacing
- oblique motion
- parallel motion
- part writing
- second relationship
- similar motion
- voice leading
- voice overlap

# CHAPTER FIVE

# Part Writing and Chorale Analysis II

The idea that a root-position triad and its inversions are one and the same harmony was foreign to composers prior to Bach's time. The figured bass system did not make that connection. Inversion serves many purposes. It varies the sound of the harmonies, it can reduce the finality and weight that root position lends a chord, and it can smooth out the bass line. Music's second most important melody is often the bass. Against the true melody, this line forms a counterpoint that is to some degree melodic and independent, and its impact can be dramatic.

**KEY CONCEPTS IN THIS CHAPTER**

- voicing and connecting first-inversion triads
- part writing the 7–6 and 2–3 suspensions
- voicing and connecting second-inversion triads

## FIRST INVERSION

### Inversion and Bass Line

Composers constantly make choices that favor either the melodic force or the harmonic, and perhaps nowhere do the opposing forces do more frequent battle than in the bass. Play or listen to Example 5-1 **a** and **b**. The melody is the same; the bass line differs. Which version do you prefer? Why?

**EXAMPLE 5-1A** J. S. Bach: "Schmücke dich, o liebe Seele"
(with a hypothetical bass)

**EXAMPLE 5-1B** J. S. Bach: "Schmücke dich, o liebe Seele" (with Bach's bass)

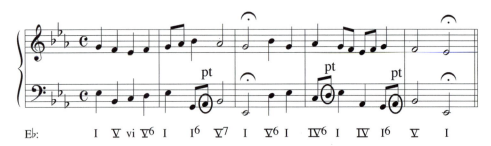

In **b**, the bass is more tuneful. With a better balance between steps and leaps, it sounds less erratic and more directed. Moreover, it's independent of the soprano, with its own rhythms and contour. Wherein lies the improvement? The passing tones in mm. 2 and 4 help, of course. Equally useful, though, is first inversion. In fact, a most important function of first inversion is to *make the bass more melodic*.

## Doubling

Recall from Chapter 4 (p. 48) that the bass is the preferred doubling in root position and second inversion and also is an option in first inversion. Because doubling in first-inversion triads is governed more by melodic factors than by concern for sonority, composers' preferences can be restated this way:

1. Any doubling option except sensitive tones (the leading tone, altered tones, and raised $\hat{6}$ and $\hat{7}$ in minor) may be employed to improve voice leading. (In major and minor triads, this will more often than not be a doubled soprano or bass.)

2. In diminished and augmented (rare) triads, the third—which, in first inversion, is the bass—is doubled.

Study the complete harmonization of the preceding chorale phrases.

**EXAMPLE 5-2** J. S. Bach: "Schmücke dich, o liebe Seele" 🔊

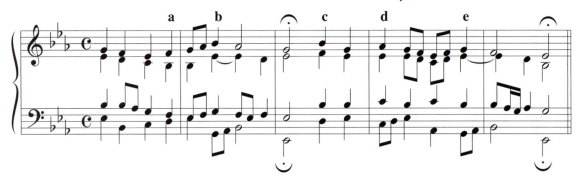

*Note*: First-inversion triads appear at points **a** through **e**. At **a** and **c**, the soprano is doubled by an inner voice. At **b** and **d**, the bass is doubled by an inner voice. At **e**, the soprano *is* the bass (soprano and bass double each other).

## Chord Connection

Little is really new in part writing that involves first-inversion triads beyond the general guidelines given in Chapter 4 (see "Review of Melodic Principles" on p. 46 and "Connecting Chords" on p. 50). Those guidelines may be summarized thus:

1. If common tones are present, retain them in the same voices and move the remaining voices in the most conjunct manner possible. If no common tones, move the soprano and, if possible, the other voices contrary to the bass.

2. Avoid large leaps, voice crossing and voice overlap.

3. Avoid consecutive perfect fifths, octaves, or unisons.

Two more-specific guidelines for first inversion can be added:

4. Step to and/or away from the bass if possible.

5. Leave the *doubled tones* in contrary or oblique motion against the soprano where possible.

The numbers corresponding to these guidelines show where they've been observed in Example 5-3.

### EXAMPLE 5-3 J. S. Bach: "Wo soll ich fliehen hin"

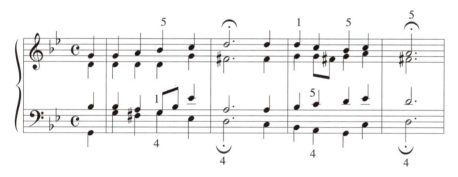

## Harmonic Weight

A second reason for using first inversion is to give less weight and finality to triads in phrase interiors. Play Example 5-1 again. In **a**, each bass note and its implied harmony has about the same "weight." This creates a blockiness absent in **b**, where "lighter" notes seem to push toward the "heavier" ones. The bass in **b** acquires a dimension beyond the melodic and harmonic in that it reflects the relative importance of the melodic tones above it. For example, m. 1, beat 4 contains a weak-beat "passing" F. A V$^6$ lends less harmonic weight to this note than would a root-position V.

## EXAMPLE 5-4

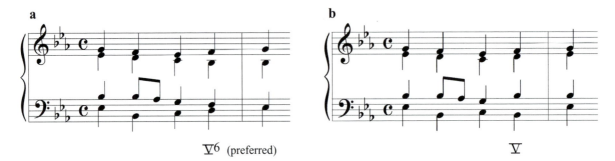

## FOR PRACTICE

In Example 5-5:

1. Identify the first-inversion triads.
2. Which pitch is doubled in each case?
3. In how many is the bass either approached or left by stepwise motion?
4. In how many is the doubled tone left in contrary or oblique motion?

**EXAMPLE 5-5** J. S. Bach: "Herr, wie du willst, so schick's mit mir"

## Suspensions

In Example 5-6, the music has been embellished with suspensions.

**EXAMPLE 5-6** Bernstein: "One Hand, One Heart" (from West Side Story)

The 9–8 should be familiar from Chapter 4 (see p. 60). In m. 69, a 7–6 suspension occurs. The "6" indicates that the resolution occurs over a first-inversion triad. Although first inversion is full of doubling options, *the resolution of a 7–6 suspension is rarely doubled* because much of the "suspense" in a suspension is siphoned off when its resolution is heard prematurely in another voice.

In Example 5-7, the soprano and tenor from Example 5-6 are interchanged.

## EXAMPLE 5-7

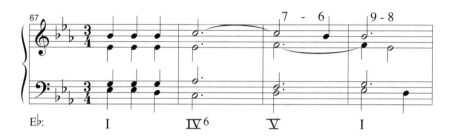

Now the V6 in m. 69 contains a doubled inner voice (F). Normally, the least preferred doubling, it's the *only* choice because the soprano (normally the preferred voice to double) carries the the suspension resolution and the bass D is the leading tone.

Bach and others used the 7–6 suspension most often over a vii°6. When doing so, they usually doubled the *fifth* of the diminished triad, probably for voice-leading reasons. (Recall that, in first inversion, almost any doubling option can be used to improve the voice leading.)

## EXAMPLE 5-8

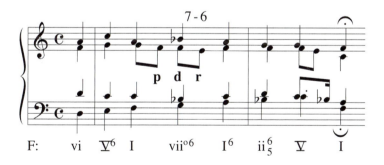

> ### CONCEPT CHECK
> What part-writing problem would be created if the tenor were to double the bass of the diminished triad? Identify the other two suspensions in Example 5-8.

One other suspension resolves over a first-inversion triad—the 2–3, or more properly, 2-$^6_3$. (Again, the "6" is an indication that the chord of resolution is in first inversion.) This **bass suspension** occurs almost exclusively over one progression: I—V⁶.

### EXAMPLE 5-9

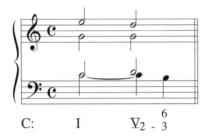

Again, the preferred doubling is the soprano. Doubling the inner voice G is also possible, although in this example it would push the tenor to its extreme high register. Doubling the bass is not recommended, for two very good reasons: it's the suspension resolution and it's the leading tone.

Example 5-10 shows Bach's treatment of the 2–3 suspension.

### EXAMPLE 5-10 J. S. Bach: "Schaut, ihr Sünder"

# PART WRITING AND CHORALE ANALYSIS II

## SECOND INVERSION

### Doubling

The second-inversion triad was historically considered a dissonant sound. Because of this, it appears much less frequently than do root position and first inversion. The common practice is to double the bass. Play Example 5-11 and compare the effect of the two endings, **a** and **b**. Which ending do you prefer? Why?

**EXAMPLE 5-11**

**EXAMPLE 5-11A/B** Beethoven: Seven Variations on "God Save the King" (theme)

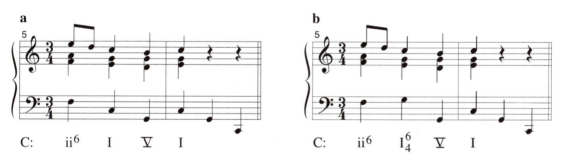

If you prefer **b**, there are good reasons. In **a**, the root-position I in m. 5 follows a ii—a rather uncommon progression. Further, this chord has about the same "weight" as the final tonic in m. 6, diluting the effect of that chord's arrival. The I in **b**, however, is in second (six-four) inversion, and the difference is dramatic. Because second inversion is less stable and "lighter" than root position, the chord no longer robs the final tonic of its impact.

## The Cadential Six-Four Chord

You're likely to hear the I chord in Example 5-11 **b** as a V with two nonchord tones (C and E) *that give it the appearance* of a I until they resolve. Herein lies the harmonic truth about the cadential six-four chord: *It looks like I but sounds and acts like V*. Think of it as V disguised as I.

### EXAMPLE 5-12  The Cadential Six-four Chord

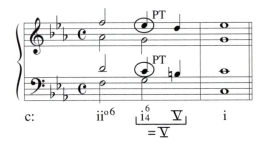

*Notes*:

1. The two passing tones (circled) mask the V by creating a chord that *looks* momentarily like a tonic (the i$^6_4$). Upon their resolution, however, the mask comes off, clearly revealing the V.

2. The bass and the tone doubling it remain stationary through the resolution to become the doubled bass in the root-position V.

---

The cadential six-four chord is the most common second inversion. These are its defining features:

- It usually (not always) occurs at cadences (hence the name).
- It spells like I but sounds like V with nonchord tones a sixth and fourth above the bass.
- It is metrically stronger than its resolution.
- The bass and the voice doubling it remain stationary while the two other voices step down.

Play and study Example 5-13 keeping these characteristics in mind.

### EXAMPLE 5-13 Beethoven: Symphony no. 9 (fourth movement)

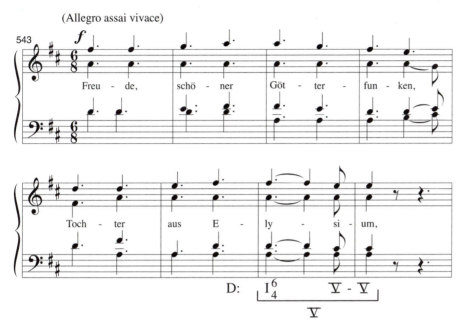

## The Passing Six-Four Chord

The passing six-four chord is usually a V connecting a I and its inversion (I—$V_4^6$—$I^6$ or $I^6$—$V_4^6$—I); occasionally, a passing I connects a IV and its inversion or a $ii_5^6$. It is usually metrically weak. The bass and the voice doubling it resemble passing tones (circled in the following example), giving the chord its name.

### EXAMPLE 5-14 Frederick W. Faber, Henry F. Henry, and J. G. Walton: "Faith of Our Fathers"

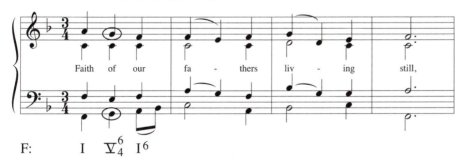

### CONCEPT CHECK

What other six-four chord occurs in Example 5-14?

Bach's chorale harmonizations, a vast repertoire for the study of so many things, do not contain many passing six-four chords. One, a $I_4^6$, is shown in Example 5-15.

### EXAMPLE 5-15  J. S. Bach: "Valet will dir geben"

*Note:* The doubled tones (bass and tenor) resemble passing tones. The chord is metrically weak.

---

Bach's voice-leading and harmonic practice were extraordinarily consistent. Compare the second phrase of Example 5-15 with the fourth phrase of Example 5-10 on p. 68.

Three of the four voices in the passing six-four chord move in a very precise and controlled manner.

## The Passing Six-Four Template

### EXAMPLE 5-16

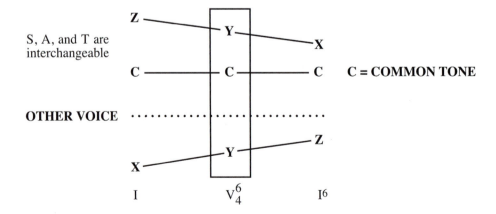

PART WRITING AND CHORALE ANALYSIS II 73

The bass and one upper voice—in this diagram the soprano—are retrogrades of each other, exchanging pitches by passing through the same tone "Y"—the doubled pitch in the passing V. One of the other voices remains stationary on the common tone "C" between the chords. (The harmonic pattern can appear in reverse as well.)

## FOR PRACTICE

In Example 5-17:

1. Identify the just-described voice-leading template in the two passing six-four chords.

2. Identify the other six-four chord in the example.

3. Complete the lead-sheet symbols.

4. Identify all nonchord tones.

**EXAMPLE 5-17** George Elvey: "Come, Ye Thankful People Come"

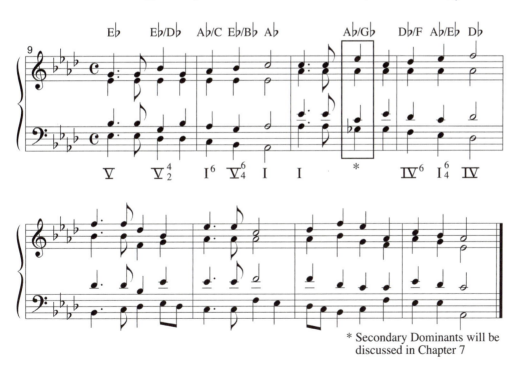

\* Secondary Dominants will be discussed in Chapter 7

## The Pedal Six-Four Chord

Occasionally, a second-inversion triad appears over a repeated or sustained bass. In Example 5-18, UNs create, if only fleetingly, a six-four chord.

**EXAMPLE 5-18** Franz Grüber: "Stille Nacht" ("Silent Night")

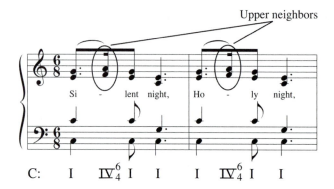

Since the bass and (usually) the doubling tone resemble pedal points, this is called the pedal six-four chord. Typically IV or I, it is usually metrically weak. Because the non-doubling tones (circled) resemble UNs, the chord is also called a "neighboring six-four."

## The Arpeggiated Six-Four Chord

The last standard type is the arpeggiated six-four chord, which results from a bass arpeggiation, usually of the tonic or dominant. It is more often metrically weak than strong.

**EXAMPLE 5-19** Sabine Baring-Gould and Arthur Sullivan: "Onward, Christian Soldiers"

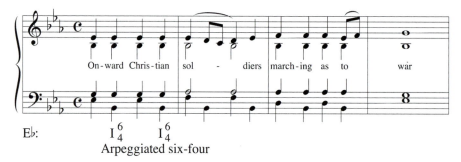

### CONCEPT CHECK

Example 5-20 contains all four types of six-four chord. Identify each and explain its characteristics.

# PART WRITING AND CHORALE ANALYSIS II

**EXAMPLE 5-20** "Michael, Row the Boat Ashore" (spiritual) 🔊

Voice leading involves spacing, doubling, and chord connection. The summary that follows subsumes and distills the guidelines presented earlier and serves well in most part-writing situations.

For triads in all positions:

1. **Spacing**: Keep each voice within its range and in its corridor, maintaining homogenrous spacing among the upper voices. Avoid voice crossing and overlap.

2. **Doubling**: Normally, double the bass (in second inversion *always* double the bass) unless it's a sensitive tone. Double a different chord member (but never a sensitive tone) to improve a melodic line or to satisfy the preceding spacing guideline.

3. **Chord Connection**:

    a.  Move the soprano and bass in contrary or oblique motion as often as possible.

    b.  Favor conjunct motion, avoid awkward melodic intervals, and resolve sensitive tones.

    c.  Where common tones between chords exist, retain them in the same voices.s

    d.  Avoid consecutive octaves, fifths or unisons between any two voices.

Additional guidelines governing triads in second inversion:

1. In the cadential and pedal six-four chords, the bass and the tone doubling it remain stationary.

2. In the passing six-four chord, the bass and the tone doubling it resemble passing tones moving in opposite directions.

3. In the arpeggiated six-four, the bass leaps to the fifth from another member of the same chord.

Each of the standard six-four chords is defined by: 1) its function in the key; 2) its metric position; 3) its bass motion.

**EXAMPLE 5-21**

| Type | Chord | Metric Position | Bass Motion | Example in C |
|---|---|---|---|---|
| Cadential | I | Strong | S - R | $^6_4$ $^5_3$ |
| Passing | V (or I) | Weak | S - S | $^6_4$  6 |
| Pedal | IV (or I) | Usually weak | R - R | $^6_4$ |
| Arpeggiated | I (or V) | Usually weak | L - L | $^6_4$ |
| S = Step; | | L = Leap; | R = Repeated | |

# CHAPTER SIX

# Part Writing and Chorale Analysis III

In Chapter One, we discussed seventh chords—their structure, classification, inversions, figured-bass and chord symbols. We'll now consider voice leading. The short rule for the voice carrying the seventh of a chord is:

- *Don't double the seventh, but do resolve it.*
- *The resolution should be stepwise downward.*

Though not without exception, this principle governs almost everything about the classical behavior of seventh chords, and it covers most part-writing situations. It also applies in a general way to jazz and popular music, although the seventh has more autonomy in these styles, at times resolving upward and sometimes not resolving at all. The remaining voices in seventh chords usually move to the nearest chord tone consistent with normal doubling.

### KEY CONCEPTS IN THIS CHAPTER

- part writing the dominant seventh chord
- nonstandard treatment of the leading tone and seventh
- part writing the diminished and half-diminished sevenths
- part writing nondominant seventh chords
- seventh chords and suspensions

## DOMINANT-FUNCTIONING SEVENTH CHORDS

The dominant seventh ($V^7$) and leading-tone seventh chords ($vii^{ø7}$ or $vii^{o7}$) possess a more urgent need to resolve than do all others because they contain *both* $\hat{7}$ and $\hat{4}$. The tritone formed by these highly charged pitches cries out for resolution, and the only chords that can provide it are I (i) and vi (VI). In Example 6-1, broken lines show the resolution of the tritone.

## EXAMPLE 6-1

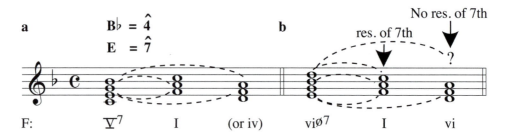

*Note*: $\hat{7}$ and $\hat{4}$ can resolve into *either* the I or the vi. However, the vi provides no stepwise resolution for the seventh of the leading-tone seventh chord (see **b**). Perhaps because of this, leading-tone seventh chords do not often progress to vi (VI in minor).

## The $V^7$

The $V^7$ has the same structure—a Mm7—in both major and minor keys. Despite its occurrence on only one scale degree—hence its name "dominant seventh"—it is the most common seventh chord, occurring freely in all inversions. Example 6-2 shows the usual voice leading *regardless of inversion*.

## EXAMPLE 6-2

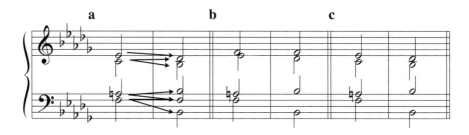

*Notes:*

1. The seventh always steps down. The other chord members have options (shown by the lines in **a**), depending on inversion, voicing, and whether the composer or arranger elects to obey the melodic or harmonic force. For example, the leading tone (A in the example) almost always resolves to the tonic when in an outer voice. When in the alto or tenor, as in **a**, it may move to the fifth of the tonic to form a complete chord.*

2. With both chords in root position, resolving $\hat{7}$ and $\hat{4}$ necessitates omitting the fifth in *either* the $V^7$, as in **b**, or the I, as in **c**. In both cases, the chord root replaces the fifth.

---

* The leading tone can be left unresolved only if in an inner voice.

The seventh can resemble any nonchord tone *that resolves stepwise downward*; those NCTs that are approached by step are the most common, particularly the PT and SUS. Whether to analyze a seventh as a chord member or a nonchord tone depends in part on its length. A generally reliable guideline is:

*A seventh as long as the chord*
*Usually belongs to the chord.*

Compare the voice leading in Example 6-2 with that in the following phrases.

### EXAMPLE 6-3A  J. S. Bach: "Vor deinen Thron tret' ich hiermit"

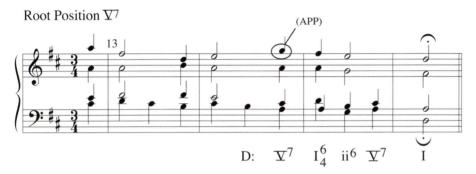

*Notes:*

1. The fifth in the first $V^7$ is replaced by a doubled root. The second $V^7$ is complete. To resolve it to a complete I, Bach chose to leave the tenor's leading tone C♯ (m. 15) unresolved.
2. The seventh of the $V^7$ in m. 14 resembles an appoggiatura.
3. To understand the voice crossing in m. 15, let's try to step into Bach's mind. Placing the bass D an octave lower would eliminate the voice crossing but change the $I_4^6$ into a root-position chord, duplicating the bass's cadence pitch and thereby sapping its weight and sense of finality. On the other hand, interchanging the bass and tenor pitches (tenor = D, bass = A) would create consecutive octaves (A–G) between the alto and bass while destroying the scalar tenor line A–B–C♯ in m. 15.

### EXAMPLE 6-3B  J. S. Bach: "Christ lag in Todesbanden"

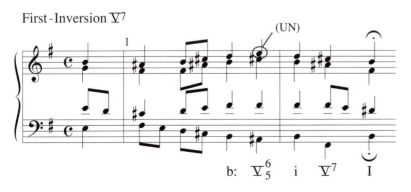

*Notes*:

1. The $V^6_5$, with less harmonic weight than the $V^7$, is consistent with the auxiliary nature of the upper-neighbor melody note E.

2. In resolving the root-position $V^7$ in m. 2, Bach again chose not to resolve the inner-voice leading tone in order to obtain a complete I.

3. In Baroque music, it was common to end a minor-key composition, and sometimes phrases within that work, with a major tonic triad. It's raised third has been dubbed the "Picardy third," probably derived from the Old French *picart*, which means "sharp" or "pointed."

### EXAMPLE 6-3C  J. S. Bach: "Gott lebet noch"

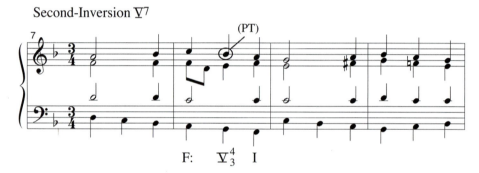

*Note*: The $V^4_3$ in m. 8 is similar to the passing $V^6_4$ in that both harmonize a melodic passing tone.

### EXAMPLE 6-3D  J. S. Bach: "Wach' auf, mein Herz"

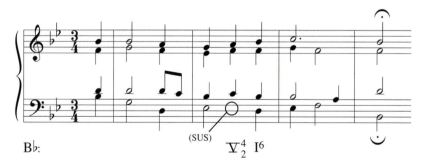

### FOR PRACTICE

In Example 6-3**b** and **c**, dominant seventh chords can be found in third inversion. Locate them and compare their resolutions.

## The Unresolved Leading Tone

As we've seen, an inner-voice leading tone is sometimes denied resolution to obtain normal doubling in the chord that follows. Example 6-4 shows this in a deceptive cadence. Both resolutions are acceptable, **a** favoring the melodic force, **b** the harmonic.

**EXAMPLE 6-4A/B** favors melodic force (A) / favors harmonic force (B)

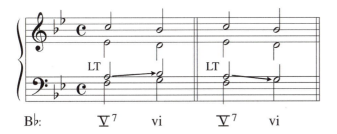

*Note*: In **a**, resolving the leading tone to the tonic creates a doubled third in the vi. In **b**, the leading tone instead descends to double the bass (G).

---

## The Unresolved Seventh

In the melodic pattern $\hat{3}$–$\hat{4}$–$\hat{5}$, scale degree 4 is often harmonized with a $V_3^4$. This is one of the few situations where the seventh routinely moves upward.

**EXAMPLE 6-5** "Prayer of Thanksgiving" (traditional Dutch air)

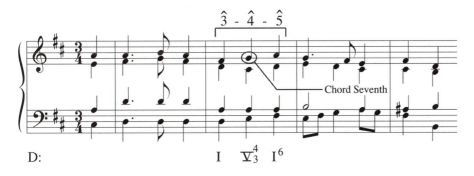

## Delayed Resolution

The resolution of the seventh is sometimes delayed or omitted entirely.

**EXAMPLE 6-6** Beethoven: Piano Sonata op. 10, no. 1 (third movement)

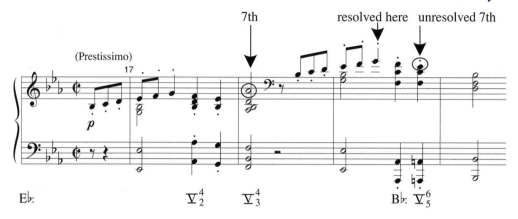

## The Leading Tone Seventh Chord

Like the dominant seventh chord, the leading-tone seventh chord appears in all inversions. As in the dominant seventh chord, the leading tone resolves up, the seventh resolves down, and the other voices move stepwise. This might or might not produce normal doubling in the tonic.

But where the dominant seventh chord has only one structure, the leading-tone seventh chord takes two forms—half-diminished in major (viiø7) and fully diminished in minor (vii°7). (You'll find the vii°7 in major keys as well. This is discussed in Chapter 8.)

**EXAMPLE 6-7** (Broken lines show resolution of leading tone and seventh)

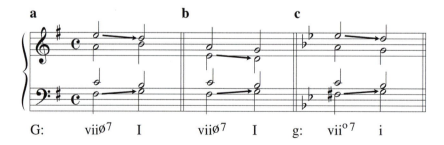

*Note*:

1. In **a,** the alto A moves upward to double the third of the tonic—B—rather than downward to double the bass, in order to avoid consecutive perfect fifths with the soprano.

2. In **b**, the soprano and alto have been interchanged so that the interval between them is a perfect *fourth*. Because consecutive fourths do not carry the same historical restriction as fifths (except in two-voice counterpoint), the A (in the soprano) resolves downward to double the bass.
3. Although the voicing of the vii°7 in **c** is identical to **a**, the alto is free to move downward to double the bass in the tonic, because the fifth formed by it and the soprano is diminished rather than perfect. Even so, it may still move upward. Notice that the vii°7 contains not one but *two* tritones. A common procedure is to resolve them both so that all voices move stepwise.

## EXAMPLE 6-8

### FOR PRACTICE

Discuss the resolution of the vii°7 in the following example. Explain the alteration to the final chord.

## EXAMPLE 6-9  J. S. Bach: "Das neugeborne Kindelein" 🔊

## NON-DOMINANT SEVENTH CHORDS

Every non-dominant seventh chord has a major-key and minor-key form. Refer to Example 1-14 in Chapter One. The "short rule of the seventh" given at the beginning of this chapter applies to them all. The following are additional points:

1. *Function:* With few exceptions, seventh chords function identically to their triadic counterparts.

2. *Resolution:* The seventh may resemble any downward-resolving nonchord tone (passing tones are the most common).

3. *Frequency:* The further removed a seventh chord is from the tonic (via the circle of fifths), the less often it appears.

4. *Inversion:* The ii$^7$ (ii$^{ø7}$) is the only non-dominant seventh chord to appear more often in inversion than in root position.

5. *Third inversion:* The seventh in the bass is often part of a descending scale.

6. *Incomplete seventh chords:* Most inverted seventh chords are complete. For voice-leading reasons, the fifth of a root-position seventh chord is often omitted and the root or third doubled.

7. *Altered forms:* Applying the melodic minor principle (involving scale degrees 6 and 7) sometimes alters a seventh chord's quality.

These points are illustrated in the examples that follow.

### EXAMPLE 6-10 (Points 1, 2, and 5) Martin Corrigan: "Cockles and Mussels"

*Note*: Every one of the seventh chords plays a role in creating the completely stepwise bass line. The I$^4_2$ and vi$^4_2$ are merely by-products of descending passing tones in the bass.

### EXAMPLE 6-11 (Points 1, 2, 4, and 6) J. S. Bach: "O Ewigkeit, du Donnerwort"

*Note*: In m. 2, the passing tone A in the alto (beat 1) creates a fleeting IV$^7$. Because the seventh is short and unaccented, it might be regarded as a passing tone rather than a full-fledged member of the chord.

Incomplete seventh chords appear in mm. 3 and 4 of Example 6-11. In each case, the chord fifth has been omitted and the third has been doubled. Let's see what happens if we add the fifth to each chord, making all three complete.

As Example 6-12 shows, the price to be paid for complete seventh chords in succession is consecutive fifths, a cost considered to be too high by Bach, and by Henry Purcell as well. Notice how Purcell omitted the fifth in the harpsichord part in the following chain of seventh chords.

### EXAMPLE 6-12

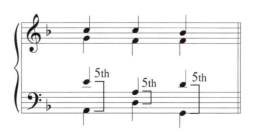

## EXAMPLE 6-13 Purcell: *Ode for St. Cecilia's Day*

### Seventh Chords and Chain Suspensions

Seventh chords can succeed each other in chain suspensions. This is especially common in circular-fifth patterns. The chords are often incomplete, with chord fifths missing. Example 6-14 shows the essential voice leading.

## EXAMPLE 6-14

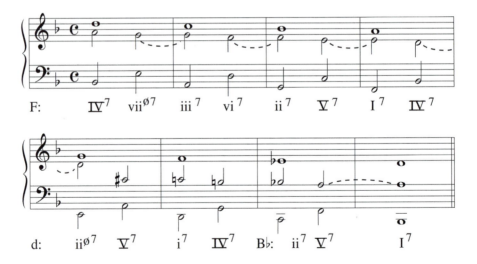

Example 6-15 shows the same circular-fifth pattern and the suspensions generated. Note the missing chord fifths.

### EXAMPLE 6-15 Mozart: Rondo, K. 494

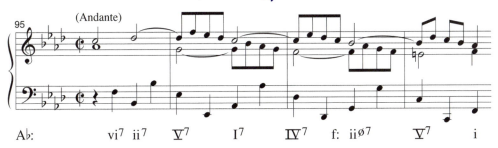

Example 6-16 shows the Mozart Rondo above in a four-voice style: **a** shows how adding the fifth to complete each seventh chord produces a string of consecutive perfect fifths; **b** shows a solution to the problem. The solution differs from Mozart's, whose answer was to write the passage for three voices only, omitting the fifth from each seventh chord.

### EXAMPLE 6-16A

### EXAMPLE 6-16B

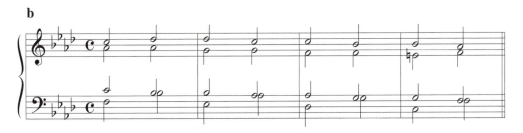

### The I⁷

Even though the rising stature of the seventh prompted composers of Mozart's time to adorn their harmonies with it ever more liberally, the one chord likely to remain dissonance-free was the tonic. In jazz and popular circles, however, the tonic is every bit as likely to include an unresolved seventh as is any other chord.

In Examples 6–17 **a** and **b**, the seventh in the tonic chord appears as a prominent melody note, clearly showing its complete acceptance as a chord tone not requiring resolution.

**EXAMPLE 6-17A** Delange, Mills, and Ellington: "Solitude" 🔊

**EXAMPLE 6-17B** Miles Davis: "Four"

*Note*: In **a**, the seventh moves upward to C. In **b**, it moves downward to D♭. In both examples, it lasts longer than a measure and is the most important melodic pitch for the duration of the tonic harmony.

---

The Voice Leading Summary from Chapter 5 is reprinted below with additions that address the practices presented in this chapter.

## For triads in all positions

1. **Spacing**: Keep each voice within its range and in its corridor, maintaining homogeneous spacing among the upper voices. Avoid voice crossing and overlap.
2. **Doubling**: Normally, double the bass (in second inversion always double the bass) unless it's a sensitive tone. Double a different chord member (but never a sensitive tone) to improve a melodic line or to satisfy the preceding spacing guideline.
3. **Chord Connection**:
   a. Move the soprano and bass in contrary or oblique motion as often as possible.
   b. Favor conjunct motion, avoid awkward melodic intervals, and resolve sensitive tones.
   c. Where common tones between chords exist, retain them in the same voices.
   d. Avoid consecutive octaves, fifths or unisons between any two voices.

## For triads in second inversion

1. In the cadential and pedal six-four chords, the bass and the tone doubling it remain stationary.
2. In the passing six-four chord, the bass and the tone doubling it resemble passing tones moving in opposite directions.
3. In the arpeggiated six-four, the bass leaps to the fifth from another member of the same chord.

## Seventh chords and suspensions

1. Don't double the seventh but do resolve it stepwise downward.
2. Omit the chord fifth when a part-writing situation requires an incomplete seventh chord.
3. Don't double a suspension dissonance. Because a suspension merely delays the resolution of a chord member, doubling in a suspension resolution should be the same as it would be in the absence of the suspension. Except for the 9–8 suspension, the note of resolution should not be present in the preceding chord.

Effective part writing requires effective melody writing for each voice. However, effective melody writing requires a sensitivity to the tendencies of the individual pitches. But the tendencies of the individual pitches depend on their harmonic context. And the harmonic context is the result of the individual lines. The circle is complete. Just as a key is a chord's context, *a chord is a pitch's context*. In the key of E♭, for example, "D" drips with tendency as the third of the $V^7$. Its tendency evaporates a bit as the fifth of the $iii^7$. Likewise, A♭ has less stability as the seventh in the $V^7$ than as the root of the IV.

In any harmony containing *both* $\hat{7}$ and $\hat{4}$, it is rarely wrong to resolve this tritone; and with seventh chords, you can rarely go astray by resolving the seventh stepwise downward. Still, a melodic tendency can be denied for the sake of obtaining a complete harmony, and an incomplete triad or seventh chord can be the acceptable result of satisfying a melodic tendency. Melodic and harmonic forces should constantly be weighed, and the balance changes with each piece.

## SUMMARY OF TERMINOLOGY

- chain suspension
- delayed resolution
- non-dominant seventh chord
- Picardy third

# Chromatic Harmony

PART TWO

| 7 | Secondary Function | 93 |
| 8 | Modulation I | 107 |
| 9 | Mixing Modes | 121 |
| 10 | Altered Pre-dominants and Dominants | 137 |
| 11 | Modulation II | 155 |
| 12 | Harmonic Extensions and Chromatic Techniques | 175 |

# CHAPTER SEVEN

# Secondary Function

Few works—especially works of appreciable length—consist solely of diatonic chords. Part Two examines ways of extending the harmonic gamut. This chapter focuses on **tonicization**—briefly endowing a chord *other than the tonic* with the aura and weight of a tonic by preceding it with a chord that functions as its V, V$^7$, vii°, or vii°$^7$ (vii⌀$^7$).

## SECONDARY DOMINANTS

In Example 7-1, the B♭ major triad in m. 2 is not diatonic. It *could* be symbolized II, the upper case indicating its quality—major. It and the chord that follows *could* be analyzed V–I if the key were E♭ major. But the key is A♭, and the two chords form a dominant-tonic relationship that is secondary to that key. For this reason, the B♭ major triad is called a **secondary dominant,** and its symbol V/V (which we read "V *of* V") reflects this (Analysis 3).

### KEY CONCEPTS IN THIS CHAPTER

- tonicization by the dominant and dominant seventh chord
- secondary leading tones and tonicizing tritones
- melodic chromaticism and harmonic sequence
- tonicization by leading-tone triads and seventh chords
- secondary function in melody harmonization

## EXAMPLE 7-1 Sir Harold Bolton: "All Through the Night"

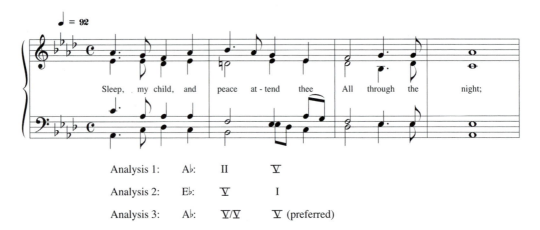

## Tonicization

The B♭ major triad **tonicizes** the E♭ major triad that follows it, causing it to sound—*for a fleeting moment*—like the tonic. In the symbol V/V, the Roman numeral left of the slash shows the function of the chord being analyzed *in relation to its chord of resolution*, which is shown to the right of the slash.

### EXAMPLE 7-2

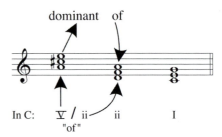

The song that follows is also in the key of A♭. The enclosed triad *could* be symbolized III (upper case because it's major). But it and the following chord (C-Fm) sound like V–I in F minor, a tonicization of vi, and the best way to express this is with the symbol V/vi.

## EXAMPLE 7-3 Elvey and Alford: "Come, Ye thankful People Come"

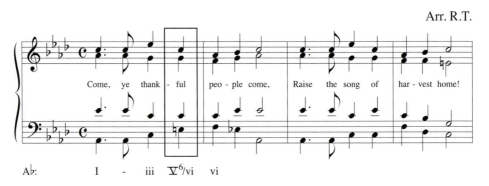

Any major or minor triad in a key can be tonicized by preceding it with a *major triad whose root lies a perfect fifth above*. The third of this secondary dominant acts as a **secondary leading tone**. In Example 7-4, asterisks mark the most common secondary dominants.

### EXAMPLE 7-4A  The second chord of each measure is a dominant of the following chord

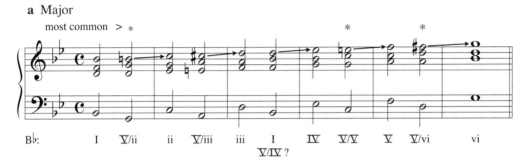

### EXAMPLE 7-4B

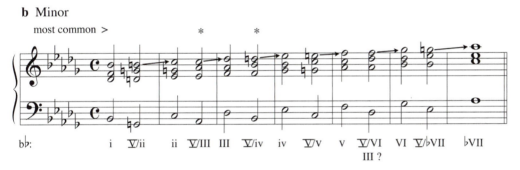

*Notes*:

1. A secondary dominant is always *a major triad* whose root is a *perfect fifth above* that of the chord it tonicizes. All secondary dominants except V/IV in major, and the V/III and V/VI in minor contain a chromatic pitch. They become major through a chromatically raised third, the secondary leading tone.

2. Diminished triads such as viio or the iio cannot be tonicized unless altered to become major or minor triads.

3. In **a**, it would be technically possible to call the I in m. 3 a V/IV; in **b**, it would be technically possible to call the VII in m. 2 a V/III and the III in m. 5 a V/VI; however, a chord really requires a chromatic note to be heard as a secondary dominant.

4. Three secondary dominants in minor (V/ii, V/iv, and V/v) are identical to their counterparts in major. The other three (V/III, V/VI, and V/♭VII) are different because they tonicize chords whose roots are a half-step lower than in major.

5. Although the V/v in minor is rare, the V/V (tonicizing the *major* dominant) is quite common.

## The Tonicizing Tritone

A major or minor triad alone offers no clue to tonality. However, the Mm7 chord, because it appears on only one scale degree, *always* suggests a tonic—the note a perfect fifth lower, and it is the way the chord has been used for centuries. The reason lies with scale degrees 4 ("fa") and 7 ("ti"). Sounded together, this "tonicizing tritone" tends toward the root and third of a tonic triad.

### EXAMPLE 7-5

When any seventh chord is altered to become a Mm7, Western ears hear "dominant seventh chord," and the triad a *perfect fifth* lower sounds fleetingly like its tonic.

When a Mm7 chord appears on a scale degree *other than* $\hat{5}$, it can be analyzed as a **secondary dominant seventh chord**. The chords in Example 7-6 could be symbolized V$^7$/G, V$^7$/B♭, V$^7$/A♭, and so on (read V$^7$ *of* G, V$^7$ *of* B♭, and V$^7$ *of* A♭).

### EXAMPLE 7-6

The D7 in Example 7-6 can *never* be a V$^7$ of anything but G. If this D$^7$ chord appeared in C major, it would be symbolized **V$^7$/V** (G being V in C). If instead the key were D minor, it would be symbolized V$^7$/iv (g being iv in that key). In E♭ it would be symbolized V$^7$/iii (g being iii in that key), and so on.

In Example 7-7, tonicizations of IV (m. 1) and V (m. 3) occur before the tonic itself (C) is heard. Even without hearing the tonic, we know by m. 4 what it is and anticipate hearing it.

**EXAMPLE 7-7** Beethoven: Symphony no. 1, op. 21 (first movement)

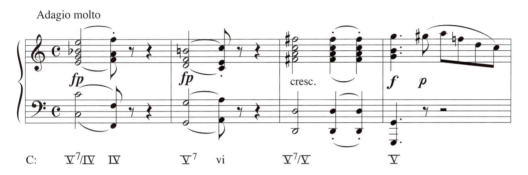

> **FOR PRACTICE**
>
> Identify the tonicizing tritone in each of the chords of Example 7-7. How do these pitches resolve?

Since the Mm7 chord more forcefully suggests a tonic than a major triad ever can, $V^7/x$ is more common than V/x. Any of the secondary dominants in Example 7-4 can become a $V^7/x$ simply by adding a minor seventh above the chord root.

**EXAMPLE 7-8** Brackets show resolution of secondary leading tone
Arrows connect chord sevenths with their resolutions (blackened notes)

## SECONDARY LEADING-TONE CHORDS

Example 7-9 begins with a tonicization of V (V$^7$/V) in m. 10 followed by a harmonic and melodic sequence a step lower. In m. 12, a diminished triad that is not diatonic in D appears. This chord is a **secondary leading tone triad**, functioning momentarily as a vii° in the key of the cadence chord, A. It is symbolized vii°/V because A (the tonicized chord) is V in the home key.

**EXAMPLE 7-9** Mozart: Piano Sonata K. 284 (third movement)

The passage in Example 7-10 is in A major. Three chords are not diatonic. The B major triad of m. 2 is a V/V. The other two chords are **secondary leading-tone chords** that function momentarily as vii°$^7$ with respect to the chords they tonicize (iii and vi).

**EXAMPLE 7-10** Schumann: Kinderszenen no. 6 ("An Important Event")

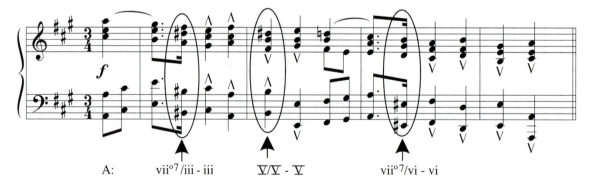

The leading-tone triad and leading-tone seventh chords contain the tonicizing tritone, just as does the V$^7$. And like the V$^7$/x, secondary leading-tone chords (vii°/x, vii°$^7$/x, and vii⌀$^7$/x) can be used to tonicize any major or minor triad. The root is always *a minor second below* the chord tonicized. (As the temporary leading tone to the tonicized chord, it *must* be.)

### EXAMPLE 7-11  Arrows show resolution of tonicizing tritone

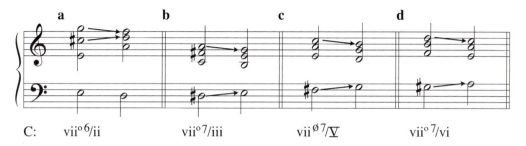

C:   vii°6/ii       vii°7/iii       viiø7/V       vii°7/vi

*Notes*:

1. The chord *must* take one of three forms: a diminished triad vii°/x, shown in **a**, a diminished seventh chord vii°7/x, shown in **b** and **d**, or a half-diminished seventh chord viiø7/x, shown in **c**.

2. The vii°/x (**a**) is in first inversion. Secondary diminished triads, like their diatonic counterparts, are commonly in this inversion.

---

The fully diminished seventh chord is the most common type of secondary leading-tone chord. *Always* the choice when tonicizing a minor triad, it's frequently used to tonicize a major triad as well.

### EXAMPLE 7-12

**a** Half-diminished:  (less common)     **b** Fully diminished: (more common)

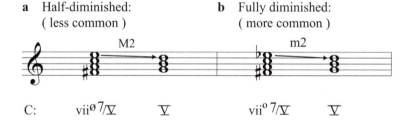

C:   viiø7/V    V       vii°7/V    V

### FOR PRACTICE

Play Example 7-13 (see overleaf). What pitch change in mm. 37 and 39 would turn the diminished seventh chords into half-diminished sevenths? Make those changes and play the passage again. Either chord (°7 or ø7) works. Which do you prefer? Why? What other secondary functions are present in the passage? What chord most likely follows m. 40? Why?

**EXAMPLE 7-13** Beethoven: String Quartet op. 18, no. 1 (third movement)

*Notes:*

1. Double suspensions are present in the first and second violin parts at the resolution of both secondary diminished seventh chords (in m. 38 and in m. 40).

2. In mm. 39–40, the vii°7/vi resolves to a chord that is itself altered—the suspension resolution F♯ turns vi major (VI).

## VOICE LEADING

- The same voice-leading practices that relate to the V, V7, vii°, vii°7, and viiø7 apply to their secondary counterparts, regardless of style or medium.

- Secondary functions behave as though they are in the key of the tonicized chord.

What these two statements mean is this:

1. The secondary leading tone is not doubled, but *is resolved,* especially when in an outer voice.

2. The seventh, if present, resolves stepwise downward.

3. The other altered tones are not doubled, and if possible, they resolve *in the direction of their inflection (up when raised, down when lowered).*

4. If it's impossible to resolve *all* tendency tones without creating doubling or voice-leading problems, *part writing should proceed as though the music were in the key of the tonicized chord.*

Example 7-14 shows these practices applied to common secondary functions in a variety of keys.

### EXAMPLE 7-14A  J. S. Bach: "Ach wie nichtig, ach wie flüchtig"

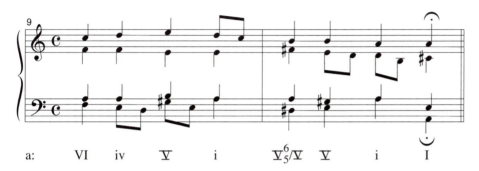

*Note*: In m. 10, the seventh of the chord (A) resolves downward to the leading tone G♯. This creates an apparent problem. The other altered tone, F♯, cannot resolve *upward* (as chromatically raised pitches normally do) without doubling the leading tone. But remember: *Secondary functions behave as if they are in the key of the tonicized chord*. In that key (E), F♯ is not an altered tone at all and so does not need to resolve upward. The problem is only an "apparent" one.

### EXAMPLE 7-14B  J. S. Bach: "Nun lob', mein' Seel', den Herren"

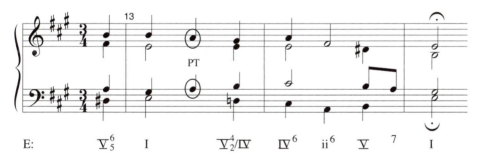

*Note*: In the V⁷/IV, the secondary leading tone is not a chromatically altered pitch. It (G♯) is resolved upward and the chord seventh (D) in the bass is resolved downward.

**EXAMPLE 7-14C** J. S. Bach: "Was frag' ich nach der Welt"

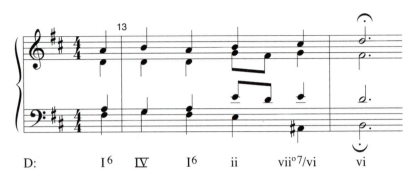

*Note*: The secondary leading tone (A♯) resolves upward, and the chord seventh (G) resolves downward. *Both* tritones in the secondary vii°7 are resolved, just as they often are in the primary vii°7.

---

**EXAMPLE 7-14D** J. S. Bach: "Herr Christ, der ein'ge Gott's sohn"

*Notes*:

1. In both the vii°7/ii and vii°7/iii, the secondary leading tone resolves upward (even though it necessitates voice crossing in m. 8). In both chords, the seventh resolves downward.

2. The V7/vi in m. 8 resolves deceptively to IV. If the key were D minor, Roman-numeral analysis would show this to be a typical deceptive cadence: V7–VI.

SECONDARY FUNCTION    103

## Secondary Function and Chromatic Lines

Secondary functions create signature linear patterns. One is a chromatic rising line formed in the bass or other voice by the secondary leading tone and the following chord's root.

### EXAMPLE 7-15  Schubert: Impromptu op. 142, no. 3

*Note*: The E natural in m. 4 (circled) is a secondary leading tone that enhances the push toward V.

Extended chromatic lines can be created by stringing together a series of secondary functions. Ascending lines are more common than descending, probably because they are generated by the normal upward resolution of the secondary leading tone, as in Example 7-16.

### EXAMPLE 7-16  Ascending chromatic bass line

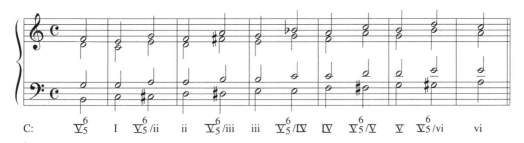

Descending chromatic lines result from **elided resolution** of the secondary leading tones, one of the few situations in which sensitive tones in an outer voice are denied their normal resolution.

## EXAMPLE 7-17 Descending chromatic soprano and bass lines

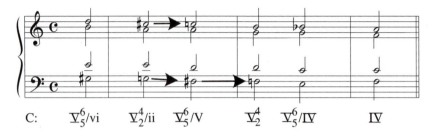

Notes:

1. The secondary leading tone in each secondary $V^7$ (except the last) omits (elides) its normal upward resolution, instead moving chromatically *downward* (shown by arrows) to become the seventh of the next chord.
2. Each seventh resolves *downward* (its normal resolution).
3. Each tonicized chord is inverted and altered to become a *new* secondary $V^7$, so that a chain of secondary dominant seventh chords tracing the circle of fifths results.

## Harmonic Sequence and Secondary Function

Secondary dominants play prominent roles in **harmonic sequences**—chord patterns that are repeated at different pitch levels.

## EXAMPLE 7-18 Friedrich Kuhlau: Sonatina op. 55, no. 5 (first movement)

*Note*: The harmonic sequence a step lower results in a descending scalar bass line.

When secondary dominants are involved in harmonic sequences, chromatic lines are often the result. In Example 7-19a, a chromatic step progression (B–C–C♯–D) results in the highest voice. In **b**, the chromatic line is in the bass.

**EXAMPLE 7-19A** J. S. Bach: Prelude no. 11 from *The Well Tempered Clavier*, Book I 🔊

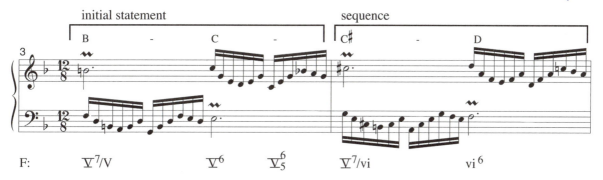

**EXAMPLE 7-19B** Handel: *Concerto Grosso* op. 6, no. 1 (Allegro)* 🔊

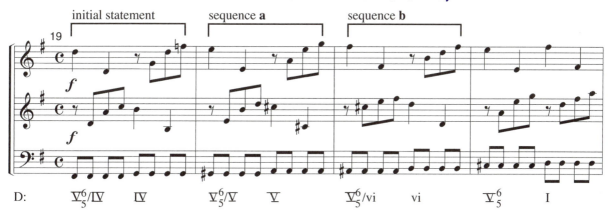

### FOR PRACTICE

Can you find the chord pattern of Example 7-19**b** in either of the patterns of Examples 7–16 and 7–17? Compare Roman numerals, not the chords themselves, as Handel's passage is in a different key.

---

* Some rhythmic elements have been omitted from this reduction to render it more easily playable. All melodic and harmonic elements are present.

Three key points to remember:

- A secondary dominant or dominant seventh is always situated a perfect fifth above (or perfect fourth below) the chord it tonicizes and is always a major triad or Mm seventh chord. **If both conditions are not present, the chord is not a secondary function.**

- A secondary leading-tone chord always has its root a minor second below the chord it tonicizes and is either a diminished triad or a diminished (or half-diminished) seventh chord. **If both conditions are not present, the chord is not a secondary function.**

- Four of the five secondary functions—V$^7$/x, vii°/x, vii°$^7$/x, and vii⌀$^7$/x—contain a "tonicizing tritone," $\hat{4}$ and $\hat{7}$ in the key of the tonicized chord. *All* contain $\hat{7}$, which is chromatically raised as the secondary leading tone. $\hat{4}$, if altered, will be chromatically lowered. These tones are "sensitive," and they demand resolution.

## SUMMARY OF TERMINOLOGY

- elided resolution
- harmonic sequence
- secondary dominant
- secondary leading tone
- tonicization

# CHAPTER EIGHT

# Modulation I

Modulation is the process of changing tonal centers. It is, along with secondary function, an important source of harmonic variety in music. While it's true that many folk songs, hymns, and traditional songs contain no modulations, even short pieces often modulate. *All* modulations, however simple or complex, fall into one of two categories: those *with* a common chord and those *without* one.

## MODULATION BY COMMON CHORD

A **common chord modulation** (also called a **pivot chord modulation**) involves a chord diatonic in both keys. If modulation is a door to a new tonality, the common chord is the "hinge." It *precedes the first chord no longer diatonic in the old key.*

### KEY CONCEPTS IN THIS CHAPTER

- modulation through a common chord
- the predominant as a pivotal point
- modulation to closely related keys
- chromatic modulation and "the rule of chromatics"
- modulation versus tonicization

**EXAMPLE 8-1** J. S. Bach: "Wach auf, mein Herz"

*Notes:*

1. The common chord precedes the new dominant, which is the first chord *not diatonic* in the old key.
2. The common chord functions as a predominant in the new key.

## Crossing the Tonal Border

Many pieces cross the "tonal border" into the new key *via* a predominant. Predominants are the most efficient vehicles for carrying music to a new key because they take the most direct route, a mere three-chord span: predominant—dominant—tonic. However, the IV and ii are not the only possibilities.

### EXAMPLE 8-2  Mozart: Symphony no. 40 in G minor, K. 550 (third movement)

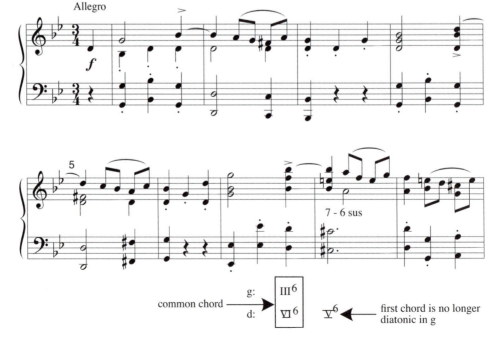

## Multiple Common Chords

In Example 8-2, the common chord is easy to identify because neither the chord preceding it (E♭) nor the chord following it (C♯°7) are diatonic in *both keys*. However, two keys may be separated by more than one chord diatonic to both.

**EXAMPLE 8-3** Anonymous: Minuet (from the *Notebook for Anna Magdalena Bach*)

Here, any chord from m. 16 through m. 19 might be considered the common chord. Perhaps hindsight (or hearing in retrospect) provides the best solution. On first hearing m. 17, the ear has no indication of a modulation. However, beyond m. 20, the ear can *retroactively* re-evaluate the entire phrase in the context of D major.

Common-chord modulations occur most often between **closely related keys**—those that differ by no more than one flat or one sharp. For a given tonality, the closely related keys consist of the relative major or minor, the dominant plus *its* relative, and the subdominant plus *its* relative.

## EXAMPLE 8-4

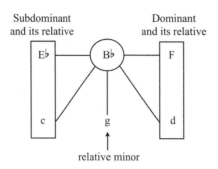 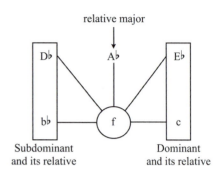

While modulation to *any* of the closely related keys is commonplace, perhaps *the most common* are modulations to the dominant and the relative major or minor key. Example 8-5 shows why this is so.

## EXAMPLE 8-5  Lines connect common chords between the keys

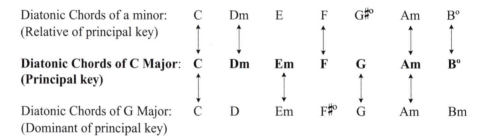

You can see why relative major and minor keys are so called. They are "relatives" by virtue of the number of chords they have in common (five). The dominant is the next most closely related key, with four chords in common. The sheer number of common chords available makes modulation to the dominant or relative both effortless and smooth-sounding.

Even more significant is the fact that the relative and dominant keys are the only closely related keys in which *both predominants* are diatonic in the home key.

*Note (Examples 8-6a and b)*: Again, predominants (ii and IV) are the prime vehicles of modulation because they lead directly to the dominant. The keys that contain both of these chords—i.e. the relative and the dominant—have been, logically, the most frequent modulatory destinations.

MODULATION I 111

**EXAMPLE 8-6A**

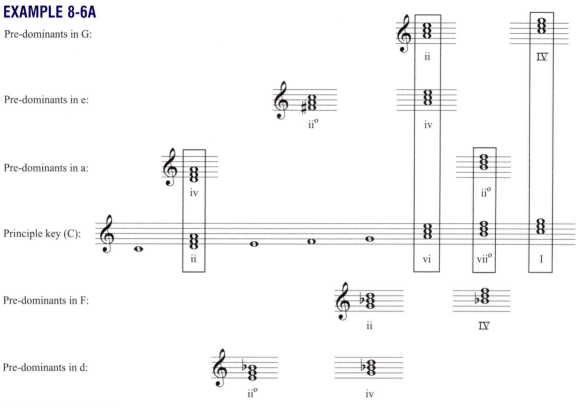

**EXAMPLE 8-6B**

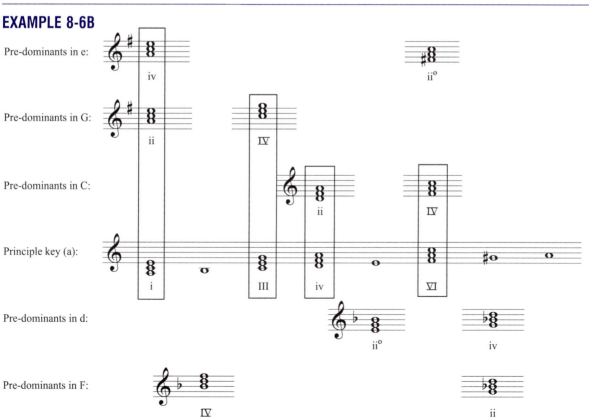

## CHROMATIC MODULATION

A **chromatic modulation** is one that does not involve a common chord. It can usually be recognized by chromatic voice leading in one or more parts at the tonal border.

### The Rule of Chromatics

Generally, *but not always*:

*A chromatically raised pitch is the new "ti" (the new leading tone).*
*A chromatically lowered pitch is the new "fa" (the new $\hat{4}$).*

"The rule of chromatics" is illustrated in the examples that follow.

### EXAMPLE 8-7 J. S. Bach: "Du großer Schmerzensmann"

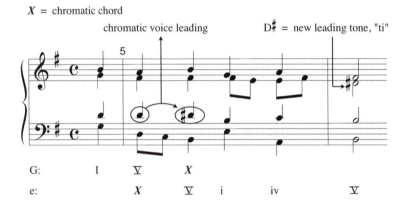

*Notes*:

1. The V in G (the old key) progresses directly to the V in e (the new key). Neither of these chords is diatonic in the other key, thus no common chord exists. The chromatically raised pitch is the new leading tone.

2. The V in G (beat 1) is also the subtonic (VII) in e. Theorists express mixed feelings about the subtonic. When is it diatonic and when is it chromatic? The authors consider it diatonic when progressing through a minor-key circular-fifth pattern and chromatic when tonicizing III or when accompanied by chromatic voice leading as here.

### EXAMPLE 8-8 Chopin: Mazurka op. 56, no. 1

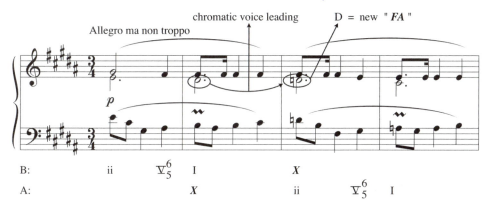

*Note*: The I in B (the old key) is followed directly by ii in A (the new key). Neither of these chords is diatonic in the other key, thus no common chord exists. The chromatically lowered pitch is the new "fa".

---

Lacking the lubrication of a common chord, chromatic modulations often sound more abrupt and perhaps for this reason are less prevalent than common-chord modulations. Just as common chord modulations occasionally involve keys *not* closely related, chromatic modulations *can* involve closely related keys (as Example 8-7). However, chromatic modulations more often lead to more distant tonalities. In most, a chord diatonic *only in the old key* is followed by a chord diatonic *only in the new key* (as in Examples 8–7 and 8–8). But sometimes a chord diatonic *in neither key* straddles the modulation. Both types are shown in Example 8-9.

### EXAMPLE 8-9A Schubert: "Kennst du das Land"

**EXAMPLE 8-9B** Stephen Sondheim and Leonard Bernstein: "Tonight" (from *West Side Story*, act 1, no. 7)

*Notes*:

1. In **a**, the *last chord diatonic in the old key* is followed directly by the *first chord diatonic in the new key* (m. 6). This is the simplest and most common type of chromatic modulation. Chromatic voice leading appears in the piano part.

2. In **b**, the last chord diatonic in the old key (m. 73) and the first chord diatonic in the new key (m. 75) are separated by a chord diatonic in *neither* key (m. 74).

In more complex chromatic modulations, *several* chords diatonic in neither key may intervene. These and other variants will be discussed Chapter 11.

## Multiple Accidentals

The more distant the modulation, the more likely that it will be signaled by multiple accidentals. To "The Rule of Chromatics" on p. 112 we can add:

> *When a modulation is signaled by the consistent appearance of more than one accidental, the one most remote from the original key often functions as the new "ti" (if raised) or the new "fa" (if lowered).*

Thus, if B♭ and E♭ appear consistently in the key of C, the E♭ (two accidentals removed from C) likely functions as "fa" and the key is probably B♭. If F♯, C♯, and G♯ appear consistently in the key of C, G♯ likely functions as "ti," and the key is probably A.

### EXAMPLE 8-10  Brahms: "Erinnerung," op. 63, no. 2

*Note*: The appearance of F♮, B♭, E♭, and A♭—all chromatically lowered pitches—signals a modulation away from G. A♭, the accidental most remote from G major, functions as the new "fa", here the seventh of the V⁷ in E♭ (m. 26).

> **FOR PRACTICE**
>
> Look again at Example 8-9, and explain how the guideline concerning multiple accidentals can aid in the determination of the new key. In **b**, remember that the guideline applies only to *consistent* accidentals. Which accidental should be disregarded when attempting to identify the new key?

## Modulation or Tonicization?

Modulations are usually not reflected by a change of key *signature* unless the new key remains in effect for a protracted length of time. How, then, to distinguish a modulation from a tonicization? In general:

1. A single secondary function does not establish a new tonal center.

2. Persistence of the same accidental(s) over several measures *may* signal a modulation.

3. A cadence in the new tonality tends to strengthen the feeling that a modulation has occurred.

4. Modulations are made more convincing by tonicizing the dominant in the new key (*e.g.* V/V –V or vii°⁶/V—V).

Sometimes it's not the persistent *appearance* of an accidental but the persistent *lack* of an accidental that signals a modulation. Example 8-11 illustrates this point along with those just made. Mozart takes a tortuous route to C major from the home key of A minor.

**EXAMPLE 8-11** Mozart: Piano Sonata K. 310 (first movement)

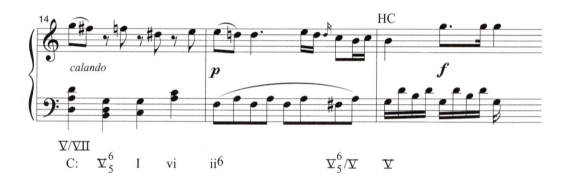

*Notes:*

Addressing each of the foregoing points in order:

1. Each tonicization is brief.
2. The presence of G natural instead of G# in mm. 12, 13 and 14 signal a modulation away from A minor.
3. A half cadence in the new key appears in m. 16.
4. The cadence chord (V) is tonicized in m. 15, solidifying the new tonic.

---

A final word: Tonicizations can be viewed as merely momentary modulations, and modulations can be seen as extended tonicizations—the difference is one of degree, not kind.

In Example 8-12, **a** contains a two-measure modulation while **b** contains a three-measure tonicization. **a** is analyzed as a modulation because it comes to a cadence in the new key, whereas **b** returns to the old key for its cadence.

**EXAMPLE 8-12A** Brahms: Variations on a Theme of Robert Schumann, op. 9

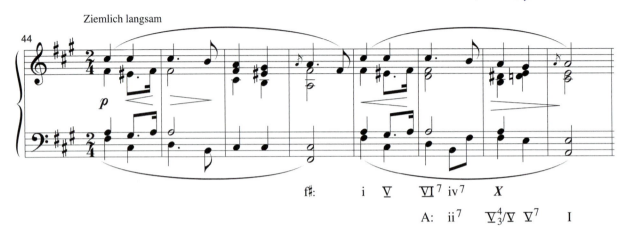

**EXAMPLE 8-12B** Schubert: Symphony no. 8 (first movement)

### FOR PRACTICE

Example 8-13 contains two tonicizations. Identify them. The chromatic chord of m. 1 appears again in m. 2 and the music appears to come to a cadence on beat 3. What is it that weakens this "cadence" and prevents us from calling this a modulation? Do you see the melodic minor principle at work in this passage?

# MODULATION I     119

**EXAMPLE 8-13** J. S. Bach: "Helft mir Gott's Güte preisen"

All modulations have what might be called a tonal border. When the music drives across, it enters a new tonality. Sometimes, the tonal border is clear—a single chord that is a signpost announcing the new key. Sometimes, the tonal border is obscured by additional chromatic harmonies that belong to *neither* tonality. The keys to understanding a modulation are (1) to correctly identify the new key from the *consistent* accidentals that signal it, and (2) to discover exactly where the tonal border is. In all but the more complex cases, the harmonies before and after the tonal border will be easily analyzable in either the old or the new tonality.

## SUMMARY OF TERMINOLOGY

- chromatic modulation
- closely related keys
- common chord
- common chord modulation
- tonicization

# CHAPTER NINE

# Mixing Modes

## VOCABULARY AND SYNTAX

The harmonic vocabulary of Baroque music consisted of all the diatonic triads and seventh chords along with the secondary functions attending each of those harmonies, in the home key and in the keys closely related. Its syntax—the way this vocabulary was used in musical phrases—involved heavy reliance on circular-fifth root movement and harmonic sequence.

The latter part of the eighteenth century witnessed the addition of chromatic elements, one important source being **mode mixture**—combining the resources of *parallel* major and minor modes. The process provided additional harmonies without entailing a modulation (change of tonal center).

### KEY CONCEPTS IN THIS CHAPTER

- change of mode
- keys related through mode mixture
- modal borrowing
- voice leading with borrowed harmonies
- common chromatic-third relationships
- voice leading in chromatic-third relationships
- chromatic-third relationship and mode mixture

## CHANGE OF MODE

**Change of mode** involves the shift from a major key to the parallel minor, or the reverse. The effect is dramatic, and if a composer seeks variety and contrast, he or she often need do nothing more than change mode. Example 9-1 illustrates the process.

**EXAMPLE 9-1** Mozart: Piano Sonata K. 332 (second movement)

*Notes*:

1. The change of mode in m. 5 effects a change of key (to B♭ minor) *without* a change in key signature.
2. The melody and harmonic pattern of mm. 1–2 are simply repeated in mm. 5–6, but in the parallel minor key.

3. The I⁶ in m. 6 (boxed) is actually an altered chord in the new key. Again a "residue" of the former key, it would more clearly appear altered if the key *signature* had changed to reflect the mode change. We'll discuss this chord further in the next section, "Modal Borrowing."

Example 9-1 shows how a change of mode can effect a change in *mood*. The mood seems to darken with the change to minor. The association of major and minor with gaiety and gloom has a history dating back to the first light of the tonal era.

## Keys Related through Mode Mixture

In addition to its mood-altering powers, change of mode provides instant access to a new set of closely related keys. If the chords of a key are likened to a tonal planetary system within a galaxy containing five other planetary systems—the closely related keys—then think of change of mode as a wormhole to a parallel galaxy.

**EXAMPLE 9-2**

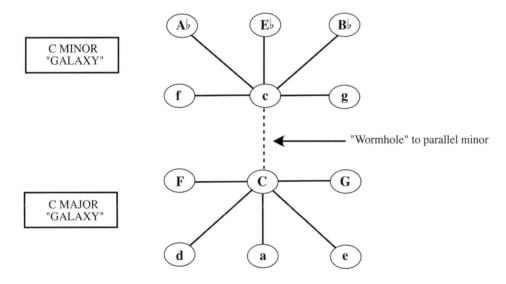

## Enharmonic Change of Mode

Occasionally, a change of mode is accompanied by enharmonic respelling. The intent usually is to place the music in a key with fewer flats or sharps.

**EXAMPLE 9-3** Beethoven: Piano Sonata op. 26 (second movement)

*Note*: The cadence in m. 8 is in C♭ major. A change of mode at this point would place the ensuing music in the key of C♭ *minor*. For this reason, the following measures are notated enharmonically in B minor, a more readable key.

# MIXING MODES

> **FOR PRACTICE**
>
> Complete the harmonic analysis of Example 9-3.

## MODAL BORROWING

While change of mode involves the *consistent and protracted* use of harmonic resources from the parallel key, **modal borrowing** involves the *brief and occasional* use of those resources. These harmonies (for better or worse) have been termed **borrowed harmonies**. You might think of them as temporarily on loan from the parallel key. Modal borrowing bears the same relationship to change of mode that tonicization bears to modulation: The former process in each case is more local in effect, the latter more lasting.

Look again at Example 9-1. In m. 5 the music changes mode to B♭ minor. However, in m. 6, the chord on beat 3 appears as it would in B♭ major. This is a borrowed harmony.

**EXAMPLE 9-4**

b♭:    I6

borrowed from B♭ major

Borrowing goes both ways. However, if you want to borrow a harmony, minor owns the bigger bank. (Recall the variable sixth and seventh scale degrees and the resulting alternative harmonies in minor.) The only harmony routinely borrowed *from major by minor* is the tonic, shown above. In fact, I, iii, and vi are the only chords from major that are not present in minor, and the latter two sound distinctly odd in a minor context.

### Common Borrowed Harmonies

On the other hand, the major mode can be greatly enriched by borrowing from the minor. Example 9-5 shows the most common borrowed harmonies from the minor mode.

**EXAMPLE 9-5**

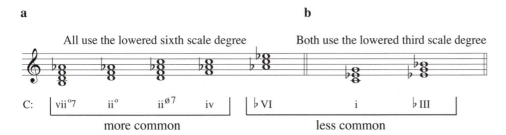

*Note*: All are "borrowed" from C minor. The most common borrowed harmonies feature the lowered sixth scale degree.

The lowered sixth degree and the harmonies that house it can lend a momentary somber cast to a major-mode work. They became favorites of the Romantic composers, whose music often involved themes of sorrow. Though somewhat melodramatic-sounding today when overused, they remain a way to lend a poignant touch to a passage.

### EXAMPLE 9-6A Brahms: "Die Mainacht"

### EXAMPLE 9-6B Gilbert O'Sullivan: "Alone Again (Naturally)"

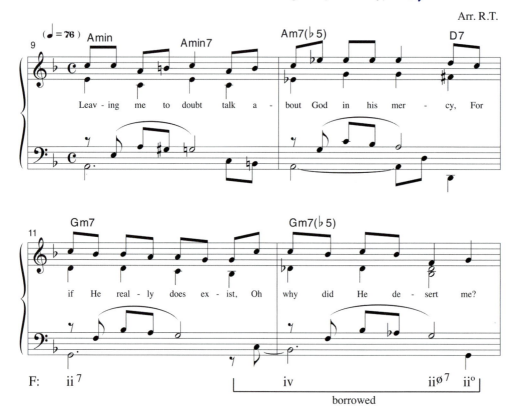

## Voice Leading

Because the minor sixth-scale degree most often resolves stepwise *in the direction of its inflection*, borrowed harmonies containing it are apt to resolve to a chord containing the $\hat{5}$ (either V or I). The resolution of the altered tone is the overriding voice-leading consideration. If ♭VI resolves first to a predominant, as in **e** below, the predominant is often borrowed as well, retaining the altered tone (♭$\hat{6}$) until its eventual resolution to $\hat{5}$.

### EXAMPLE 9-7

*Notes:*

1. Borrowed harmonies normally function identically to their diatonic counterparts.
2. The lowered sixth-scale degree (the altered tone) typically resolves downward by a half step.

---

Example 9-8 contains one of the two most common of all borrowed harmonies—iv. Observe the resolution of $\hat{6}$.

## EXAMPLE 9-8 Leslie Bricusse and John Williams: "Can You Read My Mind?" (from the movie *Superman*)

### CONCEPT CHECK

How would you symbolize the chord of m. 6? How would you expect it to resolve?

If iv is among the most common borrowed harmonies, ♭VI is probably the *least* common of those that employ ♭$\hat{6}$. The chord appears in Example 9-9.

## EXAMPLE 9-9 Brahms: Symphony no. 3, op. 90 (second movement)

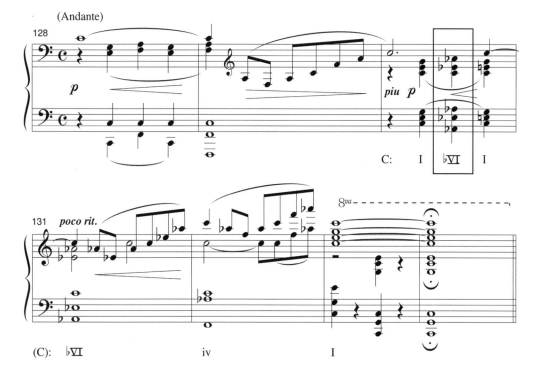

## CHROMATIC-THIRD RELATIONSHIPS

### Diatonic vs. Chromatic Third Relationship

Two triads whose roots are a third apart share two notes of the same letter name. In a **diatonic-third relationship**, these two notes are common tones. However, in a **chromatic-third relationship**, one or both common tones are chromatically altered.

### EXAMPLE 9-10

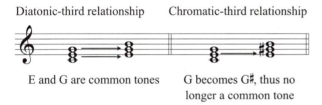

*A chromatic-third relationship exists between any two chords a third apart that do not share two common tones.* Examples are A major and C major, D minor and B minor, E♭ minor and G major, and D♭ major and E minor.

Toward the end of the eighteenth century, composers seemingly developed a fascination with the fresh sound of particular chromatic-third relationships. Beethoven—and after him Schubert, Liszt, Brahms, and Wagner—frequently juxtaposed both tonalities and chords so related.

### EXAMPLE 9-11  Schubert: "Kennst du das Land"

## The Common Chromatic-Third Relationships

The tonal relationship in Example 9-11—A major to C major—is one of the more commonly used chromatic-third relationships of the late eighteenth and early nineteenth centuries. While it might seem that the number of possible chromatic-third relationships is bewilderingly large, we'll consider only the most common four.

### EXAMPLE 9-12

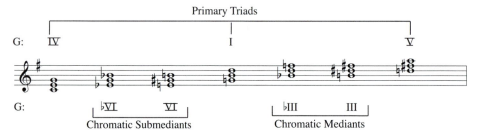

*Note*:

1. All the common chromatic-third relationships to the tonic are major triads.

2. Chromatic mediants are so called because they are the midpoint between tonic and dominant. Chromatic submediants are so called because they are the midpoint between tonic and *sub*dominant. Each chromatic mediant or chromatic submediant shares with the tonic one common tone with the second one chromatically altered.

3. Chromatic-third relationships can exist between tonal centers or between individual chords. Between chords, the seventh may be present as well (as in G-B♭7).

4. The flat sign is used to indicate a lowered chord root, whether the actual alteration involves a flat (as here) or a natural (as it would in the key of E).

5. The tonic is usually, but not always, part of a chromatic-third relationship. For example, the chromatic mediants (III and ♭III) can form chromatic-third relationships with V, and the chromatic submediants (VI and ♭VI) can form chromatic-third relationships with IV.

# MIXING MODES

> **FOR PRACTICE**
>
> Construct an illustration similar to Example 9-12, showing all common chromatic-third relationships to an A major tonic.

## Chromatic Thirds, Mode Mixture, and Tonicization

The four common chromatic-third relationships can result from processes already discussed—secondary function or mode mixture. For example, ♭III and ♭VI are borrowed harmonies in a major key, while III and VI might be tonizations (V/vi and V/ii).

**EXAMPLE 9-13**

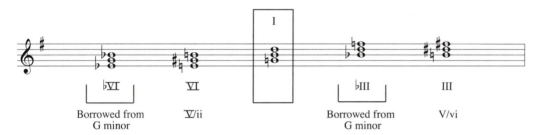

However, the chromatic-third relationship is often exploited purely for its unusual sound.

**EXAMPLE 9-14** Beethoven: Piano Sonata op. 14, no. 1 (third movement) 🔊

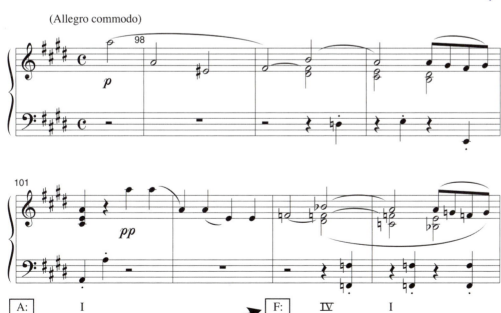

*Note*: The tonalities A and F are chromatically-third-related while the chords at the tonal border (mm. 102–103) are not. F, the lowered submediant (♭VI) in A, is the submediant (VI) in A minor, making this chromatic-third relationship a form of mode mixture.

Film composers and popular song writers seem to have rediscovered what Haydn, Beethoven, Brahms, and Wagner knew—that the sudden elevation to a new tonal plane through chromatic-third relationship is a refreshing aural change that can make a repeated phrase sound new.

Roman numeral analysis does not always directly reveal a chromatic-third relationship. Example 9-15 is such a case.

**EXAMPLE 9-15** Haydn: Piano Sonata H. XVI:34 (first movement)

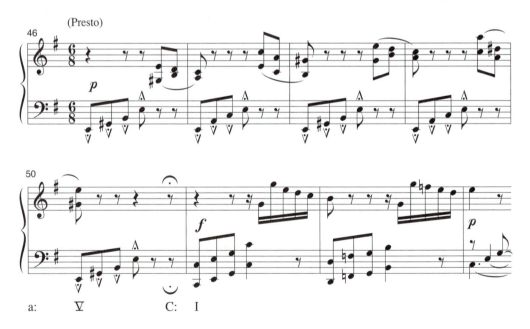

*Note*: The chords at mm. 50–51 (a: V and C: I) are chromatic-third related while the two *keys* (A minor and C major) are in a *diatonic*-third relationship (minor to relative major).

> **CONCEPT CHECK**
>
> 1. Identify the type of six-four chord that appears in this passage.
>
> 2. What secondary function appears prior to the fermata? (Look for it in an arpeggiation.)

## Voice Leading

Chromatic-third relationships were governed by less rigorous part-writing practices than were seventh chords and the like. Rather than being generated by linear processes, they were often employed for the "shock value" of their sound. Then, too, they came into frequent use in instrumental music that involved a more homophonic style, with smooth voice leading less an issue than it previously had been. Still, conjunct lines are easily attainable. When part writing the common chromatic-third relationships:

1. Retain the single common tone in the same voice.

2. Move the other voices as stepwise as possible. (Typically, one voice will move by chromatic half-step.)

3. When both chords are in root position (as is often the case), double the root in both (nothing new here) but not in the same voice. As always, contrary or oblique motion in the outer voices produces the best result.

Example 9-16 shows a typical problem when part-writing root-to-root chromatic-third relationships and a possible solution.

**EXAMPLE 9-16A** Doubling the root in the same voice (m. 1 and mm. 2–3) produces consecutive octaves against B. Parallel S and B (m. 2) lead to consecutive fifths.

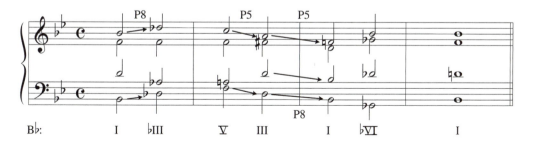

**EXAMPLE 9-16B** Doubling the root in different voices eliminates consecutive octaves. Contrary and oblique motion predominate in the outer voices. Blackened notes show doubled root. Arrows show common tones retained.

*Note*: The solution (**b**) also produces a smoother, "more singable" tenor line (and the alto, while less than enchanting, is at least easy to sing). All voices are predominantly conjunct except the bass, which "is what it is" because all the chords are in root position.

As with change of mode, chromatic-third relationships can necessitate enharmonic spellings in certain keys. This can generate unusual-looking melodic intervals. The smaller these intervals are, the better. In Example 9-17, the individual voices move largely by enharmonic half steps and whole steps.

**EXAMPLE 9-17** Dvorak: New World Symphony, op. 95 (Largo) 🔊
This four-voice passage results when the instruments doubling the lines at the octave are removed.

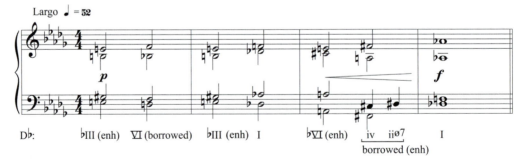

*Notes*:

1. S and B move largely in contrary motion. Doubling is, for the most part, standard (root in root position, soprano in first inversion).

2. In the four root-position triads of mm. 2 and 3, the root is doubled first by the S, then by the A, then by the T, and again by the S. This enables Dvorak to avoid consecutive octaves.

Your instructor will determine how rigorously you should apply voice-leading principles to chromatic-third relationships. Musical style and medium are factors to consider.

**Mode mixture** is a general process that combines the resources of the major and minor scales. It includes specific techniques—**change of mode** and **modal borrowing**—which differ mainly in duration.

In musical analysis, a passage might invite description in multiple ways. For example, a chromatic modulation might lead to a chromatic-third-related key, with one chord or the other described as a borrowed harmony. These multiple analytical observations are part of a complete description that addresses all facets of the passage.

## SUMMARY OF TERMINOLOGY

- change of mode
- chromatic-third relationship
- diatonic-third relationship
- enharmonic change of mode
- modal borrowing
- mode mixture

# CHAPTER TEN

# Altered Predominants and Dominants

This chapter introduces chromatic variants of three important harmonies. Their increasing use in the eighteenth and nineteenth centuries kept pace with composers' increasing fascination with mood and color.

By the nineteenth century, the four-part vocal style had lost the primacy it enjoyed in the Renaissance and Baroque eras, and composers applied those voice-leading principles—particularly in matters of spacing and doubling—in a more general way. Still, they continued to respect the two basic needs of the sensitive tones, which are: 1) to be left alone (e.g. not doubled); and 2) to do what they want (resolve).

**KEY CONCEPTS IN THIS CHAPTER**

- Neapolitan sixth chord: construction, function, and voice leading
- augmented sixth chords: construction, function, and voice leading
- altered dominants

## THE NEAPOLITAN SIXTH CHORD

The so-called **Neapolitan chord** made cameo appearances in the seventeenth century and debuted as a more central member of the harmonic cast in a type of opera centered in Naples in the first half of the eighteenth century. As its Roman numeral symbol—♭II—suggests, the chord is a major triad built on the lowered second scale degree. At least initially, the chord appeared in first inversion—called the **Neapolitan sixth chord**—reflecting its linear origin as a chromatically inflected ii$^{o6}$. As the sound became familiar, composers began to employ it in root position as well.

## EXAMPLE 10-1

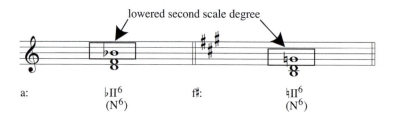

*Note*: The designation N⁶ remains unchanged whether lowering the second sale degree is achieved by a natural (as it is in sharp keys) or by a flat. For this reason, N⁶ is the preferred way to symbolize the chord.

## The Harmonic Nature of the Neapolitan

In first inversion, the Neapolitan behaves like its diatonic siblings, the ii°⁶ and iv. They are all predominants and in all:

1. The bass is doubled and *steps up to the dominant*.

2. The tone that constitutes the single pitch difference among the three chords moves *down to the leading tone*.

## EXAMPLE 10-2

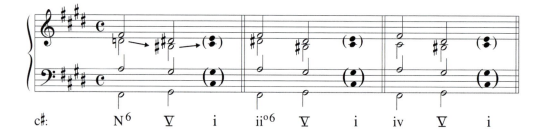

The N⁶ voiced above is present in Example 10-3. Notice that the N⁶ could be replaced by ii°⁶ or iv without altering the functional sense or voice leading of the passage.

ALTERED PREDOMINANTS AND DOMINANTS  139

**EXAMPLE 10-3** Beethoven: Piano Sonata op. 27, no. 2 (first movement)

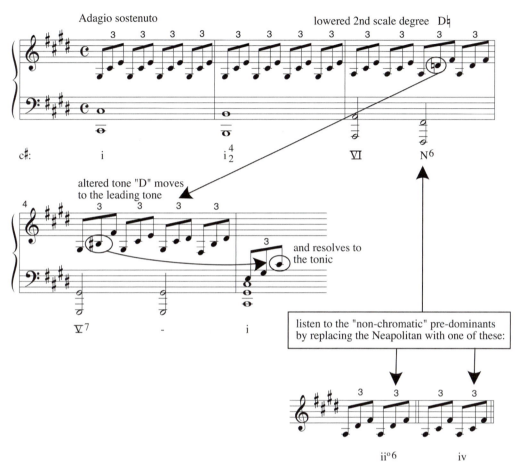

In the Neapolitan, the altered tone goes the way of all chromatic tones—undoubled, it moves *in the direction of its inflection*. The note's ultimate destination is the tonic, which is thus approached by half step *from above and below*. This motion—b$\hat{2}$–$\hat{7}$–$\hat{1}$–creates a melodic diminished third that enfolds the tonic:

The °3 that creates the wrap-around motion is one of the few non-diatonic intervals considered acceptable under the strict part-writing canon. In fact, composers seemed to relish the interval's unique sound.

**EXAMPLE 10-4**

Observe the treatment of the altered tone in the following musical examples.

### EXAMPLE 10-5A  Chopin: Prelude op. 28, no. 20

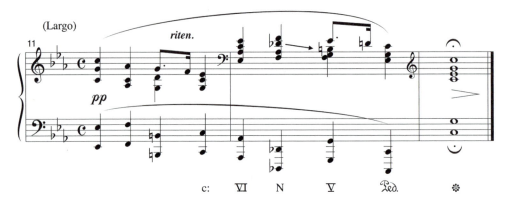

*Note*: The root-position Neapolitan typically resolves, as here, to a root-position V. Even though the bass in this passage moves from root to root, the b$\hat{2}$ in the upper voice moves downward to $\hat{7}$ and then on the tonic C, producing the "wrap-around" effect just described.

---

### EXAMPLE 10-5B  Verdi: "Stride la vampa!" from *Il Trovatore* (act 2, scene 1) 🔊

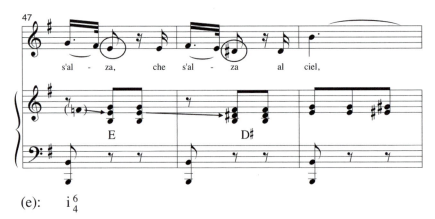

ALTERED PREDOMINANTS AND DOMINANTS   141

*Note*: The altered tone F♮ moves to the leading tone *via the tonic* E in the cadential six-four chord (see the circled tones). The leading tone then resolves to the tonic in the piano part in m. 49. The melodic motion in **b** is smoother, but the harmonic progression in **a** is perhaps more poignant.

## Insertions before V

The cadential i$^6_4$ sandwiched between the N$^6$ and V "planes out" the melodic diminished third. So does the vii$^{o7}$/V, which creates an additional chromatic passing tone in the bass. Notice, however, that the basic voice leading remains the same in all.

## EXAMPLE 10-6

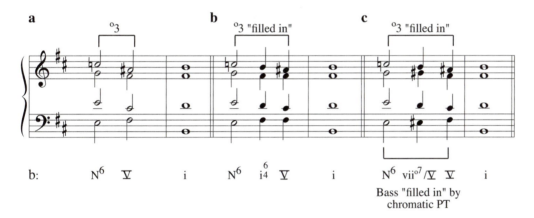

Example 10-7 incorporates both insertions. vii$^{o7}$/V is followed by i$^6_4$ before moving to V.

## EXAMPLE 10-7 Mozart: Piano Sonata K. 280 (second movement) 🔊

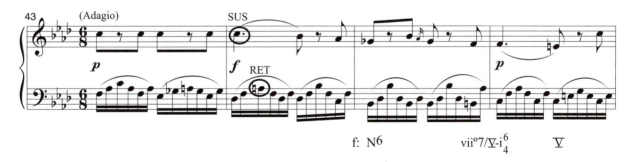

The Neapolitan lends a somber cast to most passages in which it appears. However, in Gounod's "Funeral March of a Marionette," it enhances the undertone of playful menace that perhaps prompted renowned film director and producer Alfred Hitchcock to use the work as the theme song for a weekly television show in the 1960s.

**EXAMPLE 10-8** Gounod: "Marcha Funebre de un Volatin"

d:   N⁶   i⁶₄   V⁷   i

### FOR PRACTICE

Provide harmonic analysis of Example 10-9, and discuss the treatment of b$\hat{2}$ in the passage.

**EXAMPLE 10-9** Chopin: Valse, op. 64, no. 2

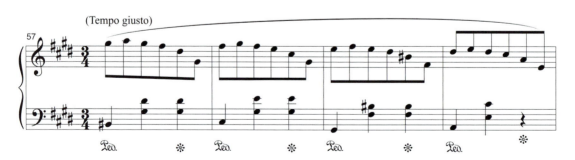

ALTERED PREDOMINANTS AND DOMINANTS 143

## AUGMENTED SIXTH CHORDS

The bass in Example 10-10 approaches the dominant G through #$\hat{4}$ followed by b$\hat{6}$, a °3 that again creates a "wrap-around."

**EXAMPLE 10-10** J. S. Bach: *The Well-Tempered Clavier*, Book I, BWV 844 (Prelude no. 1)

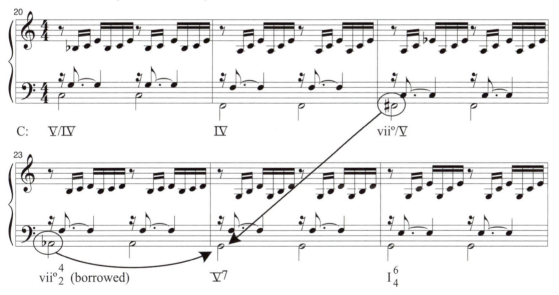

Example 10-11 shows the effect produced by these two potent melodic forces (#$\hat{4}$ and b$\hat{6}$) when contained within a single harmony. The reduction following the music shows the outer voices to be an expanding wedge from the double octave tonic to the triple octave dominant, approached by half-step from above and below.

**EXAMPLE 10-11** Beethoven: Thirty-Two Variations on an Original Theme in C Minor, WoO.80

**EXAMPLE 10-12** Reduction

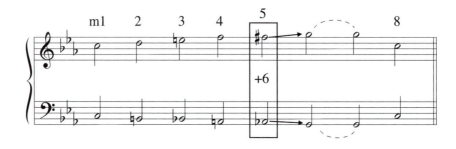

At m. 5, the push toward the dominant is enhanced through the altered tone F♯. This note and the bottom note A♭ are both a half step from the dominant G producing a double leading tone effect to the dominant. The interval they form is an augmented sixth, and the chord they frame (see m. 5 of the reduction) is called, logically, an **augmented sixth chord**. This double tendency creates an especially urgent need to resolve to the dominant note.

ALTERED PREDOMINANTS AND DOMINANTS

Two ways, both linear, of altering a predominant to create an augmented sixth chord are shown in Example 10-13.

## EXAMPLE 10-13

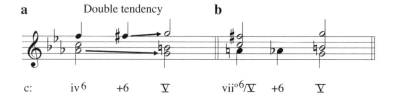

In **a** the chord results when a chromatic passing tone is inserted in a Phrygian half cadence. In **b** the chromatic passing tone is added following a secondary vii°.

## Types of Augmented Sixth Chords

Three types of augmented sixth chords are common; their aural differences are slight and their functions are identical.

## EXAMPLE 10-14

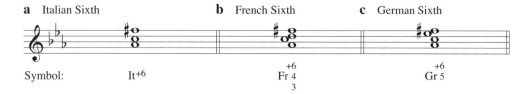

*Notes*:

1. In all three chords, the raised fourth scale degree (+$\hat{4}$) creates a leading tone below the dominant.

2. In all three chords, $\hat{6}$—the half step *above* the dominant—is the lowest tone. This bass note and +$\hat{4}$ create the *double tendency tone* to the dominant—one from above and one from below–that form the augmented sixth interval.

3. All three chords contain the tonic.

4. The French and German sixth chords have an additional tone—the French contains $\hat{2}$, the German $\hat{3}$.

5. Superscripts in the chord symbols are the ones that would appear in a figured bass to show the chord's inversion. For analytical purposes, the designations It+6, Fr+6 and Gr+6 suffice.

## Constructing an Augmented Sixth Chord

Remember the foregoing points, and you have a simple method for constructing an augmented sixth chord in any key:

In G minor:

*Step 1:* Place the dominant in the bass and any upper voice.

**EXAMPLE 10-15A**

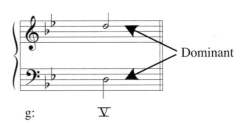

*Step 2:* Place a m2 *above* the dominant in the *bass* and a m2 *below* the dominant in the upper voice. This bit of "double-talk" might actually be easier to remember: *"Minor second above below and minor second below above."*

**EXAMPLE 10-15B**

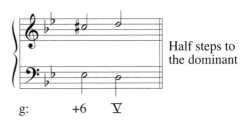

*Step 3:* Add the tonic in one of the remaining voices. Completion of this step produces an Italian sixth chord.

**EXAMPLE 10-15C**

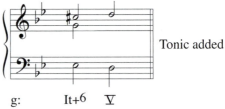

*Step 4:* For the Italian sixth: Double $\hat{1}$

For the French sixth: Add $\hat{2}$

For the German sixth: Add $\hat{3}$

**EXAMPLE 10-15D**

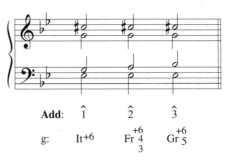

*Note:* The minor second *above* the dominant must be in the bass. The other chord members can be distributed in any upper voice.

ALTERED PREDOMINANTS AND DOMINANTS   147

Like the N⁶, the augmented sixth chords originated as minor-key sounds and gradually came into use in major keys as well. In major keys, they are more highly altered chords, because the bass note is a chromatically lowered pitch (b$\hat{6}$), as is $\hat{3}$ in the German sixth (b$\hat{3}$).

### EXAMPLE 10-16  Joplin: "The Sycamore"

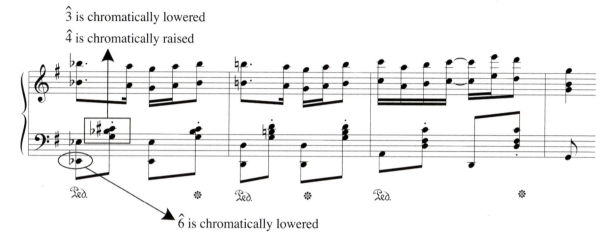

When the German sixth appears in major keys and resolves to a *major* I$_4^6$, b$\hat{3}$ is often written enharmonically as #$\hat{2}$ to reflect its *upward* resolution. (Remember that chromatic pitches resolve in the direction of their inflection.) The chord is often called an **enharmonic German sixth** (Gr+6enh) or a **doubly augmented fourth chord** (++4).

### EXAMPLE 10-17

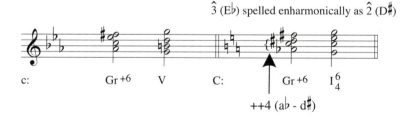

*Note*: The ++4 in the chord symbol refers to the interval created above the bass, not to +4 (in this case F#).

Following this practice, the left-hand in mm. 33–34 of Example 10-16 would be renotated as follows.

### EXAMPLE 10-18

For keyboard instruments or guitar, the doubly augmented fourth chord is a mere notational technicality. However, for instruments that can adjust their pitch, enharmonics such as D♯ and E♭ are not identical; each is nudged in the direction of its inflection.

### Voice Leading

Voice leading in an augmented sixth chord amounts to resolving the augmented sixth interval *outward to the dominant* and moving the other pitches by step.

### EXAMPLE 10-19

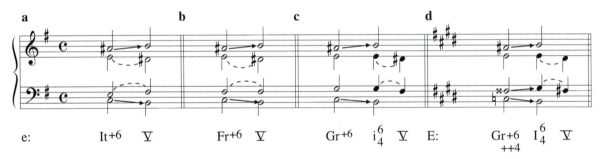

This voice leading can be studied in the examples that follow.

### EXAMPLE 10-20A  Schubert: Sonatina for Piano and Violin, op. posth. 137, no. 2

### EXAMPLE 10-20B  Mozart: String Quartet K. 421 (third movement) 🔊

### EXAMPLE 10-20C  Chopin: Etude op. 10, no. 3 🔊

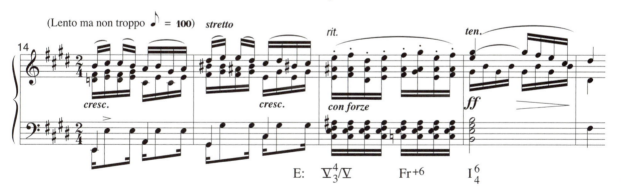

*Notes*:

1. Examples **a** and **b**, both in d minor, facilitate comparison of the Italian sixth (in **a**) and German sixth (in **b**). As shown in **b**, the German sixth often resolves by way of the i$^6_4$, since a resolution directly to V would cause consecutive perfect fifths (in this case, between the soprano (moving from F to E) and the bass (moving from B♭ to A).

## EXAMPLE 10-20D

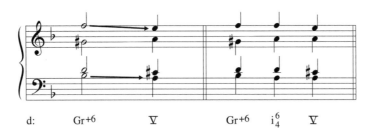

2. Examples **a** and **c** display two ways of creating an augmented sixth chord, similar to those shown in Example 10-13. In **a**, the Italian sixth is created by inserting a chromatic passing tone in the Phrygian cadence (see Example 10-13a). In **c**, a French sixth is created by the alteration of a secondary dominant (see Example 10-13b).

> ### CONCEPT CHECK
> In Example 10-21, what type of augmented sixth chord appears in m. 1 and m. 6? Discuss the resolution of the altered tones in this chord.

**EXAMPLE 10-21** Schumann: "Am leuchtenden Sommermorgen" (no. 12 from *Dichterliebe*, op. 48)

## The Neapolitan and the Augmented Sixth Chords

Did you notice that an +6 is the inversion of a °3? In augmented sixth and Neapolitan sixth chords, these intervals wrap themselves around important scale degrees, one melodically, the other harmonically. In the Neapolitan sixth chord, the °3 *collapses inward to the tonic*. In the augmented sixth chords, the +6 *expands outward to the dominant*. In this sense, the chords share a kinship beyond their harmonic function as predominants. The chords have other things in common:

- Both are linear, in the sense that they spring from chromatic voice leading, and the altered tones enhance the harmonic push toward the chord of resolution.

- Both are distinctive, highly colorful chords that appear much less often than secondary dominants and borrowed harmonies, which remain the staples of chromatic harmony.

## ALTERED DOMINANTS

The dominant was the last diatonic harmony to buckle under chromaticism's relentless advance. The only alterable member of the chord is the fifth, because modifying either the root or the third (the leading tone) would strip the chord of its defining features—its root relationship to the tonic and its major quality. **Altered dominants** are therefore a small category of chromatic harmonies that involve either raising or lowering the chord fifth:

**EXAMPLE 10-22** (Arrows show the tendency tones and their resolutions)

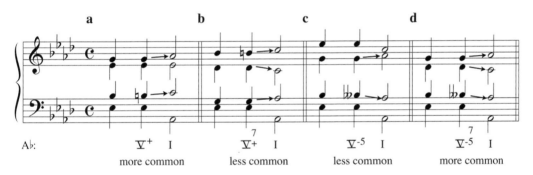

1. The altered chord fifth is normally not doubled and usually resolves as all altered tones do—*in the direction of its inflection* (**a, b, c,** and **d**).

2. Resolution of three sensitive tones—the altered fifth, the leading tone, and the seventh—results in an incomplete tonic triad—no fifth (**b** and **d**).

3. The raised fifth appears more often *without* the seventh (V+) and is found in both the Classic and Romantic periods (**a**). By contrast, the lowered fifth usually appears *with* the seventh (V-$\frac{7}{5}$) and is more common in the later nineteenth century (**d**).

4. It is common practice to symbolize the four chords as shown in Example 10-22 *regardless of inversion* since showing the inversion can necessitate an unwieldy chord symbol that actually obscures the chord's most important feature, the altered fifth.

Altered dominants are usually linear, and the altered tone can usually be analyzed as a chromatic passing tone.

## The Raised Fifth

**EXAMPLE 10-23A** Beethoven: Sonata op. 28 (third movement)

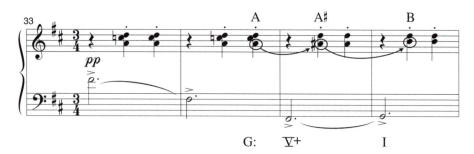

**EXAMPLE 10-23B** Chopin: Nocturne op. 27, no. 1

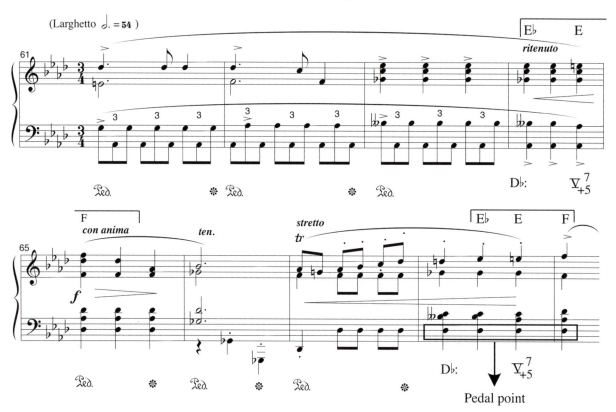

*Note*: In both **a** and **b**: The raised fifth resembles an ascending PT. The seventh resolves downward, the resolution delayed by a measure in **a**.

## The Lowered Fifth

The lowered fifth is less common than the raised fifth. It is usually accompanied by the seventh. The chord is often in second inversion, making it identical—in spelling and resolution, but *not in function*—to a French sixth chord. The two chords are analogous to homonyms (words spelled and sounding alike but have different meanings, such as *note* (a memo) and *note* (a musical symbol).

## EXAMPLE 10-24

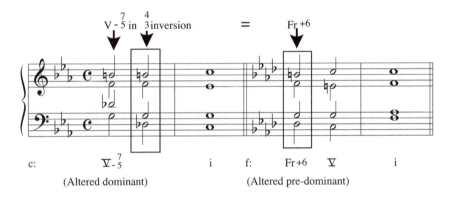

## Altered Secondary Dominants

Like their diatonic counterparts, altered dominants can function at a secondary level (V+/V and so on). In fact, the V+/IV is arguably more common than the V+.

## EXAMPLE 10-25A  Beethoven: Bagatelle no. 8, op. 119

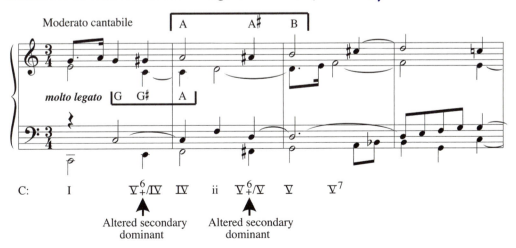

## EXAMPLE 10-25B  Wolf: "Gebet" (No. 28 from *Mörike Songs*)

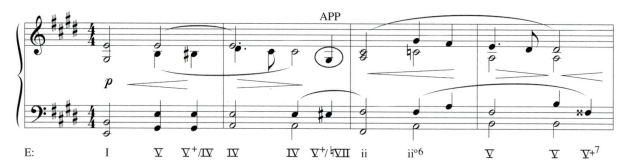

Notes:

1. The raised fifth (B♯) in m. 1 resolves upward to C♯ *by way of* an appoggiatura D♯ (m. 2).
2. The altered secondary dominant of m. 2 resolves deceptively to ii rather than to the chord it tonicizes.

Two of the harmonies discussed in this chapter are chords that approach the dominant—the Neapolitan and the augmented sixth group. The other *is* the dominant. All function identically to their diatonic counterparts. Historically, the Neapolitan and augmented sixth chords appeared earlier than the altered dominants, which were later arrivals. All were used occasionally as "color" chords, and none appear as early or as often as secondary functions and modal borrowings.

## SUMMARY OF TERMINOLOGY

- altered dominant
- altered predominant
- augmented sixth chord
- doubly augmented fourth chord
- French sixth chord
- German sixth chord
- Italian sixth chord
- Neapolitan chord

# CHAPTER ELEVEN

# Modulation II

## "IN SEARCH OF HARMONIC LOGIC"

As stated in Chapter 8, *only two basic types of modulation exist*—those with a common chord and those without. However, *every* modulation can be approached with the same two goals: (1) to identify the "tonal border"—that precise point where the music enters a new tonal region, and (2) to discover the means of transportation across it. Each chord at the tonal border is likely to function in the old key or the new in a familiar way—as a dominant seventh or secondary dominant seventh chord, a borrowed harmony, a chromatically third-related triad, and so on. These recognizable functions give the modulation harmonic logic.

### KEY CONCEPTS IN THIS CHAPTER

- clue chords
- identifying the tonal border
- chromatic pivot
- enharmonic pivot
- the enharmonic German sixth chord
- the enharmonic diminished seventh chord

## RECOGNIZING THE SIGNALS

*Chromatics, clue chords, and cadences*—these are the telltale signs of a tonality.

### Chromatic Pitches

Earlier, we discussed how the consistent appearance of accidentals signals a tonal change. A quick review:

1. A chromatically raised pitch is probably the new leading tone ("ti"). A chromatically lowered pitch is probably the fourth scale degree ("fa") in the new key, either the seventh of a $V^7$ or the fifth of a vii°.

2. With multiple accidentals, the one *most remote from the current key* probably functions in one of the ways just described. Accidentals that cannot belong in the same key signature (F♯ and B♭, for example) suggest a minor key.

## Clue Chords

Accidentals can mislead, and in short modulations, the telltale tone might appear no more than once. However, a musical passage usually offers multiple clues to its tonality. The following chords are signposts:

1. The Mm7 chord is a harmony that functions *almost exclusively* as a dominant (hence the common designation "dominant seventh"). Its consistent appearance suggests a modulation to the key whose tonic lies a perfect fifth below its root.

   If you see this:

   think A (a).

2. The °7 (diminished seventh) chord *usually* functions as a leading tone chord, suggesting a tonic a minor second above its root.

   If you see this:

   think E (e).

3. A second-inversion triad *often* functions as a cadential six-four chord.

   If you see this:

   think D♭.

4. Italian and German augmented sixth chords *almost always* function as predominants, resolving to V or i/6/4//.

   If you see this:

   think a.

(The French augmented sixth chord is not quite so categorical because the V-$\frac{7}{5}$ in second inversion is structurally identical with the Fr$^{+6}$.)

## Cadences

Because most phrases end with an authentic or half cadence, the final chord in most cadences will be I or V. Thus, phrase endings are important clues to the tonality.

These clues—*chromatic pitches, clue chords, and cadences*—will usually build the case for one tonality or another in a modulating passage.

**EXAMPLE 11-1** Brahms: "Wie Melodien zieht es mir," op. 105, no. 1

### Thinking Through a Modulation

Passages such as the preceding are easier to analyze if broken into segments:

- Mm. 14–16: These measures are entirely diatonic in A, the key implied by the key signature.

- Mm. 17–18: Despite the accidentals in m. 17, the first phrase comes to a cadence in m. 18 over a root-position A major triad. Conclusion: The music is still in A.

- Mm. 19–22: No accidentals appear consistently in these measures, but the phrase comes to a cadence in m. 22 on a D major triad. Is it I or V? If I, then m. 21 contains on beats 3 and 4 an altered dominant seventh chord. Together, the two chords produce an authentic cadence—$V+{}^7_5$–I Conclusion: The music has modulated to D.

- Mm. 22–25: No accidentals appear consistently, but the cadence chord is an F♯ minor triad (m. 25). Is it I or V? Because half cadences end on *major* (not minor) triads, this minor chord probably is the tonic. The chord preceding it is a $V^7$ in f♯, creating an authentic cadence. Conclusion: The music has traveled to the relative minor, f♯, following a short layover in D.

## THE TONAL BORDER

The harmonic logic of a modulation lies near the tonal border, where one of three circumstances will likely exist:

*Case 1: The first chord diatonic in the new key is the last chord diatonic in the old key.* This is the familiar **common chord modulation**.

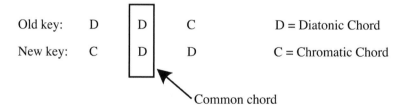

*Case 2: The first chord diatonic in the new key follows the last chord diatonic in the old key.* This is a simple **chromatic modulation**.

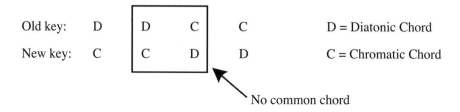

*Case 3*: *The first chord diatonic in the new key and the last chord diatonic in the old key are separated by one or more chords diatonic in neither key.* This is a more complex **chromatic modulation**. If several chromatic chords intervene, they might be tonicizing a third key.

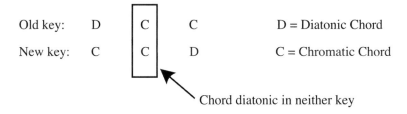

In the following discussion, we'll refer back to these three cases. Look again at the Brahms song. The last four measures begin in D and end in f♯. Example 11-2 shows the ground-level harmonic structure.

## EXAMPLE 11-2

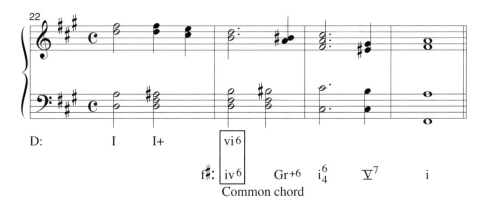

Q: Where does the modulation occur?

A: To find out, home in on the tonal border. Working backward from the cadence, the first clear indication of f♯ is the cadential six-four chord at m. 24. The chord before it (m. 23, beat 3) is chromatic in f♯ but recognizable—a Gr$^{+6}$. Working forward, everything up to this chord analyzes well enough in D. The tonal border, then, lies in m. 23.

Q: How does the music cross the tonal border?

A: The new key (f♯) takes root with the appearance of the German sixth chord. The chord preceding it (m. 23, beat 1) is common to *both keys* (b = vi in D and iv in f♯) and can therefore be considered a common chord (Case 1).

## Chromatic Modulations

If a common chord is *not* present, the chord at the pivotal point is likely to function as one of the chromatic harmonies mentioned at the beginning of this chapter. The ensuing examples show only a few of many possibilities. The discussions that follow each provide models for thinking through a modulation.

**EXAMPLE 11-3** Brahms: Quintet no. 1, op. 88

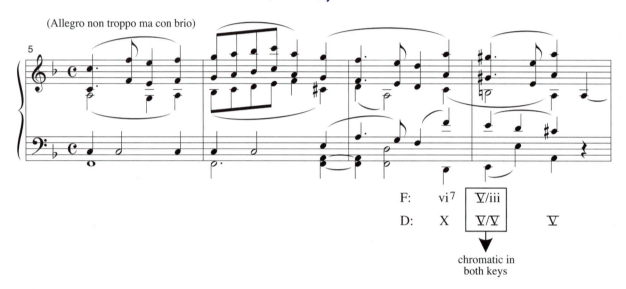

Example 11-3 typifies Case 3. A single chord (m. 8, beat 1) *follows* the last chord diatonic in F and *precedes* the first chord diatonic in D. Separating the two tonalities and chromatic in both, it's the pivotal point—the "tonal border"—in this modulation. The chord can be termed a **chromatic pivot**.

**EXAMPLE 11-4** Smith and Bernard: "Winter Wonderland"

MODULATION II    161

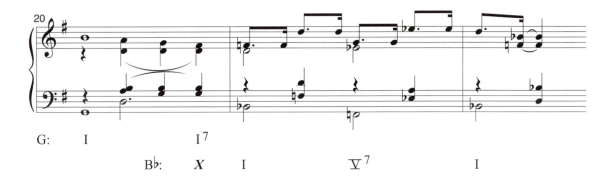

Example 11-4 illustrates Case 2, a simple chromatic modulation. In this passage, the first phrase ends in one key and the second phrase begins in another. The modulation occurs *between* rather than *within* phrases. Such modulations are sometimes termed "tonal shifts."

**EXAMPLE 11-5**  Beethoven: Sonata for Violin and Piano op. 24 
(second movement)

Gb:  i (enh.)
D:   iii           I⁶

In Example 11-5, the striking change from flats to sharps leaves little doubt about *where* the tonal border lies. Here the borrowed tonic (i in Gb) functions as iii in D (and is respelled enharmonically in that key—as f♯):

Again, this is Case 2. The two keys, incidentally—Gb and D—are enharmonically a chromatic third apart (Gb = F♯, and F♯–D = I–bVI). Modulations to bVI are frequent in music of the Romantic era (*c.* 1825–1900). Be watchful for them.

### EXAMPLE 11-6  Liszt: Consolation no. 2

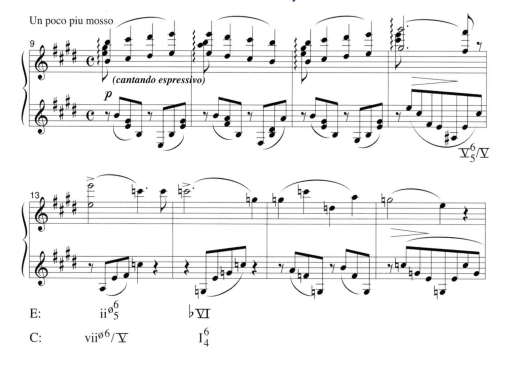

E:   ii∅⁶₅         bVI
C:   vii∅⁶/V       I⁶₄

Example 11-6 illustrates Case 3. Backing up from the authentic cadence in mm. 15 and 16 and moving forward from the beginning of the passage, we arrive at mm. 12 and 13—the tonal border. Here, the last chord diatonic in E (m. 11) and the first chord diatonic in C (m. 14) stare at each other across a harmonic divide created by two chords diatonic in *neither* key. Even so, both are recognizable chromatic harmonies in E, and the second is a common chromatic harmony in C. This chord again might be called a chromatic pivot.

Example 11-7, teeming with accidentals, looks formidable. However, it can be cut down to size by breaking it apart based on its cadences. Listen to the example and/or play it, and see if you can answer the questions posed on the music before reading the paragraphs that follow.

### EXAMPLE 11-7  Schubert: "Sehnsucht"

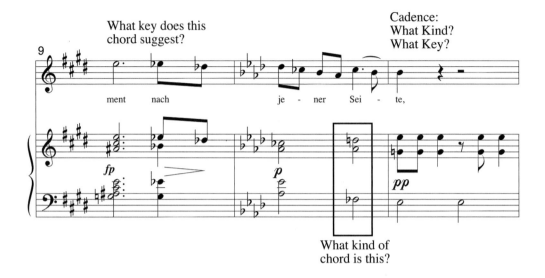

1. The song begins in A♭ and the first phrase arrives at a cadence on E♭ in m. 4. *Is the cadence chord I or V?* If I, then the music must have modulated to E♭. But the only hint of that key—the D♮ of m. 2—is offset by the returning D♭ in m. 3. Measure 4 is a half cadence—no modulation.

2. The second phrase also ends with a cadence on E♭ (m. 11). *Is the cadence chord I or V?* The Mm7 chord on beat 4 of m. 9 is a clue chord, almost always to be regarded as V$^7$. If so, it resolves to a minor tonic. So m. 11 is, like m. 4, a half cadence, and the approach chord of m. 10, beat 3—familiar from Ch. 10, perhaps—is a further clue. Measures 10 and 11 are in A♭ minor (a change of mode with respect to the beginning): i–Gr$^{+6}$–V.

3. This leaves the middle measures. The key signature of mm. 6–9 suggests either E major or C♯ minor. In C♯ minor, we would expect B♯ (the leading tone) to appear more often than B♮. This, however, is not the case, so the key is probably E, the enharmonic ♭VI of A♭.

4. On beat 3 of m. 7, a very weak cadence on a first-inversion F♯ major triad occurs. *Is this chord I or V?* You might make a case for either or both. The two following measures contain conflicting accidentals—D natural and A♯—that, when seen together, suggest B minor. And the chord of m. 9 is an A♯$^{o7}$, whose usual function is vii$^{o7}$ in B minor. It seems, then, that the music modulates first to E in m. 6, then quickly to B in m. 7, then changes mode to B minor:

|  | m. 6 |  |  | m. 7 |  | m. 8 |
|---|---|---|---|---|---|---|
| E: | I | vii$^{o6}_{5}$/ii | ii$^6$ | ii | $\underline{V^6}$ |  |
| **B:** |  |  | I$^6$ | vii$^{ø4}_{3}$/V | $\underline{V^6}$ | i |
| b: |  |  |  |  |  | i |

Notice that none of these chords are unusual or complicated when analyzed in the proper keys.

5. So how does the music swing into E? Consider m. 5. The chord on beat 4 is a Mm7 (= $V^7$ in A♭). The preceding chord is a *minor* iv. Perhaps the mode has changed to A♭ minor. If so, the $V^7$ resolves in an understandable way—*if* you think enharmonically: a♭: $V^7$-$VI_{enh}$. The modulation to E in m. 6 is by **enharmonic pivot**.

## EXAMPLE 11-8

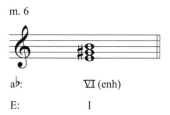

a♭:         VI (enh)

E:          I

Analysis of complex passages requires methodical thinking of this sort. You need to use what you know about chromatics, chord functions, and cadences—the three Cs. If you've trained your ear to recognize these harmonic clues, simply hearing a passage will often provide insights that elude the eye.

## ENHARMONIC FUNCTION

Chords whose functions are disguised by enharmonic spelling might be said to lead a "secret life." Two chords are particularly useful in this regard.

### The Enharmonic German Sixth Chord

## EXAMPLE 11-9

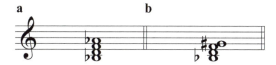

Though **a** and **b** sound identical, the two chords' spellings reflect their differing functions, **a** as a $V^7$ in E♭ and **b** as a $Gr^{+6}$ in D minor. A modulation up a half-step from d to E♭ (its Neapolitan) or the reverse can be accomplished with maximum efficiency by using this chord.

## EXAMPLE 11-10

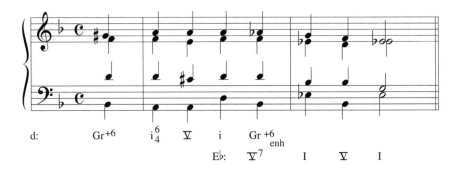

### Notes

1. Resolving the +6 interval enharmonically as a m7 transforms a German sixth chord into a dominant seventh chord, and vice versa.
2. This is a case-3 modulation.

---

### FOR PRACTICE

Respell the dominant seventh chords as German sixth chords and vice versa. Then resolve the respelled chord.

---

## EXAMPLE 11-11

The difficulty in recognizing modulations that exploit this enharmonic potential comes when composers spell the chord *in only one key.*

## EXAMPLE 11-12 Tchaikovsky: Onegin's Aria from *Eugene Onegin*

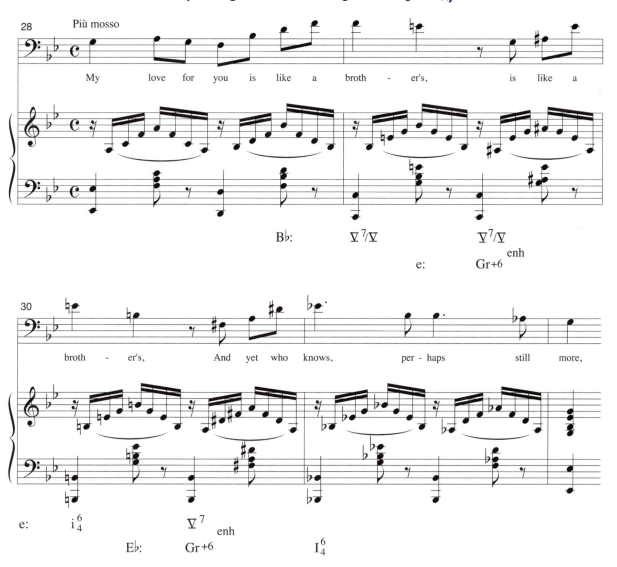

Tchaikovsky spells the chord in m. 29 in *both* the old and new keys, making clear its dual function as a $V^7/V$ in B♭ and $Gr^{+6}$ in e (note the resolution of the augmented sixth interval outward to the octave dominant B). However, he spells the chord of m. 30, beats 3 and 4, *only* in e (as a $V^7$). That spelling conceals its function as an **enharmonic German sixth chord** (a doubly augmented fourth chord, actually) in the ensuing key of E♭.

### EXAMPLE 11-13

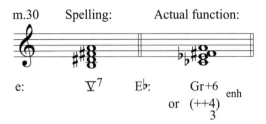

### EXAMPLE 11-14 Chopin: Fantasy in F Minor, op. 49

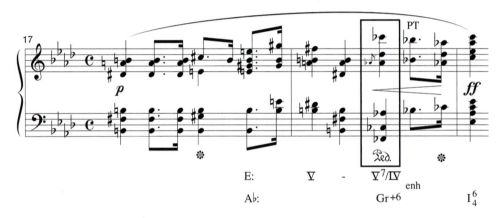

*Note*: The chord of m. 18, beat 3, is spelled as a German sixth chord in A♭ (F♭–A♭–C♭–D) rather than a doubly augmented fourth chord (F♭–A♭–B♮–D) probably because the melody descends (C♭–B♭–A♭). If the C♭ on beat 3 were to rise directly to C, it would be better spelled as B♮, creating the doubly augmented fourth chord.

## The Enharmonic Diminished Seventh Chord

The enharmonic capability of the German sixth chord pales beside that of the diminished seventh chord. This is because any one of the four chord members in a °7 can be heard as the root.

## EXAMPLE 11-15

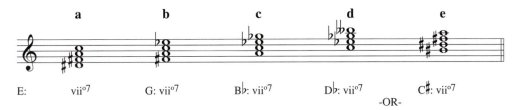

*Notes:*

1. All five chords sound identical but are spelled differently.
2. In each chord, the root functions as the leading tone in the key.
3. Examples **d** and **e** are the same leading-tone seventh chord spelled enharmonically.

Composers have exploited the enharmonic potential of the diminished seventh chord, though not as often as one might expect given its versatility. Examples follow.

## EXAMPLE 11-16  Brahms: Ballade op. 10, no. 4

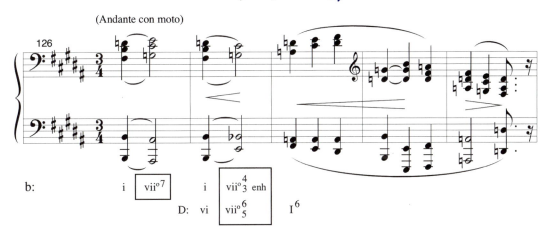

*Note*: The diminished seventh chord in m. 126 is spelled according to its function in B minor (A♯–C♯–E–G) and then, in m. 127, according to its function in D major (C♯–E–G–B♭). Aurally, the tonal border is not crossed until m. 128, but all the chords from m. 126 on are diatonic in either the old or new key. The boxed chords are enharmonic common chords, diatonic in both keys through respelling.

In the passage that follows, the enharmonic common chord of m. 135 is spelled first in the old key of g, then in the chromatic-third related key of e.

### EXAMPLE 11-17 Beethoven: Piano Sonata op. 13 (first movement) 🔊

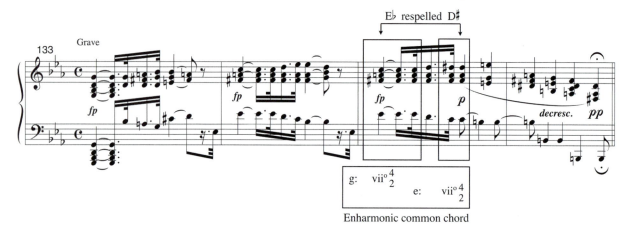

Example 11-18 shows how the chord in m. 135 of the Beethoven piano sonata might be respelled enharmonically to enable modulations to three other keys. To hear the differences, try playing through the four measures in sequence.

### EXAMPLE 11-18 🔊

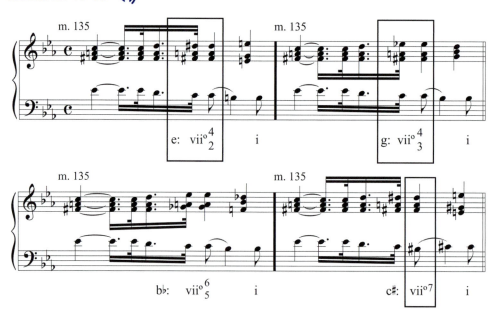

MODULATION II    171

Notice in the preceding example that lowering the C on beat 3 to B turns the diminished seventh chord into a dominant seventh chord. The same thing happens regardless of which member of a diminished seventh chord is lowered: a dominant seventh chord results.

**EXAMPLE 11-19**

In the following passage, Beethoven consolidated the steps just described, transforming a diminished seventh chord into a German sixth chord to effect a modulation to a chromatic-third related key.

**EXAMPLE 11-20**  Beethoven: Symphony no. 5, op. 67 (second movement)

The graphic that follows illustrates the versatility of the diminished seventh chord. With one or two steps you can:

### EXAMPLE 11-21 Summary: Enharmonic Juggling with the Diminished Seventh Chord. You Can:

**1** Respell the chord enharmonically so that each chord member, in turn, functions as the root.

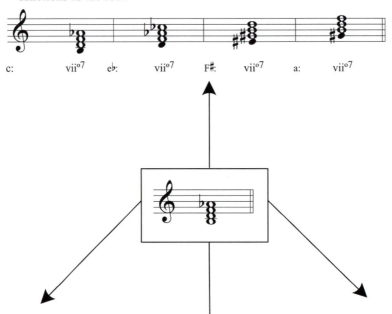

**4** Change the chord into a Gr+6 as in Step 3; then respell and resolve as ++4  
                                             3

**2** Chromatically lower each chord member, in turn, changing the chord into a $\underline{V}^7$ (enharmonic respelling of other pitches may be necessary).

**3** Change the chord into a $\underline{V}^7$ as in Step 2; then respell the m7 above the root enharmonically as an +6, turning the chord into a Gr+6.

As music approaches a tonal border, signs will normally appear—in the form of chromatically raised or lowered pitches and/or "clue chords" (major–minor seventh chords, diminished seventh chords, six-four chords, or augmented sixth chords). These signs tell us what to expect. Once in the new tonal region, we can usually look for a cadence—and we can assume the final chord of this cadence to be I or V.

When a chord at the tonal border is a German sixth chord, a dominant seventh chord, or a diminished seventh chord, consider the enharmonic possibilities. Think of every $V^7$ as a potential $Gr^6$ or $++\frac{4}{3}$, and consider how every diminished seventh chord would function with each of its other chord members as the root. Often, the enharmonic functions of these chords are the key to understanding a modulation.

## SUMMARY OF TERMINOLOGY

- chromatic modulation
- common-chord modulation
- chromatic pivot
- enharmonic diminished seventh chord
- enharmonic German sixth chord
- enharmonic pivot

# CHAPTER TWELVE

# Harmonic Extensions and Chromatic Techniques

## CLIMBING THE OVERTONE SERIES

From the tenth century to the twentieth, Western harmony has climbed the harmonic series. From the open-fifth chanting of Guido's day to full acceptance of the triad in the later Middle Ages, from the extension of the triad to include sevenths in the Baroque era to the further accretions—ninths, elevenths, and thirteenths—in the nineteenth century, each addition to the vocabulary scaled the next higher rung on the overtone ladder.

### KEY CONCEPTS IN THIS CHAPTER

- triadic extension
- linear chromaticism
- harmonic sequence

**EXAMPLE 12-1**

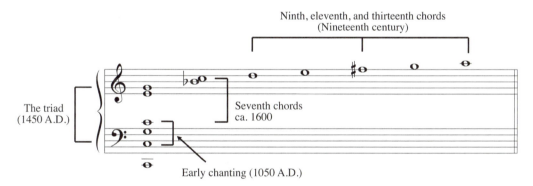

## THE DOMINANT NINTH CHORD

A **ninth chord** is a five-member sonority in which a third above the chord seventh creates a ninth above the root. Though many different ninth-chord types can be formed this way, only a few been widely assimilated into the vocabulary. The most common are the **dominant ninth chords**.

## EXAMPLE 12-2

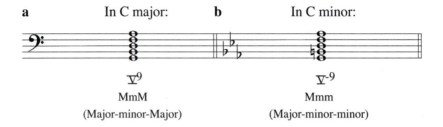

*Notes:*

1. The **dominant-major ninth,** shown in **a,** contains a major ninth above the root of a major-minor seventh chord (MmM).

2. The **dominant-minor ninth,** shown in **b,** contains a minor ninth above the root of a major-minor seventh chord (Mmm).

3. Roman-numeral symbols for **a** and **b** are V$^9$ and V$^{-9}$, respectively. Common lead sheet symbols are G9 and G7–9 or G7♭9.

In art music, dominant ninth chords typically behave in only one way—as a dominant—making it possible to refer to them by function ("dominant ninth") rather than by structure ("major–minor–major ninth," and so on). Both the ninth and seventh can usually be analyzed as downward-stepping nonchord tones. Example 12-3 shows some common voicings and resolutions. All but **d** are in root position, a reflection of actual practice.

## EXAMPLE 12-3  Arrows = resolution of 7th, 9th, and LT

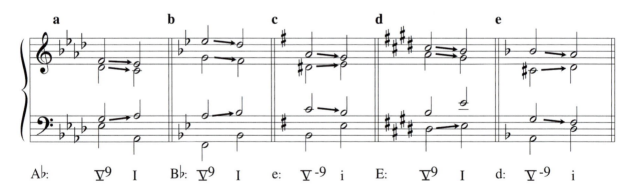

*Note:* In four-voice settings, the chord fifth is omitted.

### EXAMPLE 12-4 Chopin: Etude op. 10, no. 3

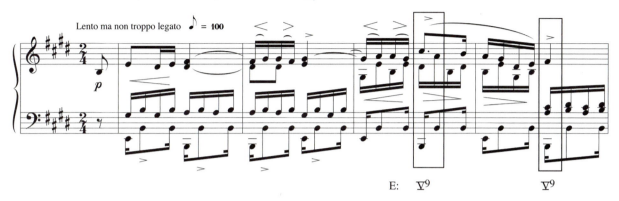

*Notes:*

1. As in this example, the fifth is often omitted. Here is the chord of m. 3, beat 2:

2. In m. 3, the ninth (C#) immediately resolves stepwise, in the manner of an appoggiatura. The seventh (A) resolves to G# in m. 4.

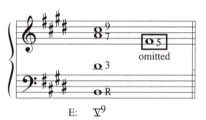

---

When the ninth resolves as it does in Example 12-4, you may wonder whether to analyze the harmony as a true ninth chord or as a seventh chord with a nonharmonic tone. Although either analysis is often valid, we can apply the same guideline to ninth chords as we did to seventh chords:

*A ninth as long as the chord belongs to the chord.*

In Example 12-5, the ninths appear not to resolve. This fact, along with their prominence, justifies their analysis as chord members.

### EXAMPLE 12-5 Tchaikovsky: Lenski's Aria from *Eugene Onegin* (act 2, scene 2)

*Notes:*

1. Three dominant-minor ninth chords appear in the passage. Their lack of an immediate or obvious resolution reflects the progressive liberation of dissonance at the pens of nineteenth-century composers.

2. One $V^{-9}$ (m. 96) is in first inversion.

## Inverted Ninth Chords

As with altered dominants, inversions of ninth chords are usually not indicated in the chord symbols because the symbols become unwieldy. Although ninth chords can be found in all inversions, the ninth is rarely, if ever, on the bottom of the chord and rarely in a lower position than the chord root.

### FOR PRACTICE

Add key signatures, voice the following ninth chords for SATB, and resolve them: $F^9$; $D^{-9}$; $V^9$ in A♭; $V^{-9}$ in A.

## EXAMPLE 12-6

## Secondary Dominant Ninth Chords

Dominant ninth chords can tonicize just as effectively as dominant seventh chords.

### EXAMPLE 12-7 Puccini: "Che gelida manina" from *La Boheme* (act one) 🔊

## FOR PRACTICE

Does the ninth of the V⁹/V in Example 12-7 resolve? In Example 12-8, one secondary dominant ninth chord and its resolution have been identified. Identify all others.

**EXAMPLE 12-8** Tchaikovsky: *Romeo and Juliet*

## OTHER NINTH CHORDS

After dominant ninth chords, the most common types are the **major ninth chord** (MMM) and **minor ninth chord** (mmM). Although rare in the nineteenth century, these chords are common in jazz. Example 12-9 shows their diatonic forms in major and minor keys.

**EXAMPLE 12-9**

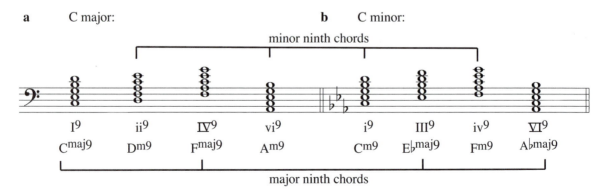

*Note*: An alternative symbol for "maj9" is "M9."

As with the dominant ninth chords, these chords are found most often in root position, and even in inversions, the ninth is normally voiced higher than the root. It may or may not resolve downward.

### EXAMPLE 12-10A Burt Bacharach and Hal David: "What the World Needs Now"

*Note:* All three of the ninth chord types shown in Example 12-9 are present in Example 12-10, along with the dominant ninth chord and a less common type (mMM). Traditional resolution of the ninth is not a priority in this vernacular style.

### EXAMPLE 12-10B

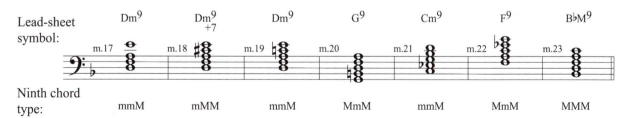

## ELEVENTH CHORDS

Eleventh chords result when a third is piled atop the ninth. These chords are found only occasionally in the nineteenth century, almost always as a dominant ($V^{11}$). They are almost never complete; the eleventh usually replaces the third.

### EXAMPLE 12-11

The upper members of this chord can be disposed in any way. However, even more often than with ninth chords, the root remains the lowest tone. Possible voicings include:

### EXAMPLE 12-12

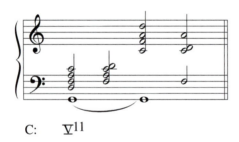

Wagner often spins long cables of dominant harmony in which the individual melodic strands intertwine to produce eleventh chords. The process often occurs over a pedal point that serves as the chord's root, as in Example 12-13.

### EXAMPLE 12-13 Wagner: "Wahn! Wahn!" (*Die Meistersinger von Nürnberg*) (act 3, scene 1)

Like non-dominant ninth chords, non-dominant eleventh chords were as rare in the nineteenth century as they are common in jazz. They are prevalent in the music of Debussy, Ravel, and some other twentieth-century composers. The most common eleventh chord, aside from the $V^{11}$, is the "minor eleventh," which can have the diatonic functions shown in Example 12-14. (When stacked as shown you can see why these chords are sometimes called "tall chords.")

### EXAMPLE 12-14

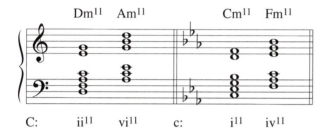

*Note*: Eleventh chords may be complete or incomplete. They almost always appear in root position, and though often stacked as shown, the upper members can be disposed in other ways.

---

### EXAMPLE 12-15 Hart and Webber: "All I ask of you" (from *Phantom of the Opera*) 🔊

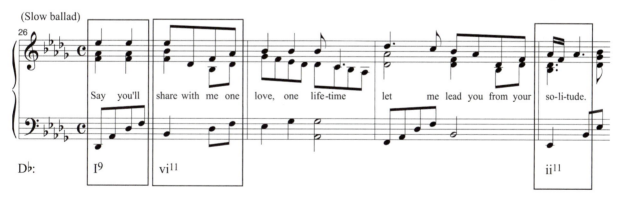

### FOR PRACTICE

Add lead-sheet symbols to Example 12-15. On the blank staff below, construct the boxed chords in simplest position, blackening the omitted chord tones.

## EXAMPLE 12-16

## THIRTEENTH CHORDS

The thirteenth chord represents the ultimate extension of the triad. Like ninth and eleventh chords, the thirteenth chord most often appears as a root-position dominant. In nineteenth-century music, the chord is incomplete, with either the eleventh or, more often, the third present (never together). In four-voice settings, the chord members critical to its identity are the root, third, seventh, and thirteenth. Possible voicings are shown below.

### EXAMPLE 12-17  Dominant 13ths in "a" minor

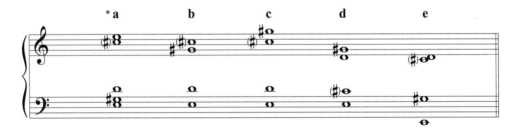

*In example a: V$^{-13}$ (with C natural) or V$^{13}$ (with C sharp)

Three of these chord members are tendency tones—the third (the leading tone), the seventh, and the thirteenth. The lowered thirteenth (C natural in Example 12-18) is enharmonically the same pitch as a raised fifth (B♯). The spelling reflects the resolution and determines whether the chord should be analyzed as V$^{-13}$ or V$^{7+5}$.

### EXAMPLE 12-18

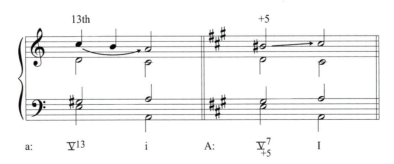

In nineteenth-century music, the thirteenth topples down to the tonic, either directly (**a**) or stepwise through the fifth of the dominant (**b**).

## EXAMPLE 12-19

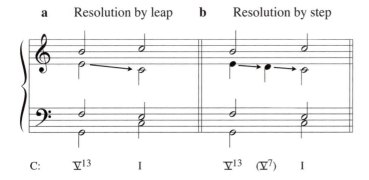

Example 12-20 contains both resolutions.

## EXAMPLE 12-20 Chopin: Nocturne op. 32, No. 1

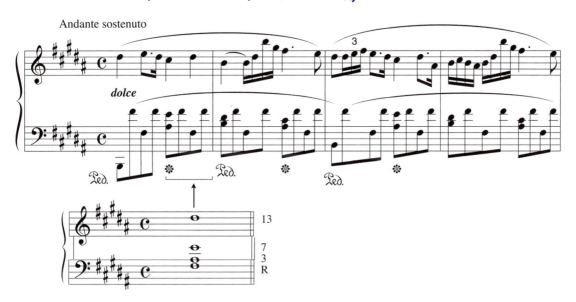

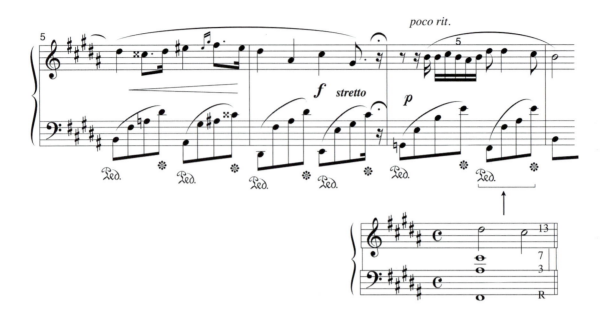

*Note*: In both cases, the chord members present are the root, the third, the seventh, and the thirteenth. In both cases, the thirteenth resolves downward—by leap in m. 1, by step in m. 7.

### FOR PRACTICE

Look again at Example 12-4. Can you locate a dominant thirteenth chord? How does the thirteenth resolve?

## LINEAR CHROMATICISM

Almost all chromatic harmonies are linear (melodic) at the core because the inflected chord members have an enhanced melodic push to the next pitch. When more than one chord member is altered—but not at the same time—the chord undergoes a *gradual* identity change that has been called **chord mutation** because the harmonies *evolve*. Because harmonies generated in this way are by-products of the voice leading, they are often nonfunctional. Roman numeral labeling may be uninformative and needlessly confusing. If Chopin was not the first major composer to experiment with chords' mutability, he produced the most renowned examples of the technique. Example 12-21 shows how a chromatic descent by each voice generates familiar chords that behave in unfamiliar ways—the V$^7$/V does not resolve to V, the vii$^{ø7}$/VI does not resolve to VI, and so on.

**EXAMPLE 12-21A** Chopin: Mazurka op. posth. 68, no. 4, 🔊
Analysis by Roman Numeral

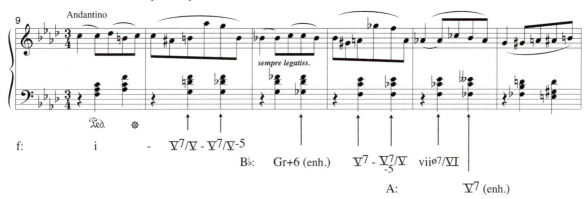

**EXAMPLE 12-21B** Chopin: Mazurka op. posth. 68, no. 4, A Practical Way

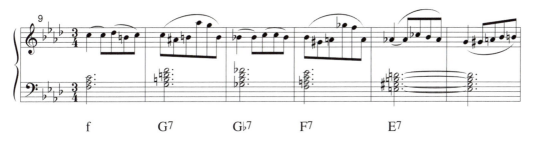

*Notes*:

1. In many cases, only a single pitch change occurs between the chords.
2. Each voice of the texture, including the melody, descends chromatically. If each voice moved downward *at the same time*, descending dominant seventh chords would result: G7—G♭7—F7—E7, as shown in **b**. Lead-sheet symbols such as these are probably more informative than Roman numerals.
3. Example **b** shows both the harmonic essence of the passage and the voice leading.

The next example is particularly well known.

**EXAMPLE 12-22** Chopin: Prelude op. 28, no. 4 🔊

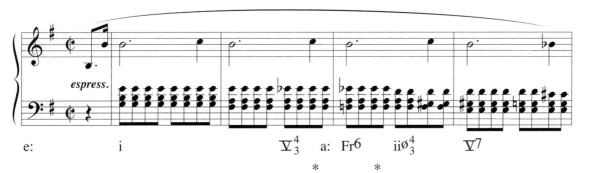

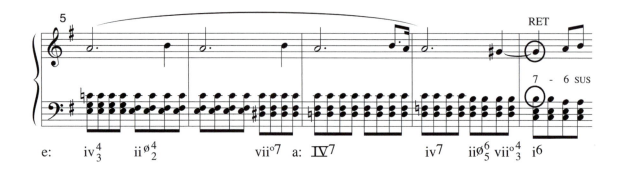

*Notes*:

1. Asterisks indicate Roman numerals that are enharmonic interpretations of the notated chords.
2. As in the previous passage, each voice in the left-hand accompaniment descends the chromatic ladder, although not in synchronization. Unlike Example 12-21, many of the harmonies generated still function in traditional ways. Measures 1 and 2 and mm. 5 and 6 make perfect functional sense in e, while mm. 3 and 4 and mm. 7 and 9 are understandable in a.

## HARMONIC SEQUENCE

In Example 12-23, the linear chromaticism in the left-hand part generates a tonicizing chord group that is repeated sequentially, tonicizing first C, then B, and finally B♭ (without ever sounding the tonicized chord). Note the way the tonicized chord groups are symbolized.

**EXAMPLE 12-23**  Chopin: Mazurka op. 17, no. 4

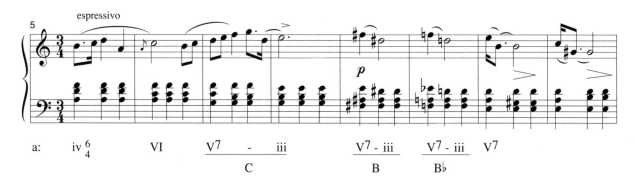

Voice leading in mm. 7–11:

## EXAMPLE 12-24

Usually, a harmonic sequence is generated when each voice of the texture forms a melodic sequence, as in the next example.

## EXAMPLE 12-25 Chopin: Nocturne op. 48, no. 2

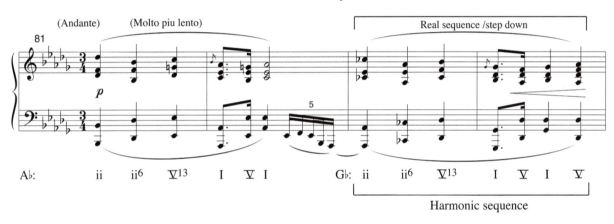

Example 12-26 shows the sequential passage that forms the basis for an entire movement. Shorter sequences are embedded within longer ones.

## EXAMPLE 12-26 Saint-Saëns: Trio in E Minor, op. 92 (third movement)

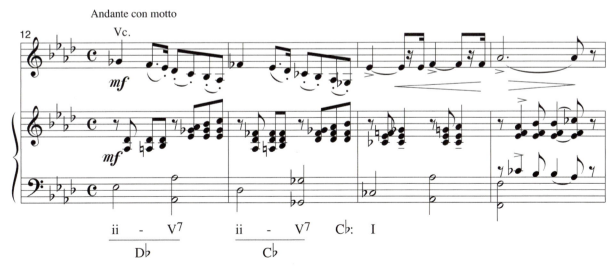

# 190  CHROMATIC HARMONY

> **FOR PRACTICE**
>
> Although in a different key and meter, and although it contains melodic chromaticism not present in Example 12-25, Example 12-26 is similar to it in some fundamental ways. Explain this. Provide a complete harmonic analysis. Identify the largest-level sequence and the embedded sequences within.

Everything discussed in Part Two involves either new vocabulary or new syntax. The triadic extensions described in this chapter represent additions to the *vocabulary*—that is, new chords (similar to new words). The linear and sequential processes spawned new *syntax*—that is, new chord order (analogous to word order). Collectively, these innovations are the harmonic stuff and substance of nineteenth-century music.

## SUMMARY OF TERMINOLOGY

- chord mutation
- dominant-major ninth
- dominant-minor ninth chord
- eleventh chord
- harmonic sequence
- linear chromaticism
- major ninth chord
- minor ninth chord
- thirteenth chord

# Form and Analysis

| | | |
|---|---|---|
| 13 | Melodic Form | 193 |
| 14 | Contrapuntal Forms | 207 |
| 15 | Small Forms | 231 |
| 16 | Sonata Form | 249 |
| 17 | Rondo | 263 |

# CHAPTER THIRTEEN

# Melodic Form

## WITHIN THE PHRASE: MOTIVE AND SEQUENCE

Identification of the phrase is essential to an understanding of musical form. However, it is not the smallest element of musical form and this, at times, is where confusion arises in defining concisely what a phrase is. A **phrase** is a melodic unit that contains harmonic motion leading to a cadence.

Two smaller units that may exist within a phrase are the motive and sequence. A **motive** is a distinctive rhythmic/melodic fragment that involves some degree of repetition within the phrase structure and beyond it:

### KEY CONCEPTS IN THIS CHAPTER

- motive and sequence
- phrases and phrase relationships
- periods and phrase groups
- cadential elision
- phrase extension

### EXAMPLE 13-1A  Chopin: Prelude op. 28, no. 20

A **sequence** is the repetition of a motive on another tonal level in the same voice. There are two types of sequence:

1. **Tonal** sequence occurs where the repetition is *diatonic*, with the interval *quality* in the repetition variable, conforming to the key.

2. **Real** sequence occurs where the repetition is *chromatic* so that the interval quality in the repetition is exact.

Both real and tonal sequences can be modified. A **modified** sequence occurs where the motivic elements remain the same but with some minor pitch or rhythm adjustments.

## EXAMPLE 13-1B

## THE PHRASE

The phrase itself normally involves harmonic motion, meaning that it contains two or more harmonies with an ending punctuated by a cadence.

## EXAMPLE 13-2A

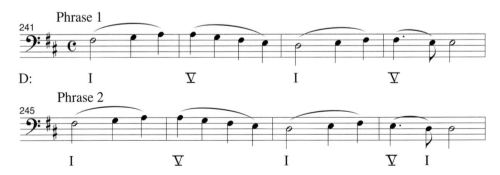

The final movement of Brahms's first symphony features a melody with phrase structure identical to that in the final movement of Beethoven's last symphony. Compare Example 13-2A with Example 13-2B.

**EXAMPLE 13-2B** Brahms: Symphony no. 1 (fourth movement)

*Notes*:

1. Each four-measure phrase states a more-or-less-complete musical idea.
2. The first phrase ends with a half cadence (m. 4), the second with an authentic cadence (m. 8).
3. Harmonic activity occurs within each phrase.

## Phrase Length

The repertory is brimming with phrases structured identically to these. However, not all are as clear about their length. In this regard, both meter and tempo must be considered. The next two passages comprise 16 beats of music. However, Mozart's unfolds in a scant ten seconds, whereas Chopin's can take 25 or so. Moreover, both passages contain multiple pauses that might be heard as cadences. Can each be regarded as a single phrase?

**EXAMPLE 13-3A** Mozart: *Eine kleine Nachtmusik*, K. 525

### EXAMPLE 13-3B  Chopin: Prelude op. 28, no. 20

The answer might depend on what follows the passage. Is it a new thought? Example 13-4 shows how Mozart continues.

### EXAMPLE 13-4  Mozart: *Eine kleine Nachtmusik*, K. 525 (continued)

Since these measures begin a new idea, it makes sense—in fact, it seems necessary—to call the first four measures (in Example 13-3A) a phrase. In fact, musicians will occasionally disagree on phrase lengths, and often, multiple views are supportable. Example 13-3B might be heard either as two-measure phrases or as a four-measure phrase. Example 13-4 is best considered a single extended phrase for two reasons: there really is no cadence until m. 10 and the incessant rhythm throughout the passage causes us to hear the singular motive as a continuous thread of music.

## Phrases and Cadences

The strongest cadences are both melodic, harmonic, and rhythmic. In Example 13-2B, the second phrase (mm. 4–8) ends melodically on the tonic, it is supported by a tonic harmony, and the rhythmic motion ceases. This creates a clear sense of repose.

Not all phrases end so definitively. In Example 13-5, the first phrase continues nonstop right through the dominant in m. 4 to begin anew in m. 5.

**EXAMPLE 13-5** J. S. Bach: "Herz und Mund und Tat und Leben" (Chorale from Cantata 147)

The four-measure phrase length is very common, but other lengths are by no means rare. And how do we distinguish two four-bar phrases from a single eight-bar phrase (as in Example 13-5)? Consider Example 13-6—is it a single 8-measure phrase or two 4-measure phrases?

**EXAMPLE 13-6** Mozart: Piano Sonata, K. 283 (first movement)

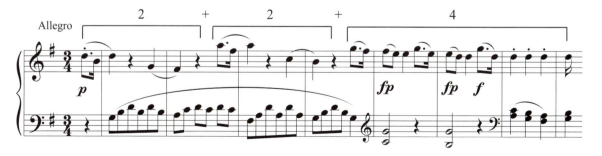

### The Musical Sentence

Either analysis is reasonable. Both 4-measure units adhere to the definition of a phrase. The question often arises with structures such as this, called **musical sentences.** A musical sentence is a type of phrase or larger unit common in the classical period that is structured in proportions of 1+1+2 (or 2+2+4), in which the first element is repeated, then followed by an expansion of the idea leading to a cadence.

### Phrase Relationships

A composer is confronted at any moment with only three choices—to repeat an idea, to vary it, or to compose something new. Since these choices pertain to melody as well as every other musical element, two phrases can be related in one of these three ways only, the relationships symbolized thus:

*Repetition:* **a a**: Octave transposition qualifies as exact repetition, but other changes, no matter how slight, do not.

*Varied repetition:* **a a′**: The second phrase is a repetition of the first with but minor modifications. Rhythmic changes, melodic ornamentation (i.e. the addition of passing tones, suspensions, and so on), sequential repetition, and even some changes in harmony qualify as minor changes.

*Contrasting phrases:* **a b**: The phrases are essentially different, melodically, harmonically, and rhythmically.

In Example 13-5, Bach chose to repeat mm. 1 and 2 of the first phrase but change the last two bars, *including the cadence.* The second phrase is similar enough to the first to be considered a variation of it, and the two would be symbolized **a a′**. If you consider Mozart's phrase structure in Example 13-6 to be two phrases (4 + 4), the first four measures are harmonically and melodically different enough from the last four measures to call these contrasting phrases and symbolize them as **a b**.

## COMBINING AND EXTENDING PHRASES

### The Period

When the second of two phrases ends more conclusively than the first, the phrases usually form a **period**. Like a question followed by an answer, the phrases of a period depend on each other for their complete meaning. The terms **antecedent** and **consequent** refer to the component phrases. Think of the inconclusive cadence that punctuates the **antecedent** as a question mark or a comma.

## EXAMPLE 13-7 Beethoven: Symphony no. 9 (fourth movement)

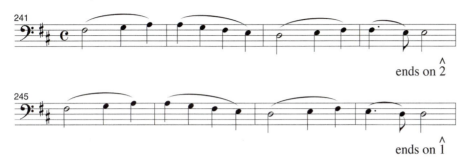

Periods are described as parallel (a a′) or contrasting (a b). A period can never be expressed as "a a" because this symbology is reserved for phrases that are identical. In such cases, the second phrase cannot end more conclusively than the first, so the period's defining feature is absent.

## Parallel Period

Example 13-7 is a **parallel period** (a a′)—a period because the consequent ends more conclusively than the antecedent, and parallel because the two phrases begin the same way (they "parallel" each other in their construction). Example 13-5 would be termed a parallel period (a a′) for the same reasons.

## Contrasting Period

In a **contrasting period**, the two phrases may share some motivic material but still differ enough to be designated "a b."

## EXAMPLE 13-8 Nikolai Rimsky-Korsakov: Scheherazade (third movement) 🔊

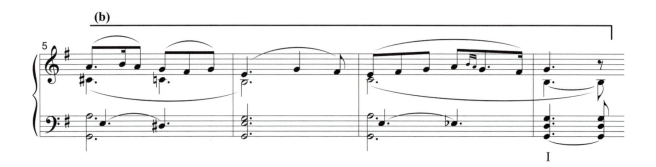

## Phrase Group

In a **phrase group**, two or more phrases that clearly belong together end *with equally conclusive cadences* and so do not display the antecedent–consequent relationship that defines a period.

Example 13-9 is a phrase group. None of the phrases ends conclusively. The lack of a conclusive cadence enhances the music's floating, ethereal effect.

**EXAMPLE 13-9** Debussy: "Claire de Lune" (from *Suite Bergamasque*)

## Double Period

A still larger melodic unit is the **double period,** comprising *two pairs of phrases,* an antecedent pair and a consequent pair. The consequent pair contains the more conclusive cadence, making the double period a *single unit*.

MELODIC FORM 201

**EXAMPLE 13-10** Beethoven: Piano Sonata op. 26 (first movement)

|  | | IAC | | **PAC** |
| :---: | :---: | :---: | :---: | :---: |
| Antecedent pair | | or | Consequent pair | |
| Phrase 1 | Phrase 2 | HC | Phrase 3 | Phrase 4 |
| a | b | | a | c |

As shown, the two phrase pairs often share the same first phrase. This is then called a **parallel double period** (Example 13-10a).

**EXAMPLE 13-10A** Beethoven: Piano Sonata op. 26 (first movement) 🔊

## EXAMPLE 13.10B  Chopin: Fantaisie-Impromptu op. 66

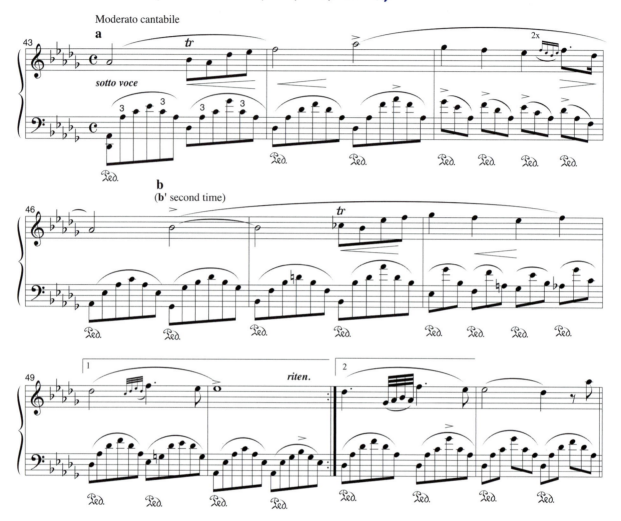

*Notes:*

1. Beethoven's op. 26 theme is a parallel double period. Although the four-measure phrases within each pair contrast with each other, the two *pairs* are parallel in construction.

2. Chopin's op. 66 is also a parallel double period. Notice, incidentally, how Chopin anticipates the opening pitch of the second phrase—B♭ (m. 46, beat 3)—giving it its own harmony, to create a syncopation and a pair of phrases that *seem* slightly asymmetric (3½ measures + 5½ measures).

3. In both examples, the final phrase ends more conclusively than all the others. Because it is a varied repetition of the second phrase (b), it is symbolized b'.

The Beethoven (a b a′b′) and Chopin (a b a b′) are symbolized in a way that reflects the parallel beginnings of the phrase pairs.

## Cadential Elision

Another technique for creating musical flow is **cadential elision**–overlapping the end of one phrase with the beginning of the next. The technique also mitigates the overly regular effect of an unbroken string of four-measure phrases.

Try this: In Example 13-11, insert this measure between m. 17 and m. 18, and observe the effect.

**EXAMPLE 13-11** Mozart: Piano Sonata, K. 309 (first movement)

The cadence you inserted completes the four-measure antecedent phrase, but it gives the passage a "blockier," repetitive sound and has a braking effect on the music. By eliding the cadence at m. 18 and directly launching a repetition of the phrase, Mozart gains momentum, mitigates the effect of the repetition, and enhances the musical flow. Film-editing techniques achieve a similar result when one image fades into the next, or when the dialogue of the coming scene is heard before the scene itself appears.

## Cadential Extension

Composers of concert music are careful to vary phrase lengths. One way is through extension. Although a phrase can be extended at any point in its course, the most common method is the **cadential extension**. This might be nothing more than a repeated cadence, or it might be more elaborate.

### EXAMPLE 13-12A Mozart: "Durch Zärlichkeit und Schmeicheln" (no. 8 from *Die Entführung aus dem Serail*)

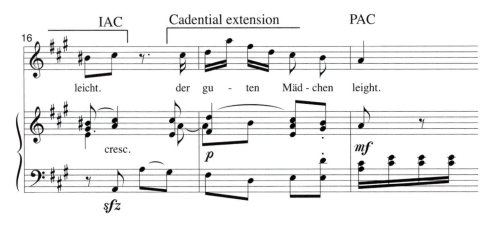

### EXAMPLE 13-12B Haydn: Piano Sonata, H. XVI: 34 (first movement)

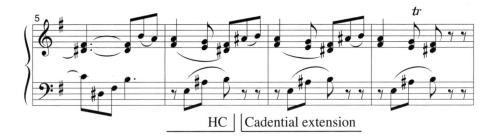

*Notes:*

1. **a** extends an authentic cadence. Notice that the cadence at m. 16 is imperfect—the melody ends not on the tonic but on $\hat{3}$ (C#). The extension ends on the more conclusive PAC.
2. **b** extends a half cadence.

---

Examples 13–12 **a** and **b** are **postcadential** extensions—that is, they *follow* the cadence. Extensions can be **precadential** as well, prolonging the *approach* to the cadence chord. They extend the cadence by *delaying* its arrival rather than *prolonging* it. Precadential passages are less obvious than postcadential. They often involve a motive that is repeated—either exactly or sequentially—just prior to the cadence.

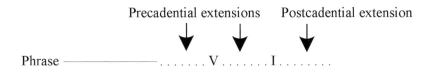

Look once more at Example 13-11. If m. 20 were to be repeated, say, twice, before coming to rest at m. 21, the repetitions would constitute a precadential extension.

Phrase analysis is tinted with shades of gray. Yet, phrasing is a significant element of style. Chopin wrote some of the most balanced, symmetric phrasing in the repertoire, while Haydn wrote some highly irregular-length phrases. Such style differences render the study of phrasing a worthwhile undertaking.

## SUMMARY OF TERMINOLOGY

- antecedent
- period
- cadential elision
- phrase
- cadential extension
- phrase group
- consequent
- postcadential
- contasting period
- double period
- precadential
- musical sentence
- parallel period

# CHAPTER FOURTEEN

# Contrapuntal Forms

## J. S. BACH'S CHORALE HARMONIZATIONS

Are Bach's chorale harmonizations **homophonic**—a melody supported by three subordinate and dependent voices—or **polyphonic**—four equal and independent voices? Any of Bach's chorale harmonizations or any piece of multiple-part music, in fact, can be described as polyphonic or homophonic to varying degrees. Compare these two passages.

### KEY CONCEPTS IN THIS CHAPTER

- general contrapuntal principles
- contrapuntal devices in Bach's two-part inventions
- implied harmony in two-voice counterpoint
- Fugal Process

**EXAMPLE 14-1A** Harmonization by Johann Crüger

**EXAMPLE 14-1B** Harmonization by J. S. Bach

*Notes:*

1. Example **a** is clearly more homophonic than **b**. Its voices lack rhythmic independence, and the inner voices also lack strongly individual contours. The soprano and bass display slightly greater melodic independence, as you would expect.

2. Example **b** is clearly more polyphonic than **a**. Its voices are rhythmically independent, and the tenor and bass display highly individual contours. Although the harmonizations are practically identical, Bach's has the added interest of independent lines gained through embellishing tones and arpeggiations.

Example 14-2 shows Bach's soprano-bass counterpoint. The notes of Crüger's bass line have been circled. Bach's bass line is primarily an elaboration of Crüger's through the addition of passing tones and extra chord tones.

### EXAMPLE 14-2 J. S. Bach: "Nun danket alle Gott" (soprano-bass framework)

*Notes:*

1. Bach's finished version is basically 2:1 counterpoint. The intervals formed on downbeats are thirds, fifths, and octaves. The embellishing tones add dissonance and rhythmic independence and "sand down" the line's rough edges. Three of the four thirds in the 1:1 counterpoint have been filled in with a PT.

2. The F♯ in m. 7 (bass) is an added chord tone, the root of a ii$^7$ (the key is E).

Most hymnlike melodies benefit from some counterpoint because of their simplicity (they were, after all, created with congregational singing in mind). More complex melodies can actually suffer from too much contrapuntal competition from the lower voices.

## BACH'S TWO-PART INVENTIONS

Although contrapuntal lines must be independent, there also must be a sense of unity. One way to accomplish this is through **imitation**—the restatement of melodic material from one voice in another voice. Imitative counterpoint is the essence of two genres of the Baroque era—Bach's Inventions and fugue.

## The Bach Inventions

Just as Bach's chorale harmonizations provide concise and uncomplicated material for studying eighteenth-century harmonic practice, his Two-Part Inventions provide a valuable microcosm of eighteenth-century imitative contrapuntal technique. Although there's no such thing as a *typical* Bach invention, the following generalizations apply:

## Motive and Countermotive

1. A **motive** is stated and then developed.

2. Typically, the motive appears in one voice and is then imitated in the other voice an octave lower.

3. A distinctive counterpoint called a **countermotive** sometimes accompanies the motive, appearing more or less consistently above or beneath it.

4. Various contrapuntal devices (to be described) may be employed.

5. Often, a modulation to the dominant (or relative major) is followed by a cadence. A middle section follows where other keys may then be tonicized. Although weak internal cadences may occur, they lack sectional affirmation before the tonic returns with the final cadence.

**EXAMPLE 14-3** J. S. Bach: Two-Part Invention no. 1 in C major., BWV 772

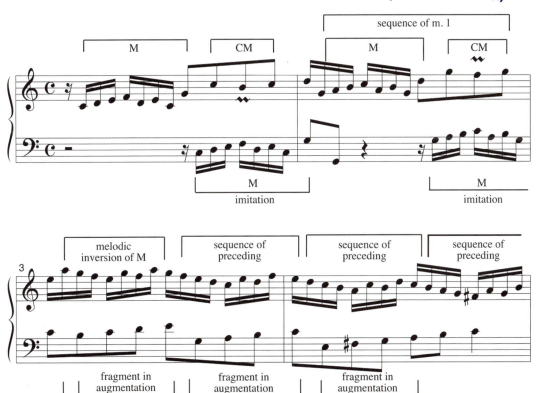

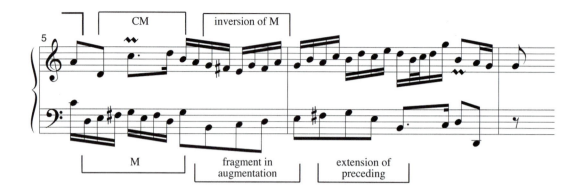

## The Devices of Counterpoint

In Example 14-3, the motive and countermotive are developed through:

- **Sequence** (present in almost every measure).

- **Imitation**: In mm. 1 and 2, the left hand imitates the right an octave lower.

- **Fragmentation**: In mm. 3 and 4, the left hand states the first four notes (a fragment) of the motive, which it then repeats in sequence, on G and then on E.

- **Augmentation**: The fragment stated in the left hand in mm. 3–4 is in longer note values than the original motive. The opposite process—**diminution** (repeating an idea in shorter note values)—is not used in this work.

- **Melodic inversion**: In m. 3 (right hand) and elsewhere, the motive is stated in contrary motion, a mirror image of its original form, with upward intervals replacing downward intervals and vice versa.

## ANALYSIS OF INVENTION NO. 6

Study the following Invention no. 6 in E major, BWV 777 by J. S. Bach. An analysis of the entire invention follows.

CONTRAPUNTAL FORMS    211

**EXAMPLE 14-4**  J. S. Bach: Invention no. 6 in E major, BWV 777

# 212 FORM AND ANALYSIS

CONTRAPUNTAL FORMS 213

## Invertible Counterpoint

Invention no. 6 relies heavily on **invertible counterpoint,** a type of *mutual imitation* where each voice states what the other just did, like this:

Higher voice:   Gesture a        Gesture b
Lower voice:    Gesture b        Gesture a

Sometimes called **voice exchange**, this cross-corridor sharing of musical material addresses two compositional concerns–unity (through repetition) and variety (through registral exchange). In invertible counterpoint, the gestures themselves are not *melodically* inverted—they're simply restated in the other voice, in *its* register. In mm. 5–8, for example, the right hand imitates the left hand of mm. 1–4 an octave higher, while the left hand imitates the right an octave lower.

> ### CONCEPT CHECK
> Locate clear examples of inverted counterpoint at two other locations.

Less obvious perhaps are mm. 51–62, which are a *transposed inverted counterpoint* of mm. 9–20 (with a few minor pitch changes).

## Sequence

After invertible counterpoint, the most prevalent device used in this invention (and in counterpoint in general) is sequence. For example, mm. 11–12 are a tonal sequence, in both hands, of mm. 9–10 a step lower.

> ### FOR PRACTICE
> Identify the sequence that begins at m. 29. In which voice does it appear, and how long does it last? What is the pitch level of the repetition? Measure 38 represents the final measure of another sequence. Where does it begin? In which voice does it appear? What is the pitch level of repetition? Locate and describe one other sequence.

## Fragmentation

Augmentation and diminution, least common of the contrapuntal devices, are not used in this invention. On the other hand, fragments of the first four-measure phrase appear throughout. The right-hand of mm. 29–32 is a sequential repetition of the figure from m. 4. Count the number of times this same figure appears. The right hand of measures 33–34 can likewise be regarded as fragmentation of mm. 1–4. And the left hand of m. 1 appears divorced from the rest of its phrase a total of seven times (in mm. 13, 17, 33, 35, 37, 56, and 59).

## Tonality

Pieces written in the Baroque era rarely breach the perimeter established by the closely related keys. Invention no. 6 modulates to the dominant, then to its relative minor, and then back to the tonic:

| m. 1 | m. 9 | m. 29 | m. 43 |
|------|------|-------|-------|
| E    | B    | g♯    | E     |

> **CONCEPT CHECK**
>
> Identify the common chord in each of the modulations. Within the g♯ tonality (mm. 29–42) two tonicizations occur. Identify them.

## Implied Harmony

As with all tonal music, two-voice counterpoint is most effective when the underlying harmonies are entirely clear. But two voices can only *imply* a harmony since two pitches do not constitute a chord. In analyzing the harmonic implications of 1:1 counterpoint:

1. Octaves, unisons, fifths and thirds usually imply root-position triads, so the lower note in these intervals can be regarded as the root.

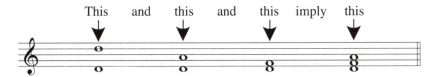

2. Sixths usually imply first-inversion triads, so the upper note in these intervals can be regarded as the root. Occasionally, a sixth will imply a six-four chord, in which case, *neither* note is the root. These chords are almost always cadential (I), passing (V), pedal (IV), or arpeggiated (usually I or V).

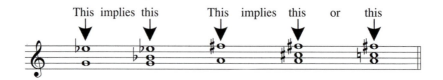

3. Tritones most often comprise scale degrees 4 and 7, which are the third and seventh of $V^7$ or the root and fifth of $vii°$. If one of the pitches is chromatic, this suggests a secondary function ($V^7/x$ or $vii°/x$).

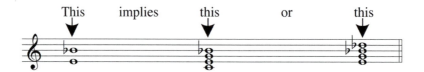

4. When one of the voices arpeggiates a complete triad, that chord is usually the underlying harmony.

5. Scalar passages contain triads filled in with passing tones. The chord tones are usually in an accented metric position relative to the passing tones.

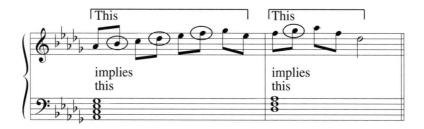

Let's apply these guidelines to Bach's Invention no. 6. Because the piece features syncopation in an almost obsessive way, where one hand lags the other by a sixteenth note, we'll need to push and pull the notes into alignment.

### EXAMPLE 14-5

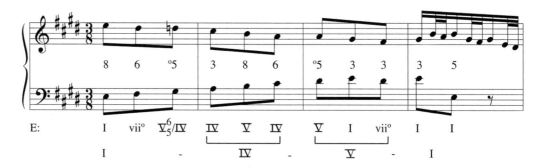

CONTRAPUNTAL FORMS    217

*Notes*:

1. Strict application of the preceding guidelines produces this harmonic analysis, which makes functional sense and sounds harmonically correct *except for m. 2, where V is pressed between two IV chords*. This chord might be better regarded as a passing I$^6_4$. Optionally, the octave Bs can be regarded as passing tones within a full-measure IV.

2. In like manner, the pitches that suggest I in m. 3 could be heard as a PT and NT within a measure-long V.

3. The four measures make perfect functional sense on a hypermetric scale. This is shown by the lower layer of Roman numerals.

---

The clearest harmonic moments in this invention are those where the underlying harmony is given a complete arpeggiation, as at mm. 9–12 (arpeggiation in both hands) and mm. 29–32 (pure arpeggiation in the left hand and embellished arpeggiation in the right hand).

Passages of two-voice counterpoint that contain successive dissonances can create harmonic ambiguity. Because of this, these moments are usually few and widely separated by passages where the harmonies are utterly clear. Measure 14 is an example.

## EXAMPLE 14-6

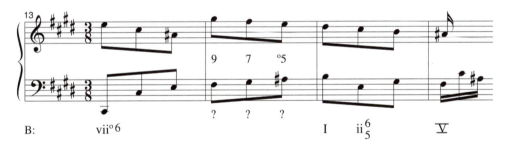

*Note*: Although the successive dissonances 9 and 7 in m. 14 are ambiguous, the tritone (°5) that follows them suggests a V$^7$ or vii°. The F♯ on beat 1 in the bass argues in favor of a V$^7$ for the entire measure, the G♯ on beat 2 a PT. The preceding and following measures are harmonically rather clear. Functionally, the succession— vii°6 | V$^7$ | I-ii$^6_5$ | V | —makes sense and it sounds right.

## Invention Analysis Checklist

1. Identify every appearance of the motive and countermotive.

2. Identify the following contrapuntal devices where present:
   Sequence
   Imitation
   Invertible counterpoint
   Fragmentation
   Augmentation and/or diminution
   Melodic inversion

3. Identify all major cadences.

4. Identify all tonalities.

# THE FUGUE

Bach's Inventions afford an excellent introduction to the **fugue** since these genres share many features. A **fugue** is a longer composition, born of imitative counterpoint, containing a fixed number of voices—most often three or four. In it, a theme, called a **subject**, is stated at the outset by a single unaccompanied voice, followed by a restatement or imitation in each of the voices in turn. In the subsequent course of a fugue, the subject returns attired in varied tonal and textural garb. The offspring of processes employed in the Middle Ages and Renaissance, the fugue reached maturity in the Baroque era and remains a viable form of composition in art music.

The fugue relies on the same contrapuntal techniques as the invention, and like the invention, it rarely contains strong sectional contrast or sharply divisional cadences. It differs mainly in its more structured opening.

## Subject and Answer

The first event in every fugue is a statement of the subject in the tonic. Although subjects average perhaps two to four measures, both longer and shorter subjects exist.

**EXAMPLE 14-7A** J. S. Bach: Fugue no. 4 (*The Well Tempered Clavier* Book I, BWV 849)

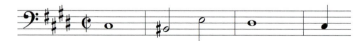

## EXAMPLE 14-7B  J. S. Bach: Fugue for Organ, BWV 578

## Real and Tonal Answers

The second event to occur in a fugue is the **answer**—the imitation of the subject, at the tonal level of dominant. Even though a dominant answer may be heard *below* the subject entry, producing the interval of a fourth below, intervallic calculations are always made ascending, and such are still considered to be "at the fifth." When all the notes of the answer are an exact transposition to the dominant (at the 5th), it is known as a **real answer**. Some answers will contain one or more pitch adjustments near the beginning, called a **tonal answer**. (The "real" and "tonal" distinction is similar to that for sequences.) Tonal answers are more common than real answers, and the effect of the alteration is to reinforce the principal tonality.

## EXAMPLE 14-8A

## EXAMPLE 14-8B

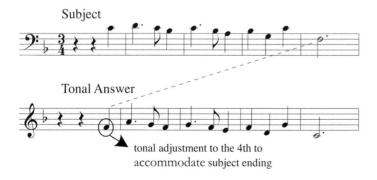

tonal adjustment to the 4th to accommodate subject ending

A tonal answer generally occurs for one of these reasons: 1) the subject ends on the tonic at its completion; 2) the 5th scale degree (the dominant) is prominent near the beginning of the subject; 3) the subject modulates to the dominant.

The following fugue subject requires a tonal answer for two of these reasons: 1) it ends on an implied tonic chord; 2) It begins on scale degree 5.

**EXAMPLE 14-9** J. S. Bach: Fugue No. 16 (*The Well Tempered Clavier* Book I, BWV 861)

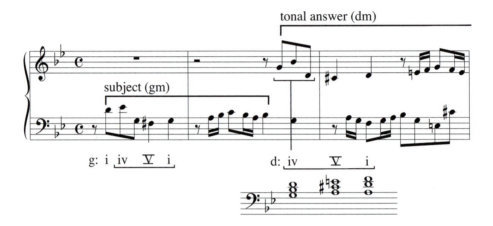

Although the implied subject progression, iv–V–i, is transposed at the 5th (minor dominant) to d minor, iv–V–I, the harmony *at the answer's point-of-entry* is still g minor—hence, the adjustment of the first note, what would be "a" to "g."

Look again at Example 14-8b. The subject begins on $\hat{5}$. It also ends on $\hat{1}$. The beginning of a fugal answer typically coincides with the end of the subject. A real answer's first pitch (G) would sound atop the subject's last pitch (F), a dissonance. (Play it to hear this.) Answering $\hat{5}$ (C) with $\hat{1}$ (F, an adjustment to the 4th) instead of with $\hat{2}$ (G, the transposition at the 5th) accomplishes two things: it avoids opening the counterpoint on a dissonance, and it creates a tonic-dominant axis that reinforces the tonality.

When a subject modulates to the dominant, as does Example 14-10a, a tonal answer is in order. Notice that a real answer (**b**) would take the music immediately to a remote key (the dominant of the dominant). Bach's tonal answer keeps the music in C.

**EXAMPLE 14-10A**

## EXAMPLE 14-10B

Real answer (modulates to D)     not a closely related key

## EXAMPLE 14-10C

Bach's answer (tonal)     ends on tonic

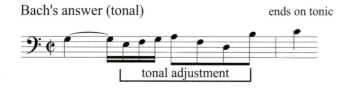

*Note*: The entire modulating part of the subject is transposed a step lower to return to the tonic.

---

The tonal level at the end of a subject or answer often determines what follows. A **bridge** is a short passage that modulates from the end of an answer to the next subject announcement. A **link** is a short passage that modulates from the end of a subject to an answer. The tonal motion of the two is opposite—from dominant to tonic (bridge) and from tonic to dominant (link). Both types of passage are usually composed of free counterpoint. **Free counterpoint** is devoid of motivic material obviously related to the subject, whereas **strict counterpoint** is based on the subject. The more common passage is the bridge, shown below in Example 14-10**d**:

## EXAMPLE 14-10D  J. S. Bach: Fugue No. 16 (*The Well Tempered Clavier* Book I, BWV 861)

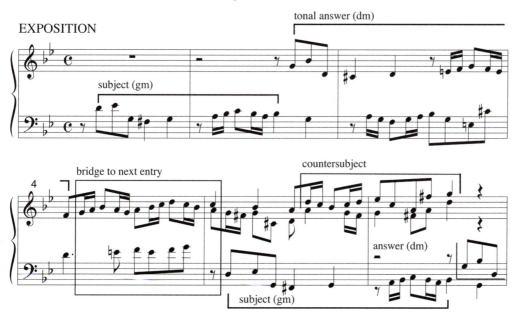

## The Exposition

The subject and answer are the first events in a fugue's **exposition**, or opening "section." The exposition comprises the **initial announcements** of the subject (or answer) in each voice in turn, and the number of these defines the number of voices in the fugue. In a three-voice fugue, three voices alternate with the subject, answer, and subject; in a four-voice fugue, four voices do so, and so on. In most fugues, the statements appear alternately in the tonic and dominant, like this:

    S (in tonic)

        A (in dominant)

            S (in tonic)

                A (in dominant)

Fugues are also defined by the *order* of entries in the exposition, the highest voice numbered "1" and the lowest voice (in a four-voice fugue) numbered "4". In Example 14-11, the highest voice states the subject in measure 9. Thus, the order of entries in this exposition is 3, 2, 1, 4. After the initial entries, a brief episode (see "Entries and Episodes" below) is heard, bringing the exposition to a close in the minor dominant.

**EXAMPLE 14-11** J. S. Bach: Fugue no. 16 (*The Well Tempered Clavier* Book II, BWV 885)

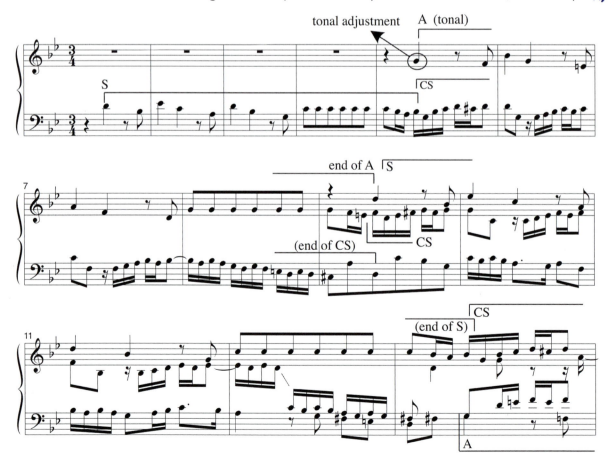

Notice in the preceding example that an identical counterpoint (labeled CS) appears with each subject (S) or answer (A) except the first. If used often against the subject during the course of a fugue, this counterpoint is termed a **countersubject** (meaning "against the subject"). It may be fashioned from motives in the subject or, as here, it may be unrelated. Typically, it makes its debut in the exposition, stated by the opening voice against the answer.

## Subsequent Entries and Episodes

Working out a musical idea is called **development**. Any or all of the contrapuntal devices listed in this chapter may be used to develop a musical idea. "Development" is what takes place in a fugue directly following the exposition. The subject reappears—either as **single entries**, in successive statements in two or more voices, termed **entry groups** (or **group entries**), and/or in overlapping statements in two or more voices, called **stretto** (meaning "tight"). Reappearances are separated by passages where the subject is absent. These **episodes** provide digressions from the main thematic material. In addition, they may develop some aspect of the subject, modulate to a new key, or provide a change of texture. *The one defining feature of an episode is the absence of a complete, intact subject.*

The next example shows the final entry in the exposition of a three-voice fugue and the ensuing episode.

**EXAMPLE 14-12** J. S. Bach: Fugue no. 12 (*The Well Tempered Clavier* Book II, BWV 881)

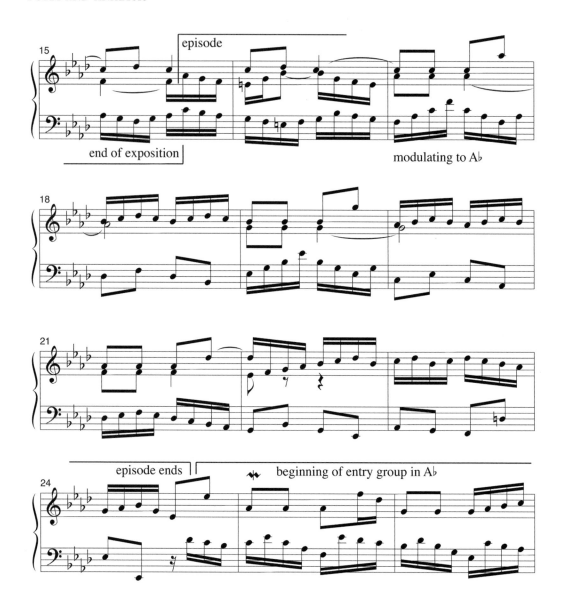

*Notes:*

1. In m. 15, the third and final voice to enter completes its statement of the subject, bringing the exposition to a close.

2. The episode provides a digression that includes a simplification of the counterpoint and a modulation to the relative major key of A♭ through sequential development of the opening eighth notes of the subject (see mm. 17, 19, and 21).

3. The episode ends with the reappearance of the subject in its entirety. The beginning of this entry group is shown (mm. 24–26).

The episode in Example 14-12 "develops" the subject through fragmentation and sequence. These, you may recall, are the most common contrapuntal devices, along with invertible counterpoint.

## The Final Statement—Closing Section

As in most compositions, fugues end in the home key, and they may do so with a single entry in the tonic, an entry group ending in the tonic, or sometimes with an episode.

## Summary

Here, then, are the essentials of the fugue:

1. A subject is stated alone and then imitated (answered) by a second voice in the key of the dominant. The remaining voices follow with statements of either the subject or its answer to complete the exposition.

2. A fugue may also contain a countersubject—a "ready-made" counterpoint that is used against ("counter to") the subject at many of its appearances. If so, its first appearance is in the exposition, against the answer.

3. The remainder of the fugue comprises reappearances of the complete subject (either single or in groups), usually in various keys and textures. These reappearances are separated by episodes, which do *not* contain the intact subject but usually develop its ideas. Often, episodes are modulatory and conclude with cadences that signal the next appearance of the subject.

4. The fugue can end with an entry, an entry group, or an episode. If it ends with an entry group, it is called a recapitulation.

## Link, Counterexposition, and Coda

In more specialized studies, you'll likely encounter a few more terms—convenient names to describe refinements or variations on the procedures just presented. Among these are:

- **Link (or Bridge)**: as previously mentioned, these are passages that connect a subject's end with an answer's beginning (link) or an answer's end with a subject's beginning (bridge).

- **Counterexposition**: an entry group that directly follows the exposition and resembles it in that it contains a complete statement of the subject by each voice (the order of entries may be different) and is in the home key.

- **Coda:** a postcadential extension at the end of a fugue (Ex. 14-13).

**EXAMPLE 14-13** J. S. Bach: Fugue no. 12 (*The Well Tempered Clavier* Book II, BWV 881)

*Notes:*

1. Codas often unfold over a tonic pedal point, as in the preceding example.
2. Codas may include a final subject statement, as in the preceding example.
3. Additional voices may be added in the coda to create a stronger ending, as in the preceding example.

## ANALYSIS

### About this Fugue

The following four-voice fugue contains a countersubject that accompanies the subject at practically every appearance. Following the exposition, entry groups containing five statements, three statements, and then five statements are separated by episodes based on material from both the subject and countersubject. Other observations follow:

1. The countersubject (mm. 3 and 4) is derived from a melodic inversion of the latter half (the "tail") of the subject (m. 2).
2. The answer (m. 2–4) is in the dominant, requiring a bridge (m. 4) to prepare harmonically for the next subject entry.
3. The exposition ends without a clear cadence (m. 8). This is typical. Fugues usually flow seamlessly from the exposition to episodes and entries.
4. The second half of the subject (m. 2) dominates this fugue in motivic fashion. Scarcely a measure passes where it is not heard in some form.

5. The subject and countersubject exchange registral positions (inverted counterpoint) throughout the fugue (as in mm. 12–16).

6. The entry group beginning in m. 28 features a three-voice *stretto* (each subject statement begins before the preceding statement has been completed).

7. The fugue ends with the "Picardy third."

**EXAMPLE 14-14** J. S. Bach: Fugue no. 16 (*The Well Tempered Clavier* Book I, BWV 861)

CONTRAPUNTAL FORMS 229

## SUMMARY OF TERMINOLOGY

- augmentation
- countermelody
- countermotive
- counterpoint
- diminution
- dissonance

- fragmentation
- homophonic
- imitation
- imperfect consonance
- implied harmony
- invention

- invertible counterpoint
- melodic inversion
- motive
- perfect consonance
- polyphony
- sequence

## SUMMARY OF FUGUE TERMINOLOGY

- answer
- bridge or link
- coda
- counterexposition

- countersubject
- development
- entry group
- Episode

- exposition
- fugue
- stretto
- subject

# CHAPTER FIFTEEN

# Small Forms

## WAYS OF LOOKING AT FORM

### Motivic Analysis

We can look at every section of music, every passage—in fact, every musical moment, and characterize it as a repetition of something, a variation/extension/development of something, or something completely new. Attempts to understand a complete composition as an outgrowth of these choices can be called **motivic analysis.** Example 15-1 can be understood, albeit a bit simplistically, in this way.

> **KEY CONCEPTS IN THIS CHAPTER**
> - musical processes
> - repetition and variation
> - binary form
> - rounded binary form
> - ternary form

**EXAMPLE 15-1** Brahms: Waltz op. 29, no. 3

*Note*: After composing two measures (C), Brahms elected to *vary* (V) his melodic idea to conform to new harmonies (mm. 3 and 4). In m. 5, he *repeated* (R) the rhythmic pattern of m. 1 but *created* a new melodic contour. Next, he chose to *vary* that material by stating it in sequence (m. 6) followed by a modified sequence (m. 7). Brahms's final compositional choice was to *repeat* the entire eight-measure phrase.

## Similarity and Contrast

Another approach to form related to the first identifies and compares the sections into which a work may be divided. At the most basic level, these sections are defined by two things: (1) cadences and (2) the similarity or contrast present in the music.

Example 15-2 shows the rest of the Brahms Waltz.

### EXAMPLE 15-2 Brahms: Waltz op. 29, no. 3

*Notes*:

1. The two halves are obviously more alike than dissimilar.
2. The element most important in defining the form is the cadence in m. 9. It divides the piece into two parts. The second most important element is probably the melody itself, which, while motivically similar throughout, is nevertheless different enough in mm. 10–17 that we do not hear it as a repetition of mm. 1–9.

## Musical Processes

A third approach to form is through identification of musical processes. At any point in any composition, the music is likely to be doing one of five things:

(1) setting the stage for what's to come (preparatory process); (2) stating a theme (thematic process); (3) moving from one section, mood, tonality, tempo, and so on to another (transitional process); (4) preparing for or extending a cadence (cadential process); (5) developing a musical idea (developmental process).

Each of these musical processes has distinct qualities that affect the listener in different ways. Short works such as the Brahms Waltz, and most popular music as well, do little beyond stating a melody (the thematic process), perhaps with extended endings (the cadential process). More complex works are likely to exhibit the other processes as well. The musical examples in ensuing parts of this chapter employ three of these processes—the thematic, transitional, and cadential—which are exemplified in an elementary way in Kuhlau's Sonatina op. 20, no. 1.

The **thematic process**: This typically involves full-blown melodies that display a unified mood, tonality, and tempo. The thematic process usually features complete phrases and periods with well-defined contours, varied but uncomplicated rhythms, and clear cadences. *Note*, however: The cadences themselves, necessary phrase-defining elements in *all* melodies, do not constitute the cadential *process*, as will be described shortly.

**EXAMPLE 15-3** Kuhlau: Sonatina op. 20, no. 1 (first movement)
Thematic Process

*Note*: Contrasting four-measure phrases are punctuated by clear cadences (both HCs). Contours are distinctive, rhythms are simple, and the tonality is stable.

The **transitional process:** A common element is a change in tonality. The term **transition** describes movement *away from* the tonic and **retransition** describes movement *back to* the tonic. Because transitional passages often connect themes, they typically lack a strong melodic character of their own, instead making ample use of scales, arpeggios, and sequences.

**EXAMPLE 15-4** Kuhlau: Sonatina op. 20, no. 1 (first movement)
Thematic Process

*Note*: Composed entirely of arpeggiations in the bass, the passage can be viewed as a melodic "non-event" that connects the thematic passage shown in Example 15–3 with the next thematic passage. A mode change (m. 12) precedes a V/V V7/V (mm. 14–15) that sets up a new tonality, the dominant.

The **cadential process:** Cadences are present within *all* the processes. However, it is the build-up to or extension of a cadence that constitutes the *cadential process*, and it can be quite lengthy. *A*pproach to a cadence usually happens through a prolonged dominant or predominant, and *e*xtension usually involves a prolongation of the final cadence chord—either I or V. Repeated cadential harmonies and short melodic figures are common.

**EXAMPLE 15-5** Kuhlau: Sonatina op. 20, no. 1 (first movement)
Cadential Process

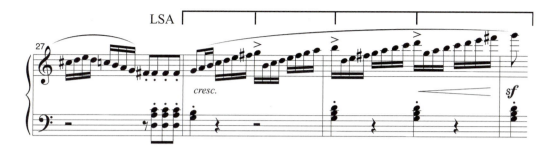

*Note*: The passage is a repeated and extended authentic cadence in the dominant (G). Like the transition in Example 15–4, it is a melodic non-event, nothing but an extended G major scale, with accents that create a large-scale arpeggiation (LSA) of the new tonic in mm. 28 and 29. Unlike the transition, it does not modulate but remains anchored in its tonality.

Kuhlau's Sonatina op. 20, no. 1, from one of his earliest sets, illustrates the thematic, transitional, and cadential processes in their most elemental form. At the pens of greater composers such as Mozart and later composers such as Beethoven, the processes are often more complex—more complex but fundamentally the same.

### CONCEPT CHECK

Identify the musical process in each of the following passages from Mozart's Piano Sonata K. 332 and explain the reasons for your choices.

**EXAMPLE 15-6A** Mozart: Piano Sonata, K. 332 (first movement) 🔊

**EXAMPLE 15-6B**

**EXAMPLE 15-6C**

## STATEMENT AND RESTATEMENT

Immediate, exact repetition is rarely reflected when describing music's form. Our topic here, then, is actually "statement and *varied* restatement." This is designated A A′. The simplest form of statement-varied restatement is the parallel period, shown in Example 15-7.

SMALL FORMS 237

## EXAMPLE 15-7 Chopin: Prelude op. 28, no. 7

*Notes*:

1. The two phrases, a (mm. 1–8) a′ (mm. 9–16), form a parallel period—*parallel* because they are rhythmically identical and built from the same idea, and *period* because only the second (final) cadence is conclusive.

2. Only one musical process is present—the thematic. Virtually all characteristics of the thematic process are on display.

3. A high point is reached in m. 12, created through a crescendo, a rise to the highest pitch, and the only chromatic harmony ($V^7/ii$) of the piece.

---

Example 15-8 is a longer, more complex form of varied restatement. The A section comprises several phrases: a (mm. 1–8) followed by its exact repetition (mm. 9–16), and b (mm. 17–24) followed by a cadential extension (mm. 25–28) and retransition (mm. 30–34).

238    FORM AND ANALYSIS

**EXAMPLE 15-8** Clementi: Sonatina op. 36, no. 1 (Vivace)

SMALL FORMS    239

*Notes*:

1. A′ begins at m. 35, identical to A for the first sixteen measures. Its b phrase is altered to remain in the home key of C, then repeated exactly, and the repetition is followed by a cadential extension (mm. 67–70). A complete diagram of the form looks like this:

| A |  |  |  |  | A′ |  |  |  |  |
|---|---|---|---|---|---|---|---|---|---|
| a | a | b | ext. | retrans. | a | a | b′ | b′ | ext. |
| m. 1 | m. 9 | m. 17 | m. 25 | m. 29 | m. 35 | m. 43 | m. 51 | m. 59 | m. 67 |

2. Three processes are present: thematic (mm. 1–24 and 35–59), cadential (mm. 25–28 and 67–70), and transitional (mm. 29–34). The cadential extensions both occur over a tonic pedal point–G at mm. 25–28 and C at mm. 67–70.

3. Example 15-8 shows how all three compositional choices—to repeat, vary, or create—can be invoked at different levels.

Example 15-8 is considerably longer and more complex than Example 15-7. Still, both are based on the same principle—statement and varied restatement (A A′). Example 15-8 clearly divides into two parts—because of its length and the elaborate cadential preparation in mm. 30–34—whereas Example 15-7 is better viewed as a one-part form.*

## THE CODA

The term **"coda"** came up in the context of the fugue in Chapter 14. When a cadential extension occurs at the end of a piece, be it a fugue, a sonata, or a song, that extension is often called a coda. Codas vary in length, from the five-measure coda in Example 15-8 to the gargantuan 129 measures that end the first movement of Beethoven's Fifth Symphony. Despite their length or musical style, all codas follow what might have been a piece's concluding cadence.

Codas normally embody the cadential process. Example 15-9 contains features that are typical in codas.

**EXAMPLE 15-9** Beethoven: Piano Sonata op. 13 (second movement)

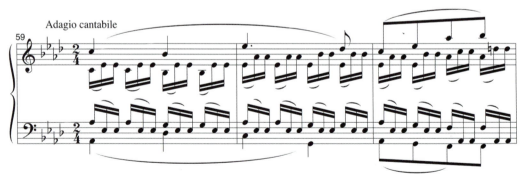

---

* It is possible to view the form of Example 15-8 in other ways. Your instructor may choose to discuss these alternatives later.

*Note*: The cadential process begins where the thematic process ends, in m. 66. From this point forward, the music scarcely departs from the tonic in repetitive melodic statements, first in eight-beat patterns, then in four-beat patterns, over $V^7$–I harmonies.

## STATEMENT AND CONTRAST/BINARY FORMS

Statement followed by contrast creates a two-part (binary) form. As with melodic phrases, the difference between A A′ and A B resides *in the degree of contrast* between the sections. In the latter, the composer's choice is not to repeat or vary, but to create something new. Even so, because composers usually seek ways to tie their ideas together, relationships between the sections are common.

Three commonly found harmonic/tonal plans are:

### EXAMPLE 15-10A

| Section: | A | | B | |
|---|---|---|---|---|
| Cadence: | | AC or HC | | AC |
| Tonality: | I<br>i | I<br>i | I<br>i | |

### EXAMPLE 15-10B

| Section: | A | | B | | |
|---|---|---|---|---|---|
| Cadence: | | AC | | | AC |
| Tonality: | I<br>i | V̲<br>v or III | V̲<br>v (III) | I<br>i | |

### EXAMPLE 15-10C

| Section: | A | | B | | |
|---|---|---|---|---|---|
| Cadence: | | AC | | | AC |
| Tonality: | I<br>i | V̲<br>v or III | Various<br>Various | I<br>i | |

### Sectional versus Continuous Forms

The main differences are tonal. **a** remains in a single key. If its A section ends in a PAC, it is termed a **sectional binary form**, meaning the first section could stand alone. If its A section ends in a HC, it is termed a **continuous binary form**, meaning the first section relies on the second for completion. **b** and **c** modulate by the end of the first section and, by definition, are continuous. **b** and **c** differ in their return to the tonic in the second section; **b** does so directly, whereas **c** explores other tonalities first.

## Symmetric versus Asymmetric Forms

Example 15-11 differs in two significant ways from the preceding forms. First, B (mm. 8–24) is vastly longer than A, creating an **asymmetric** rather than **symmetric** binary form. Second, B cannot be viewed as a varied repetition of A. Even though Bach continued to draw upon the piece's opening motive, B is substantially different. Bach clearly opted to create rather than to vary or repeat after m. 8.

This is a visual representation of the form:

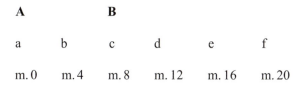

### EXAMPLE 15-11  J. S. Bach: French Suite no. 5 (Gavotte)

## STATEMENT-CONTRAST-RESTATEMENT

The restatement of original material following a contrast can be exact (A B A) or varied in any number of ways (A B A′). One of the most common ways to alter the returning material is to shorten it, although lengthening it is also possible. The principle of statement–contrast–restatement has been mined extensively. It became the basis for myriad Romantic character pieces and operatic arias, and countless popular songs.

**EXAMPLE 15-12**  Beethoven: Sonata op. 14, no. 2 (second movement)

*Notes*:

1. The overall form is A(m. 1) B(m. 9) A′(m. 13).
2. The music following the four-measure B is equal to A in length. However, four of these measures (mm. 17–20) follow what might have been the final cadence (m. 16) and sound like a cadential extension. The actual repeated material is a mere two measures (mm. 13–14).
3. B contrasts with A and A′ in its legato articulation and its initially higher register.
4. The texture is homophonic throughout.
5. The thematic process dominates.

Here is a visual representation of the form:

| A | B | A' | ext. |
|---|---|---|---|
| a | b | c | a' |
| m. 1 | m. 5 | m. 9 | m. 13 | m. 17 |
| I | I - V | I (IV) V | I |

Consider Example 15-12 in light of the three choices available to Beethoven. In mm. 1–2 he *created* an idea. At mm. 3–4 and 5–6 he *varied* it. He then *varied* m. 6 to form mm. 7 and 8. At m. 9, Beethoven *created* a new idea that he *varied* in mm. 10 and 11 (modified sequences). He *repeated* his opening at mm. 13–14, then *created* anew up to the cadence at m. 16. He again *created* in mm. 17–19, after which he *repeated* the cadence of m. 16.

## TERNARY FORMS

Ternary forms, as the name implies, have three sections that stand on their own both harmonically and proportionally. In Example 15-13, schumann creates three harmonically distinct periods of eight measures each. The first period (mm. 1-8) begins and ends with tonic in A major. The second period begins and ends with tonic in D major and, the third period is a repeat of the first period in A major. This creates a clear three-part structure, where the b "section" or period holds equal "weight" with the outer a sections in length and harmonic identity.

**EXAMPLE 15-13** Schumann: Kinderszenen no. 6 ("Wichtige Begebenheit")

## Rounded Binary versus Ternary Form

As Example 15-14 illustrates, the differences between rounded binary and ternary forms involve elements beyond the cadence structure. Typical characteristics of the full ternary include:

- An A section that ends harmonically closed without modulating.
- A strongly contrasting B that's harmonically self-contained (that is, it begins and ends in its own key, which is different from A).
- A complete return of original material.

When appearing together, these elements create the sense that B is a self-contained section distinct from A and A′.

Following is a graphic summary of the differences between the forms. It also shows their typical tonal structure. The "barlines" indicate points where strong cadential divisions occur.

## EXAMPLE 15-14

**ROUNDED BINARY**                               **TERNARY**

A     |   B    A'     Shortened       A     |   B     |   A     Full
                               return                                                return

I  -  x   |   x  -  I                          I  -  I   |   x  -  x   |   I

When the choice between rounded binary and ternary is unclear, consider this:

*The harder a distinction is to see,*
*The less significant it's apt to be.*

Put another way, if it's possible to regard a piece as one form or the other, chances are the distinguishing factors are slight and more than one viewpoint is sustainable. In these cases, agreeing on the form might be less important than understanding why or why not it might be viewed as such.

## SUMMARY OF TERMINOLOGY

- asymmetric
- binary
- coda
- continuous forms
- rounded binary
- sectional forms
- symmetric
- ternary

# CHAPTER SIXTEEN

# Sonata Form

## A BRIEF HISTORY

### Establishment, Departure, and Return

The origins of sonata form can be traced to Baroque dance movements such as those discussed in Chapter 15, especially the rounded binary form. Recall that three tonal events took place: (1) establishment of the tonic followed by a modulation to a secondary key (usually the dominant); (2) an area of harmonic instability; (3) a return of the tonic.

### KEY CONCEPTS IN THIS CHAPTER

- cadential process
- developmental process
- exposition
- tonic-dominant polarity
- transition and retransition
- recapitulation
- coda

### EXAMPLE 16-1

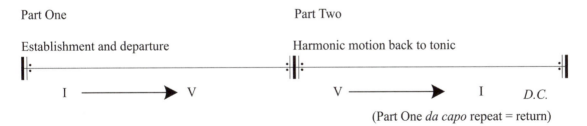

Over time, distinctive thematic material came to mark the two tonalities of Part One, and the beginning of Part Two was given over to developing the themes' potential and exploring additional tonalities. The resulting harmonic instability of this area was balanced by an extended return of the intact themes but remaining in the tonic, thereby reconciling the tonal conflict of Part One and providing a satisfying sense of closure.

Over the years, musicians began to observe consistencies in these compositions that led to a theoretical description of the form. While studying sonata form, think of it not as a mold into which composers poured their ideas but rather as a general way of proceeding. Each example of sonata form differs from others in ways that make it unique.

## MOZART: *EINE KLEINE NACHTMUSIK* (FIRST MOVEMENT)

### The Exposition

The **exposition** involves the establishment of two tonal areas (tonic and dominant) that consist of **primary thematic material** and **secondary thematic material** respectively. The thematic process may begin immediately or follow an **introduction** that is typically in a slow tempo.

### Primary Tonality and Theme

In *Eine kleine Nachtmusik,* the primary theme (mm. 1–18) begins without introduction. It consists of four phrases that form a double period. While all are four-measure phrases "at heart," the second (b) is extended to six measures and the fourth (c') is truncated to three measures. While listening to this part of the movement, take note of its tonal stability and strong melodic identity.

**EXAMPLE 16-2**  Mozart: *Eine kleine Nachtmusik* (primary thematic/tonal area)

SONATA FORM     251

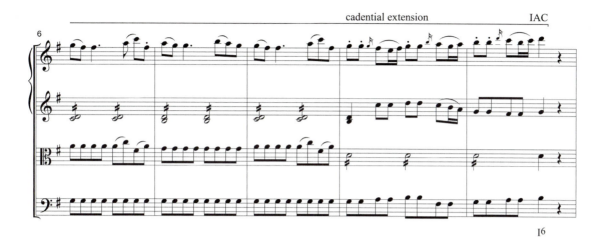

*Note*: Phrase a = mm. 1–4 ending with HC. Phrase b—mm. 5–10 ending with IAC. Phrase c = mm. 11–14 ending with IAC. Phrase c′ = mm. 15–18 ending with PAC.

## Transition

The primary thematic area is usually followed by a **transition**, characterized by an increase in rhythmic activity and tonal instability. The transition facilitates a modulation to the dominant, or in minor keys, to the relative major (III). In *Eine kleine Nachtmusik*, the transition begins in m. 18 with a dramatic *sforzando* and increased rhythmic activity in the lower strings. The transition ends in m. 27 with a half cadence in D major.

**EXAMPLE 16-3** Mozart: *Eine kleine Nachtmusik* (transition)

## Secondary Tonality and Theme

A new and often contrasting theme marks the secondary tonal area, or "polar key." In *Eine kleine Nachtmusik*, as in much of Mozart's music, the new theme is quieter and more lyrical. Note, incidentally, the more polyphonic interplay between the upper and lower strings. This theme consists of a parallel period (mm. 28–35) followed by a contrasting period that repeats in measures 43 through 50.

**EXAMPLE 16-4**  Mozart: *Eine kleine Nachtmusik* 🔊
(secondary thematic/tonal area)

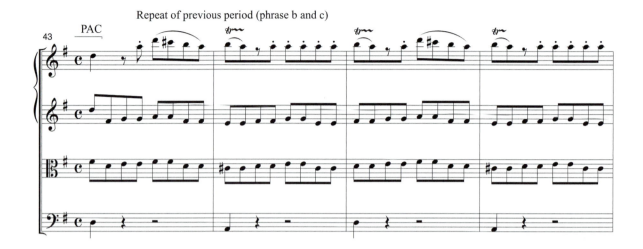

## Closing Area

The exposition usually concludes with a closing area, in which the *cadential process* described in Chapter 15 prevails. If this material has a strongly thematic character, it's called a **closing theme**. If it's purely cadential, it is more correctly termed a **codetta**. In *Eine kleine Nachtmusik,* a short cadential extension (mm. 51–55) follows an elided cadence (mm. 51) and wraps up the exposition in the dominant, D major.

### EXAMPLE 16-5 Mozart: *Eine kleine Nachtmusik* (codetta) 🔊

## Development

The **developmental process** involves the working out of musical ideas presented earlier. These ideas may be combined contrapuntally. Thematic fragmentation, unstable harmonies, rapid modulation, and increased textural complexity are common. One idea, one dynamic level, or one texture may quickly yield to the next, creating a capricious quality. In developmental passages, change is the one constant, and it is often dramatic. In *Eine kleine Nachtmusik*, the development begins with a restatement of the opening fanfare-like motive. Then follow tonicizations of D Major, C Major, A Minor, and G minor, during which the thematic material beginning at m. 35 is stated sequentially.

### EXAMPLE 16-6 Mozart: *Eine kleine Nachtmusik* (development) 🔊

## Retransition

"Retransition" literally means "moving back to." At the end of the development, a harmonic preparation for the returning tonic usually occurs. This often occurs over a dominant pedal point or other **dominant prolongation**. In *Eine kleine Nachtmusik*, the retransition occurs in mm. 70–75. (See Example 16-6.)

## Recapitulation

The most significant aspect of a recapitulation (or "return") is the re-establishment of the tonic. Typically, the primary and secondary themes return in the same order but may undergo some revision with some phrases shortened, lengthened, or omitted altogether.

The most significant change is that the secondary thematic area is heard in the *tonic* instead of the dominant, often necessitating changes in the transitional area. Composers have dealt with that passage in the following ways:

- *Transposition*: The transition may be simply transposed so that it remains in the tonic.
- *Recomposition*: The transition may be rewritten in part or in whole, to exclude the original modulation.
- *Repetition*: If the original transition did not modulate, then it may simply be repeated.
- *Omission*: The transition may be omitted entirely.

In *Eine kleine Nachtmusik*, the primary thematic material is restated, followed by a transition partially repeated and slightly recomposed to end on a half cadence in G rather than in D.

**EXAMPLE 16-7** Mozart: *Eine kleine Nachtmusik* (recapitulation)

SONATA FORM 259

The secondary thematic material follows, in the home key of G but otherwise unchanged.

**EXAMPLE 16-8** Mozart: *Eine kleine Nachtmusik* (recapitulation continued) 🔊

## Coda

The coda is the final bit of cadential music in a sonata-form movement. If present, it typically occurs after the cadence that terminates the closing area—*the cadence that otherwise would end the movement*. Its length can vary considerably, but in most cases, the musical process is cadential throughout, never straying very far from the tonic, which it prolongs.

**EXAMPLE 16-9**  Mozart: *Eine kleine Nachtmusik* (coda)

## SUMMARY OF *EINE KLEINE NACHTMUSIK* (FIRST MOVEMENT)

**The exposition** begins without introduction in G major.

- The primary theme is a double period.

- The secondary theme (in D, the dominant) begins in m. 28, comprises two symmetrical periods (contrasting and parallel) with a repetition of the second, and ends with a short closing section.

**The development** begins with a statement of the opening phrase in the dominant, and immediately takes on a developmental character (harmonic fluctuation and thematic fragmentation).

- E minor is tonicized in m. 59 (note the leading-tone D♯), but a deceptive resolution effects an abrupt modulation to C major (m. 60).

- Fragments of the thematic material from m. 35 and beyond are heard in C, A minor (note the leading tone G♯ in m. 65), and G minor (suggested by its dominant in measure 67 and the continuing presence of B♭ and E♭ through m. 71).

- The mode changes quickly to G major in m. 74 when the B♭ changes to B♮ in a cadential six-four chord (mm. 74–75).

- Compared to the exposition, the development is relatively short with only three keys explored and two themes heard.
- The retransition (m. 70) is equally brief.

**The recapitulation** begins exactly like the exposition.

- Because the recapitulation remains in the home key, the transition is altered—shortened by two measures, the last two cleverly rewritten to introduce the secondary thematic area in the tonic.
- The secondary thematic area and **closing section** are almost exact transpositions of the original passages.

**The Coda:** Any music that is **added** after the completion of repeated music signals the end of the recapitulation and the beginning of a closing section known as the **Coda**. It is a cadential extension that may or may not use thematic/motivic material.

---

### Additional pieces for study

Beethoven: Piano Sonata op. 10, no. 1 (first movement)
(Turek/McCarthy: *Theory for Today's Musician* Workbook)

Haydn: Piano Sonata H. XVI:37 (first movement)
(Turek/McCarthy: *Theory for Today's Musician* Workbook)

Mozart: Piano Sonata K. 332 (first movement)
(Turek: *Analytical Anthology of Music*)

Haydn: String Quartet op. 20, no. 5 (first movement)
(Turek: *Analytical Anthology of Music*)

Beethoven: String Quartet op. 18, no. 1 (first movement)
(Turek: *Analytical Anthology of Music*)

Beethoven, Piano Sonata op. 53 (first movement)
(Turek: *Analytical Anthology of Music*)
Mendelssohn, Octet for Strings op. 20 (first movement)

---

## SUMMARY OF TERMINOLOGY

- closing area
- codetta
- developmental process
- dominant prolongation
- exposition
- primary thematic/tonal area
- recapitulation
- retransition
- secondary thematic/tonal area

# CHAPTER SEVENTEEN

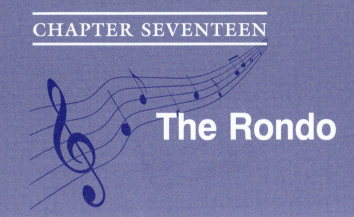

# The Rondo

## PERSPECTIVE

### Refrain and Episode

Along with sonata form, another popular format for extended movements in the classical period and beyond was the **rondo**. Rondos are of two principal types—the five-part (A–B–A–C–A) and the seven-part (A–B–A–C–A–B–A). Both types can be found with another B refrain in place of C: A–B–A–B–A, and A–B–A–B–A–B–A.

**KEY CONCEPTS IN THIS CHAPTER**

- episode and refrain
- rondo form

The rondo principle involves a theme that recurs as a **refrain** interspersed with contrasting sections called **episodes**. Refrains and episodes may be connected by transitions (from the refrain in the tonic to an episode) and retransitions (from episode to refrain), and the piece or movement may end with a coda. In the classical style, refrains are often folk-like melodies with balanced phrases that produce symmetrical periods. While episodes tend to be in related keys and may display developmental features, the refrain typically remains in the tonic and undergoes very little transformation. This makes it the most stable and immediately recognizable feature of the form and an anchor that keeps the music from drifting into remote tonal waters. The two intervening episodes ("B" and "C") are harmonically explorative, often in mediant relationships to the refrain.

In this study, we'll consider a **five-part rondo,** the second movement of Beethoven's "*Pathétique*" Sonata op. 13. This staple of piano literature with its decidedly *unfolk-like* refrain, closely parallels the norms in the treatment of the rondo form of the middle and latter classical period.

## BEETHOVEN: PIANO SONATA OP. 13 (SECOND MOVEMENT)

### The Rondo Theme (A)

The theme in this movement is a beautifully lyric melody marked "Adagio cantabile," consisting of two four-measure contrasting phrases, the first ending with a HC, the second ending with a PAC. The eight-measure period is repeated an octave higher with textural enhancement in the alto.

**EXAMPLE 17-1** Beethoven: Piano Sonata op. 13, (second movement)

THE RONDO 265

## The First Episode (B)

We encountered the term episode in our study of the fugue. Here, as there, the episode's function is to provide a digression (tonal and otherwise). Episodes may be rhapsodic and even developmental, consisting of scalar passages, motivic fragments, and arpeggiations. More often, episodes are thematic, as this one is. Its structure differs from the refrain, a single seven-measure phrase that begins abruptly in the relative minor (a tonal shift) and modulates to the dominant E-flat followed by a two-measure cadential extension (mm. 23–25). The extension, repeated, becomes a retransition, returning to the home key at the very last moment at the end of m. 28.

**EXAMPLE 17-2**

### The First Refrain (A′)

The return of the refrain is an exact restatement of the first eight measures, labeled A′ because the second eight measures are not present. It leads directly to the second episode. (Refrains are often abbreviated and sometimes varied, but almost always remain in the tonic.)

### EXAMPLE 17-3

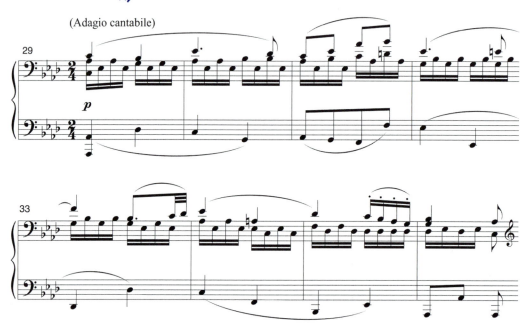

### The Second Episode (C)

The second episode is the longest of the movement and also the most rhythmically active, introducing a new element—the sixteenth-note triplet. It provides the most distant tonal digression, beginning without transition in the parallel minor (A♭ minor) and modulating to E. It ends with a three-measure retransition (mm. 48–50) to the final refrain.

### EXAMPLE 17-4

## The Second Refrain (A′)

Beethoven provides a complete restatement of the theme, retaining and enhancing the triplet accompaniment introduced in the C episode to create a sense of continuity and growth.

## EXAMPLE 17-5

## The Coda

A seven-measure coda follows the third refrain. A clear example of the cadential process, it extends the tonic of m. 66 through a repeated $V^7$–I harmonic motion. Notice how the pattern first unfolds over two measures (mm. 67–68 and mm. 69–70) and is then compressed into four beats (mm. 70–71, 71–72, and 72–73).

**EXAMPLE 17-6**

## Summary

This movement is a concise five-part major-key rondo with episodes in the relative minor and parallel minor, no transitions from refrain to episode, and brief retransitions (mm. 27–28 and mm. 48–50) from the episodes to the refrains. A diagram comparing the form of this movement to a "fully loaded" five-part rondo follows:

## EXAMPLE 17-7

**a  Five-part rondo with all elements present**

| Intro. | A | tr. | B | ret. | A | tr. | C | ret. | A | Coda |
|---|---|---|---|---|---|---|---|---|---|---|

**b  Beethoven Piano Sonata op. 13 (second movement)**

| Section: | A | B | ret. | A | C | ret. | A | Coda |
|---|---|---|---|---|---|---|---|---|
| Measure: | 1 | 17 | 27 | 29 | 37 | 48 | 51 | 66 |
| Length: | 16 mm. | 12 mm. |  | 8 mm. | 14 mm. |  | 16 mm. | 8 mm |
| Tonality: | A♭ | f-E♭ |  | A♭ | a♭-E |  | A♭ | A♭ |

tr. = transition;   ret. = retransition

## SUMMARY OF TERMINOLOGY

- episode
- rondo
- refrain
- rondo theme

# PART FOUR: The Twentieth Century and Beyond

| | | |
|---|---|---|
| 18 | Syntax and Vocabulary | 273 |
| 19 | New Tonal Methods | 289 |
| 20 | Non-Serial Atonality | 301 |
| 21 | Serial Atonality | 319 |

# CHAPTER EIGHTEEN

# Syntax and Vocabulary

Although art music in the twentieth century represented in many important respects the continuation of past practices, much of it reflected an unprecedented reassessment of the nature and function of melody, harmony, rhythm, form, sound, and even the meaning of music. A sizable catalogue of new techniques was introduced to music by a relatively small group of twentieth-century composers. This chapter considers some of the more important innovations in harmonic vocabulary and syntax, chiefly by Claude Debussy.

> **KEY CONCEPTS IN THIS CHAPTER**
> - nonfunctional harmonic syntax
> - planing
> - modality
> - new melodic and harmonic building blocks

## SYNTAX

**Syntax** refers to the order in which elements are strung together. In grammar, meaning depends not only on word *choice* but on word *order*. In music, meaning depends not only on chord *choice* but on chord *order* (and much more).

During a 20-year period, Claude Debussy (1862–1918) created a musical language of harmonic succession in which nonfunctional relationships became the norm. In the example to the right it is clear that much of Debussy's harmonic language is tertian. Beyond that, many of the harmonic norms of tonal progression have been abandoned in a way that, at the time, were quite unfamiliar. For example, what is harmonically unusual about this passage?

**EXAMPLE 18-1** Claude Debussy: *Pour le piano* (Sarabande), mm. 1–2

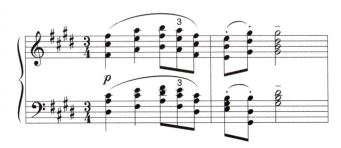

Perhaps the most noticeable harmonic feature of this excerpt is its cadence—the movement of the E major triad to G♯ minor. By either major or minor standards, it's unusual—in E it's a cadence on iii and in c♯ it's a half cadence that ends on a *minor* dominant. Leading to the cadence is a succession of seventh chords that function in a non-traditional way—in E, a vii°7 followed by a ii7 (a retrogression) and a V7. A little further along, we encounter this:

**EXAMPLE 18-2**  Debussy: *Pour le piano* (Sarabande), mm. 9–10

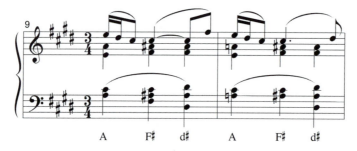

Again, nonfunctional successions of chords produce chromatic and diatonic third relationships: A—F♯—d♯—A—F♯—d♯.

## Planing

Debussy was the great liberator of the triad, freeing it from an obligation to behave in prescribed ways—hence the term **nonfunctional**. However, freedom can lead to chaos. Debussy's control—as was Chopin's and Liszt's—was linear voice-leading.

**Planing** refers to the parallel melodic motion of two or more musical lines. In Debussy's music, we can distinguish two types:

1. **Diatonic planing**: Each line moves in parallel motion with the others, by intervals of the same numeric value but not necessarily the same quality. Like a tonal sequence, the precise intervallic motion is *diatonic to the key*. In so doing, the harmonic structures are *variable*.

**EXAMPLE 18-3**  Debussy: *Pour le piano* (Sarabande), mm. 37–38

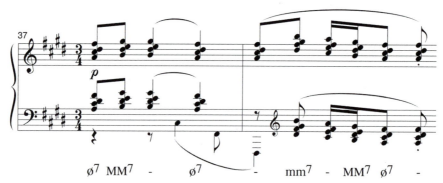

2. **Chromatic planing**: This is a bolder type in which each melodic line moves at *precisely* the same size interval, yielding a chromatic series of *identical* harmonic structures that are *chromatic* in the key.

**EXAMPLE 18-4** Debussy: *Pour le piano* (Sarabande), mm. 11–12

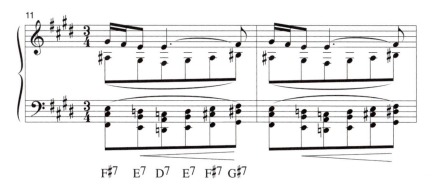

F♯7   E7   D7   E7   F♯7   G♯7

### FOR PRACTICE

On the staff below, show both diatonic and chromatic planing (first chord given) beneath the given melody notes.

**EXAMPLE 18-5**

## The Non-Functional Mm7 chord

The functional behavior of the dominant seventh chord is the resolution of the chord 3rd upward and the chord seventh downward—the collapsing of the tritone within the chord to the root and the third of the tonic respectively. Each chord formed beneath the melody in Example 18-4 is a Mm7 chord. However, these chords are non-functional, and the short-hand name we've been using—"dominant-seventh"—suggests a function they do not perform.

Perhaps following Debussy's lead, other composers ventured into new syntactic realms, relating traditional chords in non-traditional ways.

> **CONCEPT CHECK**
>
> Compare the three passages of Example 18-6. What harmonic structures are featured in each? Which type of planing—diatonic or chromatic—is present?

**EXAMPLE 18-6A** Debussy: *Pour le piano* (Sarabande), mm. 56–57

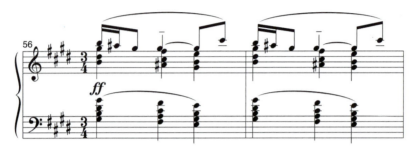

**EXAMPLE 18-6B** Richard Rodgers: "Slaughter on Tenth Avenue"

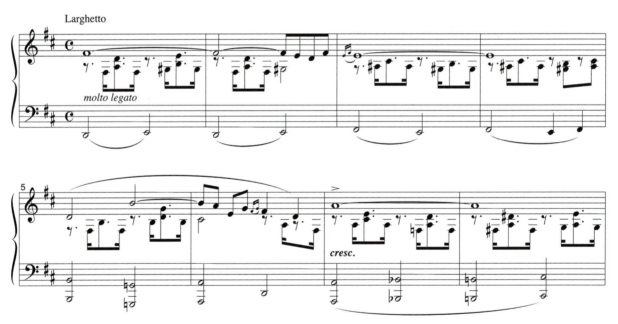

**EXAMPLE 18-6C** Prokofiev: Classical Symphony op. 25 (third movement)

Long the stepchild of functional harmony, the augmented triad found a loving home in Debussy's music. Again, he tethered its use to planing. Passages such as the next are less tonally anchored than the preceding ones owing to the tonal ambiguity of the augmented triads in the right-hand part.

**EXAMPLE 18-7** Debussy: "*Minstrels*" (Preludes, Bk. I, no. 12), mm. 37–43

## MODALITY

### The Church Modes

Debussy's fascination with the **church modes** probably helped form his approach to syntax since modally based music pre-dated major–minor tonality and its associated harmonic functions. The church modes can be compared to the major and minor scales.

### EXAMPLE 18-8A

**Major modes**

| | | | | | | | |
|---|---|---|---|---|---|---|---|
| Ionian (major scale): | C | D | E | F | G | A | B |
| Lydian: | C | D | E | F♯ | G | A | B |
| Mixolydian: | C | D | E | F | G | A | B♭ |

### EXAMPLE 18-8B

**Minor modes**

| | | | | | | | |
|---|---|---|---|---|---|---|---|
| Aeolian (natural minor scale): | C | D | E♭ | F | G | A♭ | B♭ |
| Dorian: | C | D | E♭ | F | G | A | B♭ |
| Phrygian: | C | D♭ | E♭ | F | G | A♭ | B♭ |

*Note*: Only one of the modes—Lydian—retains the leading tone and is therefore capable of producing a *major dominant*.

---

Look again at Examples 18–3 and 18–6a. In the first, the $\hat{5}$–$\hat{1}$ motion in the bass creates the feeling that F♯ is the tonal center, suggesting Dorian mode.

**F♯ Dorian**

The melodic cadence on G♯ in the second perhaps implies Aeolian mode.

**G♯ Dorian**

During the seventeenth century, Renaissance modal practice gradually gave way to functional harmonic syntax. Three hundred years later—in a bit of irony, perhaps—functional harmonic syntax fell victim to Debussy's use of the modes.

Each mode has a distinctive character, and composers have used modes to produce particular *affects* (emotional states).

### EXAMPLE 18-9A  Carlos Chavez: Ten Preludes (no. 1) 🔊

### EXAMPLE 18-9B  Ralph Turek: "Carnival Days" (from *Songs for Kids*) 🔊

*Notes*:

a   is E Phrygian. The mood is tinged with melancholy. The second degree a half step above the **final** ("tonic") gives Phrygian the darkest aura of any mode. Do you recall the lachrymose sound of the Neapolitan? Formed on the lowered second scale degree, it's diatonic in the Phrygian mode.

b   is C Lydian. The mood is playful. Because it is the only mode to retain the leading tone, and because the raised fourth degree acts as a leading tone to the dominant as well, Lydian is the brightest mode.

## Modal Cadences

**Modal cadences** are two-chord phase endings that contain modal inflections. As with tonal cadences, the final chord is likely to be heard as tonic or dominant, even though the chord succession leading to the cadence may be non-functional. Debussy's music is filled with such moments.

**EXAMPLE 18-10A** Debussy: *"Hommage a Rameau"* (Images, Book I) 🔊

G♯ Phrygian: ♭II$^6_4$ - i$^6$

**EXAMPLE 18-10B** Debussy: *"Les collines d'Anacapri"* (Preludes, BK. I, no. 5) 🔊

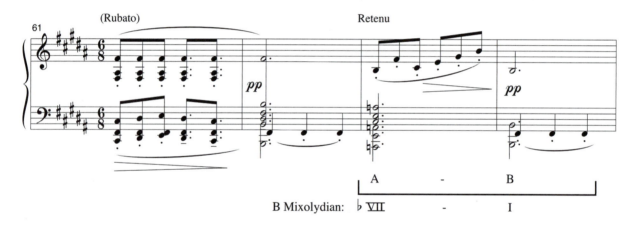

B Mixolydian: ♭VII - I

## NEW MELODIC AND HARMONIC STRUCTURES

The following melodic passage appears in Debussy's *Sarabande*:

**EXAMPLE 18-11A** Debussy: *Pour le piano* (Sarabande), mm. 63–66

The melody consists of five different pitches that huddle around G♯. Here are the pitches placed in the form of a scale:

### EXAMPLE 18-11B

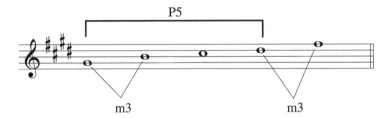

In the broadest sense, any five-tone scale is a **pentatonic scale.** The types most commonly used by composers have characteristics identical to the preceding one:

- They contain no half steps (thus no leading tones).
- They contain no more than two whole steps in succession.

These two characteristics assure two others:

- A minor third occurs at two points.
- No tritones are present.

With no leading tone, any pitch in this scale might be made to sound like a tonic by sheer emphasis, registral placement, and so on. In practice, composers have favored the two pitch arrangements that allow a major or minor triad to be constructed above the lowest tone.

### EXAMPLE 18-12

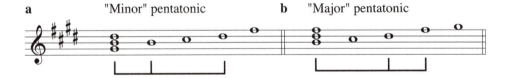

> **CONCEPT CHECK**
>
> Write the pitch material found in Example 18–13. What scale is this? Which pitch sounds like a "tonic?" Why?

### EXAMPLE 18-13 Debussy: *"Voiles"* (Preludes, Bk. I, no. 2) 🔊

Melody and harmony are often woven with the same thread on Debussy's loom. That "thread" may be a mode or other type of scale. Examples 18–13 and 18–10a are cases in point.

## Quartal and Quintal Harmonies

A structure inherent in the pentatonic scale is the **quartal harmony**—a structure of fourths. In the pentatonic scale, all the fourths are perfect. As a result, the chords built on each scale degree have a similar sound.

### EXAMPLE 18-14A

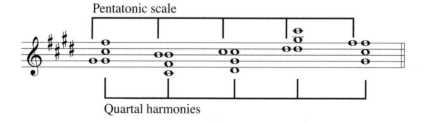

Each note of the pentatonic scale is a member of a quartal harmony built from pitches in the scale. In fact, the entire pentatonic scale can be stacked to form an extended quartal harmony:

### EXAMPLE 18-14B

A quartal harmony can be restacked as a **quintal** harmony—a stack of fifths. The sounds are intrinsically related:

## EXAMPLE 18-14C

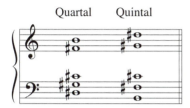

The middle section of Debussy's *Sarabande* features quartal harmonies moving in parallel motion (planing) beneath a partly pentatonic melodic line.

## EXAMPLE 18-15  Debussy: *Pour le piano* (Sarabande), mm. 23–28

In Example 18-16, alternating quartal and quintal harmonies are implied by the counterpoint. ("Q" is used here to symbolize *both* quartal and quintal harmonies.)

## EXAMPLE 18–16  Hindemith: Ludus Tonalis (Fugue no. 5)

> **FOR PRACTICE**
>
> Which "Qs" mark quartal harmonies and which mark quintal? How many additional quartal or quintal harmonies can you find in Example 18-16? How many can you discover implied in the melodic lines? What Baroque voice-leading principle does Hindemith eschew in this passage? What traditional methods of melodic organization do you observe?

## The Whole Tone Scale

Debussy used other scalar patterns as a basis for his pitch material, among them the **whole tone scale**—a succession of six whole steps.

### EXAMPLE 18-17

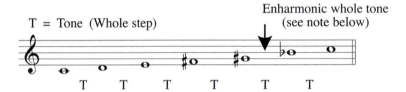

*Note:* The enharmonically spelled whole tone is a necessity at some point in the whole-tone scale. It can occur between any two pitches, such as F♯–A♭, or A♯–C, and so on.

Regarding the whole-tone scale:

1. There are no half steps in the whole-tone scale (hence the name) and therefore no leading tones.

2. The whole-tone scale contains six rather than seven pitches. One letter name must be omitted in its spelling, so that one of the whole tones is spelled enharmonically.

3. The scale may be transposed upward by a half step only once before the pitch content of the original is duplicated.

### EXAMPLE 18-18

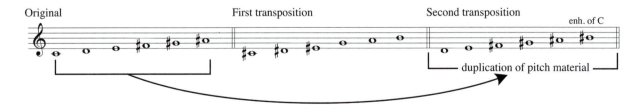

4. Only one of the four basic triad types can be formed—the augmented triad. It can be constructed on every degree of the scale.

### EXAMPLE 18-19

5. The whole-tone scale contains abundant tritone relationships but no possibilities for their resolution.

Perhaps Debussy was intrigued by this scale's lack of leading tones and tonic-dominant relationships. Example 18-20 shows the opening of "Voiles," a ternary form in which the outer sections are based melodically and harmonically on a single transposition of the whole-tone scale. (Example 18-13 was from the middle of this prelude, which by contrast is constructed entirely on the pentatonic scale.)

### EXAMPLE 18-20  Debussy: *"Voiles"* (Preludes, Bk. I, no. 2)

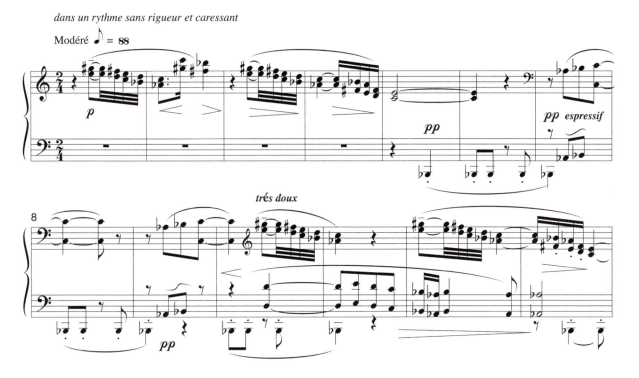

## Other Scales

Other scales make occasional appearances in Debussy's music. One such scale comprises two identical tetrachords. It might be viewed as a Phrygian mode with raised third and seventh degrees.

### EXAMPLE 18-21A

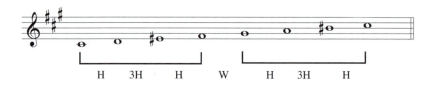

### EXAMPLE 18-21B Debussy: "Soirée dans Grenade" (Estampes, no. 2)

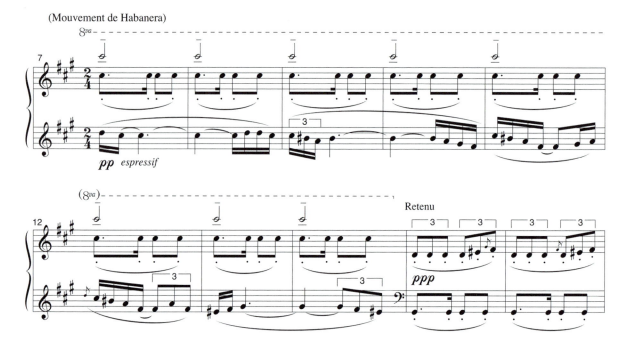

A scale that has been used more extensively throughout the century is the **octatonic scale.** This eight-tone scale comprises alternating half steps and whole steps, with several features that have appealed to composers. Chief among them are its limited transpositional capabilities. It can be transposed only twice before the pitch content of the original is duplicated. The first and fourth lines in Example 18-22 illustrate this.

## EXAMPLE 18-22

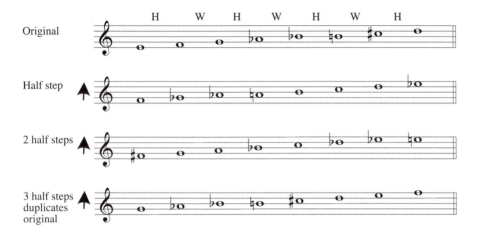

Example 18-23 illustrates one characteristic of the octatonic scale that results from its symmetrical interval structure. A major triad can be formed starting on every other pitch. This is true also of a minor triad, a diminished triad, and a "dominant seventh" chord. A diminished seventh chord can be formed beginning on *every* pitch.

## EXAMPLE 18-23A

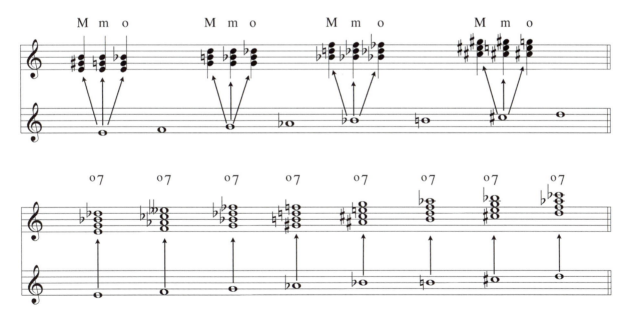

### EXAMPLE 18-23B  Debussy: *"Feuilles mortes"* (Preludes, Bk. II, no. 2)

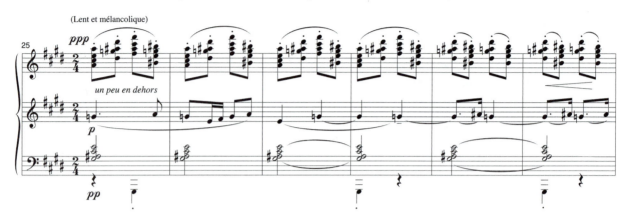

Ravel, Scriabin, Stravinsky, and Messiaen are prominent among twentieth-century composers who have employed the octatonic scale. We'll encounter it again in Chapter 19.

Claude Debussy was a countercultural fellow. Caught in the rising Wagnerian tide and the general mania for things German that deluged his native land, he swam vigorously against the current and found his way to a distant shore. Some of his comments are anecdotal. After attending a performance of Wagner's *Ring*, he reportedly said, "My God, how tiresome these people in skins and helmets become by the fourth night . . ." In the middle of an orchestra concert, he reportedly whispered to a friend, "Let's go, it's beginning to develop."

Debussy's "distant shore" provided solid footing for the likes of Stravinsky, Bartók, Copland, George Crumb, Bill Evans, and countless film composers. The music represented in the next two chapters—indeed, much of the music of the twentieth century—follows either the way pointed by Wagner or the way pointed by Debussy.

## SUMMARY OF TERMINOLOGY

- church modes
- final
- modal cadences
- modality
- octatonic scale
- pentatonic scale
- planing
- quartal
- quintal
- syntax
- whole-tone scale

# CHAPTER NINETEEN

# New Tonal Methods

The examples in this chapter consist of harmonic techniques similar to Debussy's but less traditional. Whether a piece asserts or lacks a pitch center is a question that can elicit different answers from different listeners. In fact, some examples in this chapter might seem to some to be lacking a tonality altogether.

**KEY CONCEPTS IN THIS CHAPTER**

- quartal and quintal harmonies
- polychords
- polytonality
- bimodality
- dual modality
- ostinato
- implied polymeter

## NEW TONAL VENTURES

### Quartal Harmonies

Debussy's occasional use of quartal harmonies were more fully integrated in the harmonic vocabulary of Paul Hindemith (1895–1963). In Hindemith's music, triadic harmonies surface mainly at cadences, with more complex harmonies residing in interior phrases. In Example 19-1a, some triadic harmonies result when a melodic pitch is compatible with the accompanying quartal sonority because it can be seen to exist lower in the quartal structure (see Example 19-1b). Most of the melodic pitches can, in fact, be viewed as extensions above or below the quartal sonorities formed by the lower voices. These voices move in parallel motion for the greater part of the phrase. Béla Bartók, too, was attracted to the rootless sound of quartal harmonies as demonstrated in Example 19-1c.

## EXAMPLE 19-1A Hindemith: "Un cygne," from *Six Chansons* (1939)

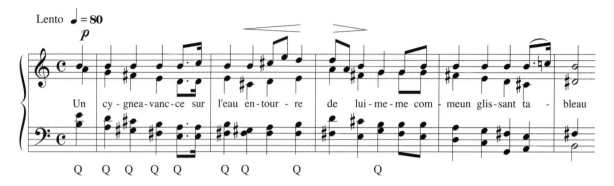

## EXAMPLE 19-1B

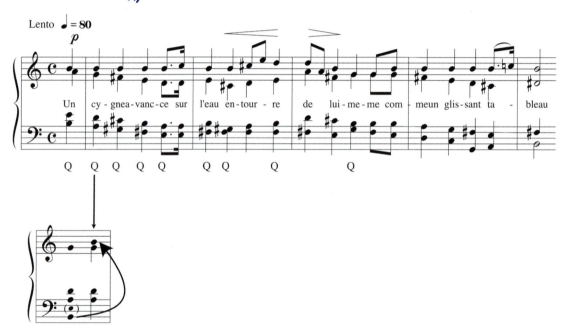

## EXAMPLE 19-1C Bartók: *Fourteen Bagatelles* op. 6, no. 11 (1908)

NEW TONAL METHODS    291

Quartal harmonies such as those in Example 19-1 owe their unique sound largely to their lack of tritones and minor seconds. The effect is only mildly dissonant, and their "rootless" quality comes from the stacking of equidistant intervals. (Recall that the diminished seventh chord and the augmented triad heard *in isolation* are likewise rootless.) However, quartal and quintal harmonies can be stacked in other ways, as shown in Example 19-2.

## EXAMPLE 19-2

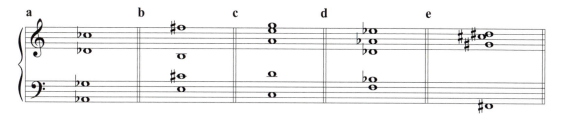

### FOR PRACTICE

Restack the harmonies of Example 19-2 in either fourths or fifths.

## Polychords

**Polychords** are harmonies that can be heard as two (rarely more) discrete chords. To be heard this way requires some spatial separation and/or timbral distinction (dissimilar sound sources). The absence of common tones between the component chords also aids in separating the sounds. The chords may be of the same or different type. Although no widely accepted way of symbolizing these structures exists, a possibility is to indicate the component structures, as shown in Example 19-3.

## EXAMPLE 19-3

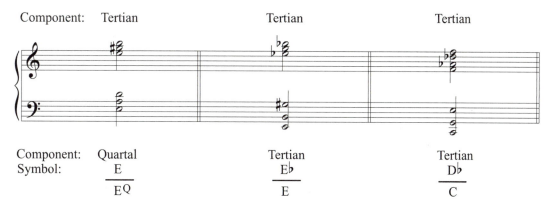

*Note*: The upper and lower components of each polychord are separated by an octave or greater distance. Although this much registral separation does not always occur, it helps to render the component chords aurally distinct.

292    THE TWENTIETH CENTURY AND BEYOND

The upper and lower components share few if any common tones. Polychords can be even more distinct when played by contrasting sound sources, such as oboes and trombones.

In some cases, polychords can be analyzed alternatively as extended triads or mixed-interval chords. Few musical examples are as overtly polychordal as Example 19-4a. Example 19-4b is less clearly polychordal but more typical.

### EXAMPLE 19-4A  William Schuman: *Three Score Set* (second movement) (1943)

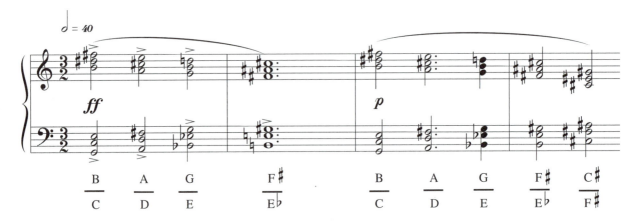

### EXAMPLE 19-4B  Vincent Persichetti: *Harmonium* op 50, no. 3 (1959)

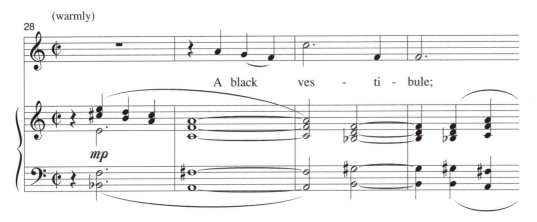

*Note*: In **b**, the complete triads in the right-hand part seem to provide the harmonic basis for the melody while the left-hand part consists mostly of sixths that follow their own course. Analysis as polychords (the left hand as incomplete triads) seems a logical way to analyze the passage.

#### FOR PRACTICE

In a manner similar to Examples 19–3 and 19–4, add chord symbols that reflect the polychordal components in the passage that follows. Besides the polychords, what other compositional techniques are employed in the passage?

**EXAMPLE 19-5** Honegger: Symphony no. 5, first movement (1950)

## Polytonality

**Polytonality** suggests that two (or more) tonalities exist simultaneously in a passage. The technique has been used to a limited extent, possibly because it's difficult to project multiple tonal centers effectively without keeping the harmonic structure extremely elementary. Examples 19–6a and b, like the previous examples, illustrate both more and less straightforward applications of the technique.

**EXAMPLE 19-6A** Ravel: "Blues" (Sonate pour Violon et Piano, 1897, second movement)

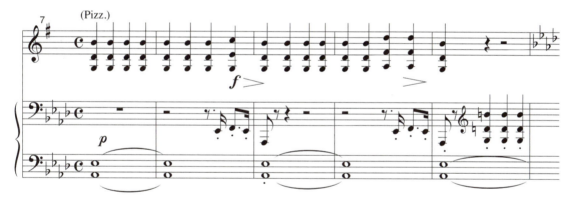

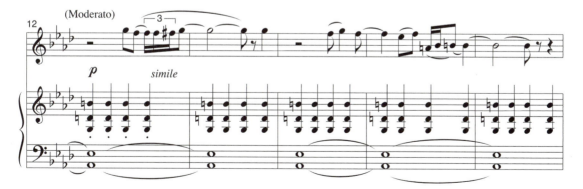

*Note*: G major is juxtaposed against A flat major.

**EXAMPLE 19-6B** Stravinsky: *The Rite of Spring*, "The Sacrifice" (1913) 🔊

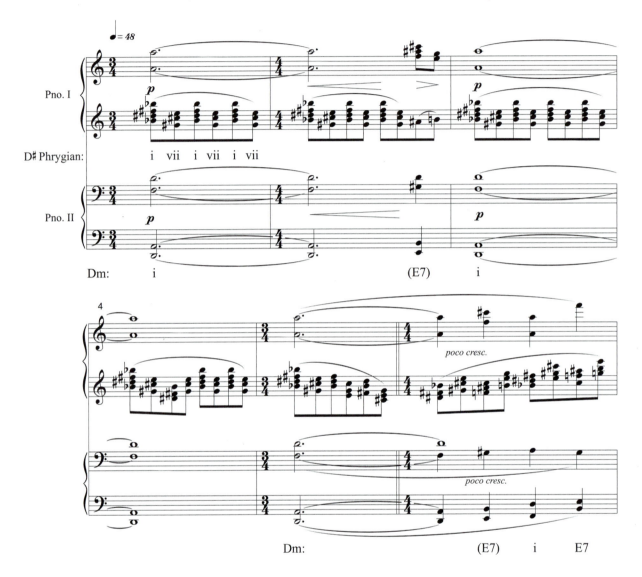

*Note*: Casting aside enharmonic spellings reveals alternating triads in the Piano I—D♯m and C♯m—with D♯ sounding vaguely like the final in D♯ Phrygian. This occurs over a Piano II part solidly anchored in D minor (with G♯). Example **b** is somewhat less overt in its polytonality than Example **a**.

## Bimodality/Dual Modality

Perhaps a more accurate term than polytonality for the Stravinsky passage is **bimodality**—the use of two modes simultaneously. When both modes are centered on *the same* final, the term "dual modality" is preferred by some.

**EXAMPLE 19-7A** Bartók: "Major and minor" no. 59 (from *Mikrokosmos* vol. II)

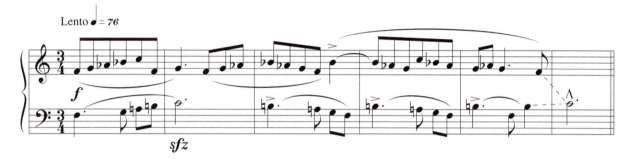

**EXAMPLE 19-7B**

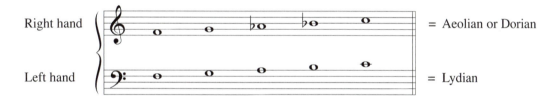

## Pandiatonicism

**Pandiatonicism** is the use of pitch material diatonic to a given scale or mode with few or no chromatic pitches. For the most part, functional harmonic relationships are not present, so that any diatonic pitch can occur against any other diatonic pitch. Because of this pitch equality, harmonic tension is minimized, and cadences are often produced more by rhythmic means than harmonic. Often the texture is polyphonic, and the harmonies show little consistency because they are the mere byproducts of the moving lines.

**EXAMPLE 19-8** Dello Joio: Piano Sonata no. 3 (first movement) (1949) Variation IV

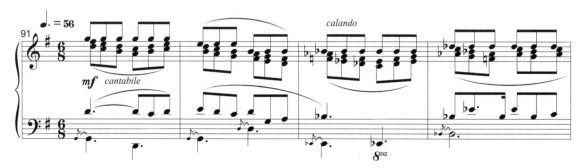

*Note:* Pandiatonicism can range from purely to partly so. This passage is pandiatonic alternately in G and A♭ (or E♭ Dorian if you interpret the bass as $\hat{1}$ and $\hat{5}$). Because of the tonic–dominant feel of the bass, the passage has a stronger tonal focus than **a.**

## STRAVINSKY

### The Rite of Spring

Over nearly sixty years, Igor Stravinsky (1882–1971) traveled practically every important musical byway, from Russian post-Romanticism and Neoclassicism to serialism and free atonality. Although his methods (and the country in which he chose to reside) changed, his Russian roots remained audible in everything he wrote. His *Rite of Spring*, a depiction in music and dance of an ancient Russian fertility ritual, contains at some point every technique we've discussed, often in a distilled and subtle guise. Although its first performance met considerable hostility, *Le Sacre du Printemps* has come to be regarded as a masterpiece of twentieth-century music. Excerpts appear below.

**EXAMPLE 19-9** Stravinsky: *The Rite of Spring* (introduction)

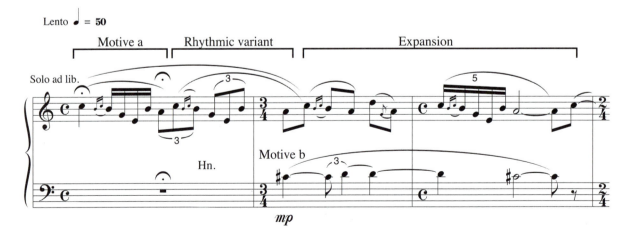

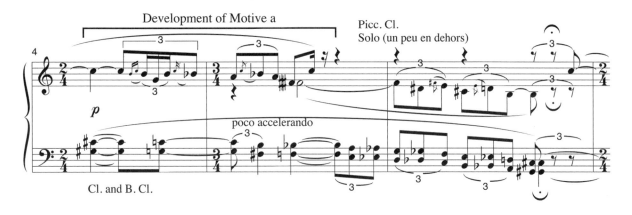

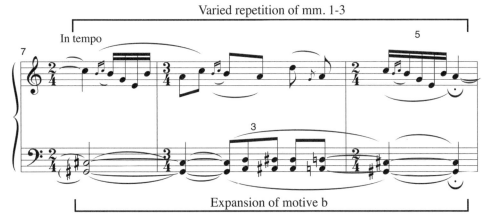

*Notes*:

1. The opening bassoon melody might be viewed either as C major pentatonic or A minor pentatonic with an added B.

   Stravinsky's approach to melodic development—repeating small fragments, adding minor pitch and rhythm changes at each repetition—is illustrated here.

2. Stravinsky sets a chromatic motive centered on C♯ against the prevailingly diatonic bassoon solo to create a vaguely bitonal quality. This motive grows into parallel-moving lines (planing) at m. 4 that descend an octave to land once more on C♯ in m. 7.

**EXAMPLE 19-10** Stravinsky: *The Rite of Spring* ("Spring Rounds")

One of Stravinsky's favorite compositional techniques—the **ostinato**, a repeating melodic/rhythmic pattern (from the same root word as "obstinate")—provides the foundation for this passage.

> ### FOR PRACTICE
>
> 1. On what mode or scale is this passage based?
> 2. What techniques of melodic development are similar to those in Example 19-9?
> 3. Compare the melodic material on each of the staves.

## BARTÓK

### *Mikrokosmos, Book V*

Béla Bartók (1881–1945) pursued a multifaceted career as a composer, concert pianist, and ethnomusicolgist. His interest in the folk music of his native Hungary is evident in his own compositions. Although a catalogue of his techniques would be remarkably similar to one compiled for Stavinsky, Bartók's music has an individuality that owes much to the character of his native folk music and to his more traditional approach to development and counterpoint.

In his *Mikrokosmos*, a six-volume set of 153 piano pieces of graded difficulty, we have a compendium of nearly all Bartók's techniques.

In Example 19-11, a pentatonic melody unfolds, using the pitches E♭, G♭, A♭, B♭, and D♭ (the black keys on the piano, over a quartal ostinato). At m. 15, the ostinato yields to a string of arpeggiated quartal harmonies in the left hand, built on a bass that descends almost a complete octave to A at m. 21. The completion of this descent occurs in m. 24, which marks the major dividing point in the piece. The ostinato then begins anew, transferred from the left hand to the right.

**EXAMPLE 19-11** Bartók: "Boating" (from *Mikrokosmos* vol. V (1939))

> **FOR PRACTICE**
>
> Note the extent of the melodic repetition in the first fourteen measures. How is the opening phrase expanded? Compare this to Stravinsky's melodic process.

Measures 15–23 contain entirely white-key pitches in the upper voice: A B C D E F G. The focal pitch appears to be A, since the melody begins and ends on that pitch and returns to it numerous times. The mode suggested is A Aeolian.

Throughout the piece, a hemiola is produced by the gently rocking ostinato, which suggests a 6/8 meter.

### EXAMPLE 19-12

Together, the melody and its accompaniment create an **implied polymeter**—two different but simultaneous sounding meters notated in a single meter signature. The two hands produce a polytonal effect, black keys against white keys throughout.

As you played and studied the music in this chapter, it may have struck you that most, if not all of it is triadic, quartal, scalar, or modal at its core. What else is possible? A few composers have experimented with "clusters," as harmonies built of seconds are called. But the larger answer to the question "What else is possible?" resides in the music we'll consider next.

## SUMMARY OF TERMINOLOGY

- bimodality
- implied polymeter
- ostinato
- pandiatonicism
- polychord
- polytonality
- dual modality

# CHAPTER TWENTY

# Non-Serial Atonality

## PERSPECTIVE

The music we've studied to this point embodies a principle held sacrosanct for hundreds of years—that music must be organized around tonal centers. In the early twentieth century, the Austrian composer, Arnold Schoenberg (1874–1951), faced what he considered the impasse of traditional tonality due to the high degree of chromaticism reached at the end of the nineteenth century. He sought a music in which pitches would not be members of a tonal hierarchy but rather would be equally important within the chromatic total.

If Debussy was the great liberator of the triad, Schoenberg was the great liberator of dissonance, treating all harmonic combinations as equally viable. His music garnered a huge following and influenced practically every composer of art music in the twentieth century. Yet, his methods have not proved to hold the future of all music. Composers have been finding ways back to various aspects of tonality, and Schoenberg's methods are taking an appropriate place in the musical mainstream among those already available.

### KEY CONCEPTS IN THIS CHAPTER

- pitch-class sets
- set type
- normal order
- best normal order
- prime form
- interval-class vector
- set class

## ATONALITY: TOOLS AND TERMINOLOGY

For better or worse, Schoenberg's early style has been dubbed "atonal," meaning without tonal center. This music might better be termed "pantonal," as it distributes tonal significance more equitably among the chromatic total than does traditional tonal music. A process and corresponding terminology have been developed for its analysis.

## Tools for Atonal Analysis

1. **Octave and enharmonic equivalence**: Absence of traditional harmonic function in this music permits pitches of the same note name in any octave or enharmonic spelling in any octave to be considered identical.

2. **Pitch class** (PC): Any given pitch and all its octave transpositions and enharmonic spellings belong to the same pitch class. Pitch class incorporates both octave equivalence and enharmonic equivalence.

**EXAMPLE 20-1** All notes are the same pitch class

All Notes are the same Pitch Class

3. **Pitch-class interval** (PCI): The number of semitones (half steps) between two pitch-classes. A PCI is simply represented by an upper-case letter **I** with a superscript numeral indicating the number of semi-tones between the two pitch-classes. A table of traditional interval and PCI labels is listed below:

   m2 = $I^1$, M2 = $I^2$, m3 = $I^3$, M3 = $I^4$, P4 = $I^5$, Aug.4/dim.5 = $I^6$

   P5 = $I^7$, m6 = $I^8$, M6 = $I^9$, m7 = $I^{10}$, M7 = $I^{11}$, P8 = $I^{12}$

4. **Ordered pitch-class interval**: A pitch-class interval designated by its exact semitone content *and* by its contour with a plus (+) for ascending contour, or a minus (−) for descending contour. Such designations refer to intervals as they are found in the "surface" of a composition (exactly how the composer wrote them):

**EXAMPLE 20-2**

I +22      I −22

5. **Unordered pitch-class interval**: The distance between two pitch classes *without reference to its contour*.

## EXAMPLE 20-3A

6. **Modulo 12 (Mod 12):** In atonal music, 12 is a crucial number since Western music is a twelve-note system and atonality seeks equity within the chromatic total. In Mod 12, compound intervals are converted to their simple equivalents and the shortest distance between two notes can be found by applying simple arithmetic. For example, intervals larger than an octave "wrap around" the octave (12 half steps) like a clockface, meaning 12 = 0, 13 = 1, 14 = 2 and so on. Thus, any interval larger than 12 (any compound interval) can be reduced to its simple equivalent by subtracting 12:

$$I^{18} - (Mod\ 12) = I^6$$

## EXAMPLE 20-3B

Any two pitch-class intervals that add up to 12 (0 Mod 12) are considered to be **complements**, such as a perfect fourth—$I^5$ and a perfect fifth—$I^7$ ( 5 + 7 = 12 ). In other words, an interval and its inversion are **complementary** and span 12 semitones (an octave).

7. **Interval class (IC):** An interval class is the smallest distance between two PCs. Thus, the IC of any interval is its smallest complement. For example, the IC of the perfect fifth from $C^4$ to $G^4$ ( 7 half steps ) is that of its complement, the perfect fourth ($C^4$ to $G^3$), which is the shortest distance between the two PCs (5 half steps). Likewise, a major sixth (9 half steps) is an $IC^3$—its complement (12 − 9 = 3). No IC exceeds 6 semitones or $I^6$ since a larger interval will invert to its smaller complement.

## EXAMPLE 20-4

*Note:* All are Interval Class 3 (IC3), meaning they can be rearranged to span three half steps.

8. **Index numbers**: Index numbers are fixed integers assigned to each pitch-class, making it possible to use arithmetic formulas in interval and set calculations. It is analogous to "fixed-Do" solfege. Pitch class "C" is identified by the fixed integer zero (C = 0), C♯/D♭ = 1, D = 2, and so on. An example of its application can be demonstrated by calculating the interval distance between two pitch classes such as E-flat and B. Using index numbers (E♭ = 3 and B = 11), the interval descending from PC B$^4$ (11) to E♭$^3$ would be 11 − 3 = I$^8$. The interval descending from E♭ $^4$(3) to B$^3$ (11) (adding Mod 12 to PC "E♭" since we are moving counter clock-wise past C zero), the formula would be 15 (3 + 12) − 11 = I$^4$, the complement of I$^8$. The index table is listed below (enharmonic equivalents apply):

   **Pc**: C = 0, D♭ = 1, D = 2, E♭ = 3, E = 4, F = 5, F♯ = 6, G = 7, A♭ = 8, A = 9, B♭ = 10, B = 11

9. **Ordered pitch-class set**: An ordered PC set is a collection of pitch-class intervals as they are heard in a musical composition or in the "surface" of the music. An ordered PC set forms the basis of an atonal work's pitch organization. It is thus similar to a motive, with this important difference: a motive is usually a melodic/*rhythmic* unit, while a PC set is a melodic/*harmonic* unit that can appear in any rhythmic pattern, in any melodic order, in any transposition, and with its PCs in any octave and any spelling. It can appear as a melodic figure, a single harmony, or a partly melodic and partly harmonic figure.

## EXAMPLE 20-5

Ordered Sets:

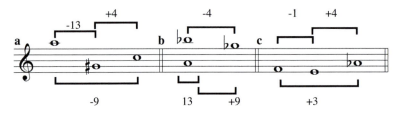

*Note*: While the PC sets in a, b, and c contain different pitch classes, the PC *interval content* for all are the same: IC1, IC3, and IC4.

---

10. **Unordered PC sets**: Unordering seeks to find the shortest distance of the set from top to bottom. Example 20-6 demonstrates the sets from Example 20-5 unordered.

# EXAMPLE 20-6

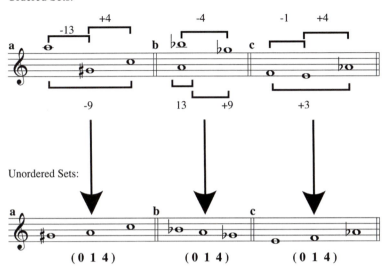

11. **Set Names**: A means of naming sets according to the number of pitch-classes they contain (the above sets are called "tetrachords"). Since Western music is based on twelve pitch-classes, sets are usually arranged in divisions of twelve; 3-note, 4-note, and 6-note sets. However, they can be found in any numerical arrangement, typically one through nine with the following names:

- Dyad (2-note set)
- Trichord (3-note set)
- Tetrachord (4-note set)
- Pentachord (5-note set)
- Hexachord (6-note set)
- Septachord (7-note set)
- Octachord (8-note set)
- Nonachord (9-note set)

## UNORDERED SET ANALYSIS

The following passage, from one of Schoenberg's earliest atonal compositions, demonstrates a trichord set in several of its transformations (bracketed or enclosed).

### EXAMPLE 20-7  Schoenberg: Klavierstücke, op. 11, no. 1

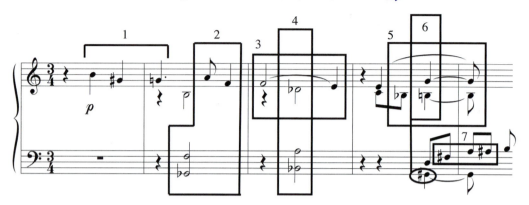

> **CONCEPT CHECK**
>
> Play each of the bracketed/enclosed note groups and observe their aural similarity. This is because they all have identical IC structure. They all contain an IC1, an IC3, and an IC4.
>
> 1. PC set: B–G♯ = IC 3; G♯–G = IC 1; B–G = IC 4
> 2. PC set: G♭–F = IC 1; G♭–A = IC 3; F–A = IC 4
> 3. PC set: F–D♭ = IC 4; D♭–E = IC 3; F–E = IC 1
> 4. PC set: B♭–A = IC 1; B♭–D♭ = IC 3; A–D♭ = IC 4
> 5. PC set: B♭–B = IC 1; B♭–G = IC 3; B–G = IC 4
> 6. PC set: G♯–B = IC 3; G♯–G = IC 1; G–B = IC 4
> 7. PC set: F♯–A = IC 3; A–A♯ = IC 1; F♯–A♯ = IC 4

The melodic–harmonic engine driving Schoenberg's *Klavierstücke*, op. 11, no. 1 is a consistent PC trichord, each containing an IC 1, IC 3, and an IC 4. At this point, the question is often asked if Schoenberg was aware of these details when composing. Although it's certain that he was, it is likely that he used a mixture of theoretical awareness and intuition, sculpting both melodic lines and harmonies from selected intervals according to the dictates of his ear.

## Normal Order

Set analysis begins with finding the **normal order** of a PC set—the ascending order of a set with the smallest interval from the lowest pitch, known as the *reference* pitch, to the highest pitch. To begin this analysis, use the first pitch in the set as the reference pitch and organize the set in ascending order within one octave. Analyze the set's **ambitus**—the range from the reference pitch to the highest pitch. Next, perform a **gap rotation** analysis. Find the two pitch-classes with the largest gap and use the second pitch in the gap as the next reference pitch and organize a new set ascending from that pitch. Analyze each set's ambitus and compare it to the previous set and so on. The set that yields the smallest ambitus is the **normal order** of the set. An ordered set and a gap rotation analysis for finding normal order are shown below.

## EXAMPLE 20-8

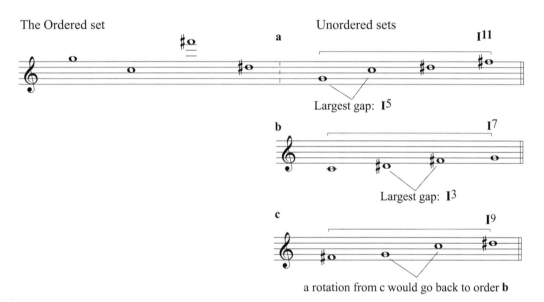

- The set is organized in ascending order within an octave (order **a** in Example 20-8).

- In Example 20-8a, the set's ambitus from the reference pitch g to the highest pitch f-sharp is $I^{11}$. To perform the first gap rotation, the largest gap is found between the PC g and C. The second PC in the gap, C, is used for the first rotation in Example 20-8 where the set's ambitus is $I^7$.

- For the next rotation, two gaps are equal—C to D♯ and D♯ to F♯. In such a case, preference is given to the gap followed by the smaller interval, D♯ to F♯, since F♯ is followed by G, a semitone above it. The set rotated above the reference pitch F♯ has an ambitus of $I^9$.

- Since set order **b** has the smallest ambitus ($I^7$) from the referemce pitch C, *order b is normal order of the set.*

## ANALYZING THE SET TYPE

The **set type** is identified by a numeric list (with or without parentheses) of the set's semitone content measured from the reference pitch (= 0) to each successive PC in the set.

### EXAMPLE 20-9

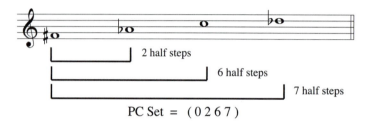

### FOR PRACTICE

Find the normal order for each of the PC sets below and give their set types.

### EXAMPLE 20-10

### Best Normal Order

A set may be further refined so that the smaller intervals appear to the left, rendering the set's most compact identity. This involves finding the set's **best normal order,** possibly requiring that the set be inverted and then again placed in in ascending order. Unlike triad inversion in tonal music, when a PC set is inverted, every upward interval is replaced by a downward interval of the same size. Known as **melodic inversion**, it's like doing pushups on a mirror. Keep in mind, however, that the set may *already* be in best normal order. You will find out by comparing the set type of the inversion with that of the non-inverted form.

Through inversion, the pitch-classes C–D♯–F♯–G (Example 20-11a) become C–A–F♯–F (Example 20-11b). The *pitch-class* changes resulting from inversion are irrelevant since determining interval content is the sole objective of inversion. When the set is placed back in ascending order (**c**), the set type changes:

NON-SERIAL ATONALITY 309

## EXAMPLE 20-11

**a**: Normal Order  **b**: Inversion

( 0  3  6  7 )

**c**: Resulting Set from Inversion

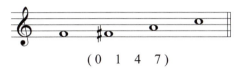

( 0  1  4  7 )

It is necessary to choose only one of these PC sets to represent best normal order. This can be done by comparing the interval content of set types in Examples 20–11a and c. Example 20-11c is best normal order of the set since it begins with the smaller interval, "0 1," as opposed to the set in Example 20-11a beginning with "0 3."

## Another Way

You might see other ways of determining best normal order such as choosing the set with the lowest sum of all the intervals in the set type: (0 3 6 7) = 16 (PC set **a**) compared to (0 1 4 7) = 12 (indicating that PC set **c** is best normal order). Another way to apply inversion is to use subtractions of the set type numerals in reverse: In this case, 7 – 6 = 1, 7 – 3 = 4, and 7 – 0 = 7: (0 1 4 7) .

## Prime Form

Best normal order, however, is only the process of placing the pitches in their most compact order—and, a set put in normal order may *already* be in best normal order. Once best normal order of a PC set is determined, we analyze it as a set type. The resulting *numerical expression of a PC set's best normal order* is known as the set's **prime form**. The best normal order of that set in Example 20-11 are the pitch-classes ordered **F, F#, A, C**. The prime form of the set is **0 1 4 7** (parentheses are not necessary in displaying prime form). You might think of prime form as atonal music's "chord symbol" or a kind of figured bass, although it's more than that. It's the harmonic label we use to refer to all melodic and harmonic units that have the same intervallic content and therefore is an indispensable tool for discovering the harmonic unity that underlies an atonal work.

### FOR PRACTICE

Name the trichord responsible for much of the passage below and bracket as many instances of it as you can find. Then, determine its prime form.

# EXAMPLE 20-12 Schoenberg: "Nacht" from *Pierrot Lunaire*

## Inversional Symmetry

In the process of finding a PC set's best normal order, you might find that the inversion of its normal order yields an identical set type. Therefore, both the normal order and its inversion are the set's best normal order, a condition known as **inversional symmetry** or **inversional equivalence** (also known as "invariance"). An inversionally symmetrical set is analogus to a palindrome—in words such as "MOM," and "DAD." Such a set is demonstrated in the hexachord below:

### EXAMPLE 20-13 Inversional Symmetry

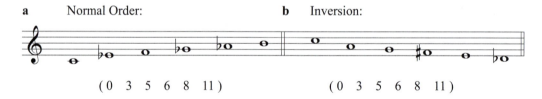

> **FOR PRACTICE**
>
> Create three tetrachords that are inversionally symmetrical.

## EXAMPLE 20-13A

## The Interval Class Vector

While some atonal compositions are based on a single prime form set, others appear to be based on two or more. Closer analysis reveals that such sets are related on a deeper intervallic level than their prime forms may indicate. This information is important to understanding the "harmonic" unity in such works, especially in works where rhythmic motives play only a minor role. A tool useful in this regard is the **interval-class vector** or **interval vector**. A set's interval vector reveals the total of all intervals heard in the interior of a melodic line or sonority in a kind-of "score board" notation of numerals.

The interval vector (IC vector) contains six numerals that indicate the number of times each interval class occurs in a set—hence, its limitation to six numerals. The first numeral indicates the number of times IC1 occurs, the second, the number of times IC2 occurs, and so on. *The interval vector differs from prime form in that all interior intervals are accounted for, not just those measured ascending from the reference pitch.*

You can think of a vector analysis as creating a set type from every pitch class in the set. In the vector, every interval higher than IC6 is inverted to its complement. For example, to find the number of IC1s in the set of Example 20-14, count the occurrences of the numeral 1 AND THE NUMERAL 11 (the complement Mod12 of 1). To find the number of IC4s, count the occurrences of the numeral 4 AND THE NUMERAL 8 (the complement Mod 12 of 4). And so on. Enter these totals in the interval vector.

## EXAMPLE 20-14

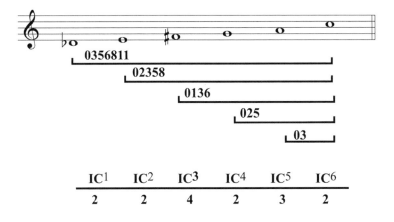

The analysis is placed between two arrows:     < 2 2 4 2 3 2 >

The complete analysis of this hexachord is:     0 3 5 6 8 11     < 2 2 4 2 3 2 >

## The Z-Relationship

In our discussion of the interval vector, we discovered that pitch collections can have similarities in the way they sound despite having different prime forms. In fact, sets having differing prime forms can be found to have identical interval vectors. Such sets bear the **Z-relationship**. In Example 20-15, the two tetrachord gestures 0 1 4 6 and 0 1 3 7 might appear to have only an $I^1$ in common. But analyzing them vectorally (for their interval vectors) demonstrates that they share the identical interval-class vector of < 1 1 1 1 1 1 > . Therefore, the prime forms 0 1 4 6 and 0 1 3 7 bear the **Z-relationship**.

**EXAMPLE 20-15**

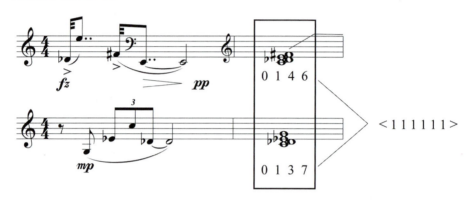

> **FOR PRACTICE**
>
> Place the following set in Best Normal Order, and construct its IC Vector.

**EXAMPLE 20-16**

## The Set Class

With the numerous ways in which PC sets are analyzed, identified, and compared, a singular labeling system was developed by the twentieth-century music theorist Allen Forte (Yale University). **Set class** (also known as **set name** or **Forte number**) is a label that systemically defines each extant set by a cardinal number (the number of pitch-classes in the set) and an ordinal number (the hierarchy of the set in a list according by its interval content) followed by the set's prime form and interval vector.

The set lists begin with dyads, followed by trichords, tetrachords, and so on. In each cardinal category, sets are ordered according to their interval size from left to right, with the most compact sets appearing at the top of the order. For example, tetrachord ordering begins in this manner:

*Set Class*

| | | |
|---|---|---|
| 4—1 | ( 0 1 2 3 ) | < 3 2 1 0 0 0 > |
| 4—2 | ( 0 1 2 4 ) | < 2 2 1 1 0 0 > |
| 4—3 | ( 0 1 3 4 ) | < 2 1 2 1 0 0 > |
| 4—4 | ( 0 1 2 5 ) | < 2 1 1 1 1 0 > |
| 4—5 | ( 0 1 2 6 ) | < 2 1 0 1 1 1 > |
| 4—6 | ( 0 1 2 7 ) | < 2 1 0 0 2 1 > |
| 4—7 | ( 0 1 4 5 ) | < 2 0 1 2 1 0 > |
| 4—8 | ( 0 1 5 6 ) | < 2 0 0 1 2 1 > |

The hierarchy of sets progresses as the interval sizes increase as they move across the right of the set. All sets are listed in descending order until all prime forms are exhausted. Then, the next cardinal sets are listed.

## APPLICATIONS IN ANALYSIS

The IC vector can give a general sense of the harmonic character of a set. The higher the IC numbers in positions 1, 2, and 6 in a set's vector, the more dissonant will be the sonority based on it. A vector can also show how two sets not obviously related are similar in other ways. This can help explain the harmonic unity and diversity present in certain atonal works.

The two opening gestures (set "y" and set "z") in Daniel McCarthy's "Visions and Apparitions" (for flute, vibraphone and percussion) share an important degree of unity. We can simply compare the set types to observe the intervallic similarities between these sets. But a comparison of the vectors in each set demonstrates a unity not always immediately obvious when comparing prime forms. In Example 20–17, we'll concentrate on creating the IC vector for set "z."

**EXAMPLE 20-17** Daniel McCarthy: Visions and Apparitions (second movement) 🔊

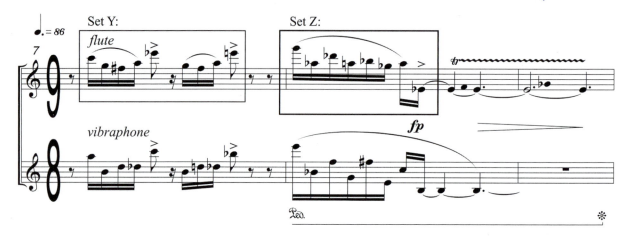

**EXAMPLE 20-17A** Set Z in prime form

Using set types to determine the IC vector of Set Z:

1. Create six set types, one beginning on each successive pitch in the "Z" collection—first from Gb, then from G, then from Ab, and so on.

2. Scan the 6 sets and count the times each number AND ITS COMPLEMENT appear. For example, the number "1" appears in 4 of the set types and thus "4" becomes the first number of the IC vector, meaning an IC1 is formed among 4 pairs of PCs (Gb-G, G-Ab, Ab-A, A-Bb). The number "2" occurs in 4 of the set types as well and thus becomes the second number in the vector. Remember that the number 9 is tallied in the vector as an $IC^3$, 8 is entered as an $IC^4$, and 7 is entered as an $IC^5$.

## EXAMPLE 20-18

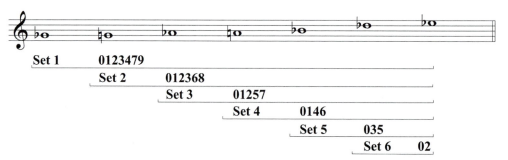

*Set Z IC Vector:*

| $IC^1$, | $IC^2$, | $IC^3$, | $IC^4$, | $IC^5$, | $IC^6$ |
|---|---|---|---|---|---|
| 4 | 4 | 4 | 3 | 4 | 2 |

The vector for Set Y is determined similarly using its prime form, [0 1 3 4 6 9]. When comparing the prime forms of Y [0 1 3 4 6 9] and Z [0 1 2 3 4 7 9], some surface similarities are immediately apparent—both have a normal order span of $I^9$ and both begin with the interval content of an $I^1$, for example. We can further see that both contain the $I^3$ and $I^4$. The distinction seems to be that set Y has an $I^6$ in its set type while Z has the $I^7$. But their vectors reveal that there are more similarities than these.

For example, while set Z appears not to contain an I6 as does set Y, the relationship between set Z's $I^1$ and $I^7$ reveals that an $I^6$ does exist in its interior (7 − 1 = 6). This is where the vector analysis is most revealing. Not only does it show what commonalities exist but which do not exist.

IC Vector for Set Z:     < 4 4 4 3 4 2 >

IC Vector for Set Y:     < 2 2 5 2 2 2 >

From the vector analysis above, we can see (and hear) that set Z is a more dissonant set with 4 IC 1's, but both sets share 2 IC6's, and both are also saturated with IC3's.

When attempting to discover the pitch basis of an atonal work:

1. Consider identifiable melodic-rhythmic figures. Sets most likely involve three or four PCs, because in general, the larger the set, the less useful it is as a unifying device per se.

2. Sets containing six or seven PCs may actually be a combination of smaller sets.

3. Create the set classses (in prime forms) of all sets you identify, and mark their occurrences at various key points in the work–beginnings, endings, important section changes, and so on.

4. As in tonal music, consider pedal points and ostinatos apart from the rest of the texture.

5. Remember that the order of the PCs in a set is not very significant. Interval relationships are what provide unity and pitch organization in this music.

### Set and Superset

The 0 1 4 trichord is integral to David S. Bernstein's *Three Silhouettes for Guitar*. The set is heard at the beginning (G–B♭–B) and several times throughout the piece without transposition. However, larger sets occur that contain 0 1 4 with added intervals. These expansions are known as **supersets**. For example, measure three opens with a 0 1 4 trichord but the addition of the F♮ expands the trichord into a 0 1 2 4 tetrachord. Another superset expands 0 1 4 on beat 3 of measure six into a 0 1 4 5 8 pentachord.

**EXAMPLE 20-19** David S. Bernstein: Three Silhouettes for Guitar (second movement)

> ### FOR PRACTICE
> 
> In mm. 7 and 8, what set is formed by the lower line (stem-down notes)? How does the music above this line relate to the original set?
> 
> Analyze the superset on beat 1–2 in measure 10.

### Another Way

Despite the numerical bent of this chapter, there is nothing wrong with understanding and describing music such as in Example 20-19 in traditional musical terms, as long as you remember that traditional harmonic function does not apply. For example:

- *Three Silhouettes for Guitar* features major and minor thirds and the minor-second clashes that result from their combination.

NON-SERIAL ATONALITY 317

- Sets constructed of perfect fourths and fifths and the major seconds and minor thirds that attend their combination—i.e. (0 2 7) and (0 2 5 7)—can produce a mildly dissonant, opening-sounding music reminiscent of Copland.
- Sets containing only major seconds, major thirds, and tritones, such as (0 2 6), can produce music with many "dominant-ninth-sounding" sonorities reminiscent perhaps of Debussy.

### CONCEPT CHECK

The opening of the second movement of Daniel McCarthy's "An American Girl" ("II. Siobhan in Colonial Williamsburg") has two distinct "harmonies" that lend themselves both to set theory analysis and traditional methods. Describe the music in both ways.

**EXAMPLE 20-20** Daniel McCarthy, An American Girl (second movement)

## SUMMARY OF TERMINOLOGY

- Enharmonic equivalence: Any notes of the same pitch are equivalent regardless of spelling (p. 302)
- Octave equivalence: Enharmonically spelled notes are also equivalent regardless of octave (p. 302)
- Pitch class: A singular pitch and its enharmonic and octave equivalents (p. 302)
- Pitch-class interval: The semitone distance between two pitch classes (p. 302)
- Ordered pitch-class interval: The exact semitone distance and contour between two pitch classes as written in the surface of a composition (p. 302)
- Unordered pitch-class interval: The shortest distance between two pitch classes (p. 302)
- Modulo 12: A modular arithmetic system of integers where the semitones in a pitch-class interval and its inversion (complement) equal the sum of twelve (p. 303)
- Complement: The inversion of a PC interval, which, added to the original interval, equals Mod 12 (p. 303)
- Index numbers: Fixed integers given to every ptich class from which arithmetic interval calculations are made (p. 304)
- Interval class: The shortest semitone distance between two pitch classes (p. 303)
- Pitch-class set: A collection of pitch classes (p. 304)
- Set type: A list of numerals given to a set demonstrating its semitone content from the lowest pitch class to each successive pitch class (p. 308)
- Normal order: A pitch-class set in ascending order with the smallest distance from the lowest to highest pitch class (p. 306)
- Melodic inversion: A set that is reordered in reverse intervalic contour (p. 308)
- Best normal order: A normal ordered set with the smallest intervals packed to the left (p. 308)
- Prime form: The set type for best normal order (p. 309)
- Inversional Symmetry (Invariance): A pitch-class set that has the same set type for both normal order and its inversion (p. 310)
- Interval vector: A six-digit analysis for occurrences of all interval classes in a set (p. 311)
- Z-relationship: Two sets of differing prime forms with identical interval vectors (p. 312)
- Set class: The hierarchical ordering of pitch-class sets developed by Allen Forte (p. 312)

# CHAPTER TWENTY-ONE

# Serial Atonality

## SERIALISM

Feeling that non-serial atonality lacked the organizing power to sustain larger musical works, Schoenberg developed the aggregate chromatic pitch-class system known as twelve-tone or serial composition. His approach to this method was gradual, as can be seen in Example 21-1, Schoenberg's last composition using a freely atonal approach—in his words, "composing with the notes of the motive."

**KEY CONCEPTS IN THIS CHAPTER**

- twelve-tone row
- series
- row forms
- matrix
- derived set
- Hexachordal symmetry

**EXAMPLE 21-1A**  Schoenberg: *Fünf Klavierstücke*, op. 23, no. 4, mm. 1–3

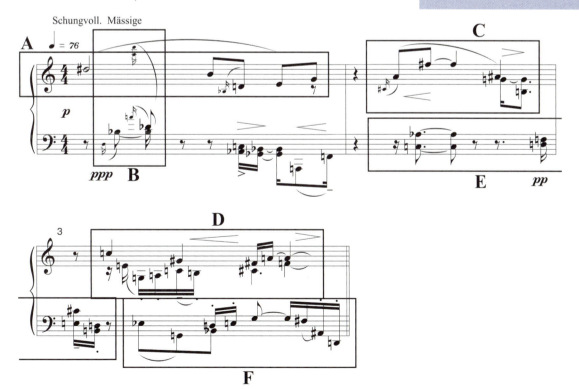

**EXAMPLE 21-1B** Schoenberg: *Fünf Klavierstücke*, op. 23, no. 4, mm. 24–26

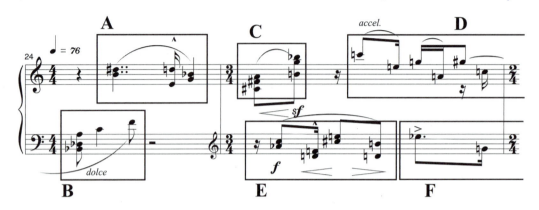

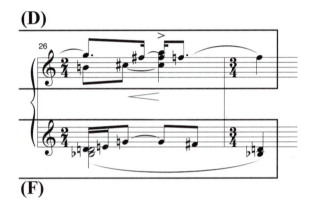

*Notes*:

1. A comparison of the two passages (comparing Box A to Box A, Box B to Box B, and so on) reveals some concern for preserving the ordering of PCs and also a tendency to use all twelve PCs in close succession, two techniques basic to the twelve-tone method.

2. The [0 1 4 5] set and its subsets—[0 1 4] and [0 1 5]— are embedded in the majority of the melodic figures, imparting a similarity to them that also unifies the piece as a whole.

---

Certain techniques basic to the 12-tone method are present in Schoenberg's treatment of sets in his earlier works, with this important difference: Ordering is the essence of a 12-tone row's identity. As we discuss the method, it may be helpful to think of the row as a "theme" that is subject to all the traditional techniques of development.

Schoenberg set forth the following "rules," then proceeded to break every one (so much for theory):

1. The pitch material for a composition is derived from a discrete ordering of all twelve PCs.

2. No PC is to be sounded out of order.

3. No PC is to be repeated (except for immediate repetition) until all other members of the row have been sounded.

A composer can decide how strictly or casually to apply these principles. Beyond that, flexibility resides in the method as follows:

1. A PC can appear in any octave.

2. The row can appear in any or all of four basic forms:
   - Prime (P): the original series.
   - Retrograde (R): The series in reverse order.
   - Inversion (I): The series in melodic inversion.
   - Retrograde Inversion (RI): The reverse order of the inversion.

A row and its four basic transformations, called row forms, are shown in Example 21-2.

## EXAMPLE 21-2

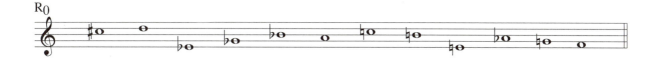

*Note*: The subscripts indicate the transposition level in semitones measured above the first pitch of each row form. In the case above, there is a zero level of transposition for each.

3. Any of the four row forms (series) can be transposed eleven semitones.

**EXAMPLE 21-3** (Prime series transposed one half step higher)

4. The members of the row may be assigned any durational value and may be used in any rhythmic or harmonic configuration.

5. One or more forms of the row may be used simultaneously. For example, one row form may provide the melodic line while another provides a subsidiary line or supporting harmonies, or the same row may be distributed between both the melody and its supporting harmonies.

Example 21-4a shows the beginnings of two possibly very different compositions based on the P0 series of Example 21-2 and a single transformation. As you can see, the twelve-tone method can be used to produce any kind of music the composer wishes to create while providing a "built-in" means of unification. The numerals indicate each pitch's position in the series.

**EXAMPLE 21-4A** Ralph Turek: Three by Twelve (first movement)

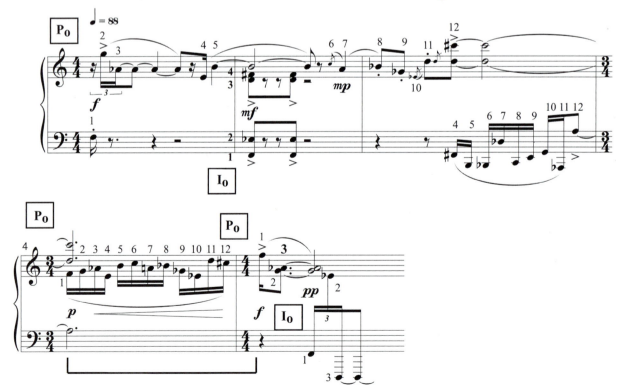

*Row Deployment*:

m. 1: P0 is distributed between the right-and left-hand parts.

m. 2: The melodic line is a continuation of P0. The first four pitches of I0 occur in the left-hand part as a chord. (Note its immediate repetition.)

m. 3: The left-hand part is a continuation of I0. The right hand completes P0.

m. 4: A new P0 statement takes place "inside" a sustained harmony by members of both P0 and I0.

m. 5: The right-hand part begins a new P0 statement. The left-hand part begins a new I0 statement.

**EXAMPLE 21-4B** Ralph Turek: Three by Twelve (second movement)

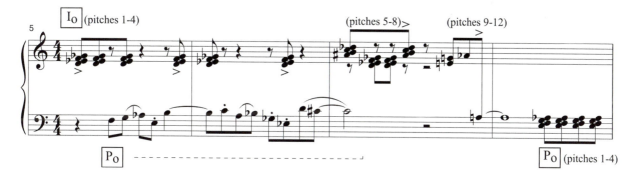

*Row Deployment*:

mm. 1–4: The first four pitches of P0 occur vertically in the left-hand part as a rhythmic pedal point. The right-hand part contains a complete linear statement of I0.

mm. 5–6: The first four pitches of I0 occur vertically in the right-hand part as a rhythmic pedal point. The left-hand part contains a complete linear statement of P0.

## THE MATRIX

Composers routinely use the prime, retrograde, inversion, and retrograde inversion forms of their rows in multiple transpositions (P11, I7, R4, RI9, and so on), making it difficult to recognize row variations in analysis. In order to aid identification, theorists use a matrix, which orders all the rows and their transpositions into a "grid."

To construct a matrix, draw a table of 48 squares, twelve in a row from left to right and twelve in a column from top to bottom. In the top row, enter the note names of the P0 row form from left to right. In the left column from top to bottom, enter the note names of the I0 row form. Since both P0 and I0 share the same note name at the beginning of the row, they share the same note name at the upper left-hand corner of the matrix. For this matrix, we'll use the P0 series (row) from Example 21-2.

### EXAMPLE 21-5

| F | G | A♭ | E | B | C | A | B♭ | F♯ | E♭ | D | C♯ |
|---|---|----|---|---|---|---|----|----|----|---|----|
| E♭ | | | | | | | | | | | |
| D | | | | | | | | | | | |
| F♯ | | | | | | | | | | | |
| B | | | | | | | | | | | |
| B♭ | | | | | | | | | | | |
| D♭ | | | | | | | | | | | |
| C | | | | | | | | | | | |
| E | | | | | | | | | | | |
| G | | | | | | | | | | | |
| A♭ | | | | | | | | | | | |
| A | | | | | | | | | | | |

Notice that the second row begins on E♭—10 semitones above the F that begins P0. Therefore, the prime row form beginning on E♭ is labeled P10. (Row forms are indexed above, not below, P0.)

Since the first note of P10 (E♭) is one step lower than the first note of P0, the P10 row form can be completed by entering every note one full step lower than the note directly above it. Although this seems to be the easiest way to complete a row form, errors can compound so be sure to check your accuracy. Similarly, the third prime row form, beginning on D, now named P9, is one semitone lower than the row directly above it, P10. Each note of P9 will thus be one half-step lower than the corresponding note of P10. (You are free to spell pitches enharmonically.)

If you proceed correctly, the beginning note of P0 and I0 appearing at the top left corner of the matrix—in this case, F—will run diagonally through the matrix from the top left corner to the bottom right corner, as the arrow indicates.

## EXAMPLE 21-6

|  | I0 |  |  |  |  |  |  |  |  |  |  |  |
|---|---|---|---|---|---|---|---|---|---|---|---|---|
| P0 | F | G | A♭ | E | B | C | A | B♭ | F♯ | E♭ | D | C♯ | R0 |
| P10 | E♭ | F | F♯ | D | A | B♭ | G | A♭ | E | C♯ | C | B | R10 |
| P9 | D | E | F | C♯ | A♭ | A | F♯ | G | E♭ | C | B | B♭ | R9 |
|  | F♯ |  |  |  |  |  |  |  |  |  |  |  |
|  | B |  |  |  |  |  |  |  |  |  |  |  |
|  | B♭ |  |  |  |  |  |  |  |  |  |  |  |
|  | D♭ |  |  |  |  |  |  |  |  |  |  |  |
|  | C |  |  |  |  |  |  |  |  |  |  |  |
|  | E |  |  |  |  |  |  |  |  |  |  |  |
|  | G |  |  |  |  |  |  |  |  |  |  |  |
|  | A♭ |  |  |  |  |  |  |  |  |  |  |  |
| P4 | A | B | C | G♯ | E♭ | E | C♯ | D | B♭ | G | F♯ | F | R4 |
|  | RI0 |  |  |  |  |  |  |  |  |  |  |  |

> **FOR PRACTICE**
>
> Complete the matrix above following the steps just described.

## Indexing the Matrix

Once the matrix is complete, all rows running left to right are labeled P for "Prime" forms (not to be confused with the term used for the prime form of a set), indexed with a subscript according to the distance in semitones of the first pitch above the initial pitch of P0. All columns running from top to bottom are labeled I forms (inversion), indexed according to the distance in semitones of the first pitch above the initial pitch of I0. For example, columns 1 (beginning on F) and 2 (beginning on G) are labeled I0 and I2, respectively. Rows running from right to left are labeled R forms (retrograde) and columns running from bottom to top will be labeled RI forms.

Retrogrades share the same index number with their corresponding prime form, and retrograde inversions share the same index number with their corresponding inversion. (The retrograde of P7 will be I7, and the retrograde of I4 will be RI4, and so on.)

> **FOR PRACTICE**
>
> Index the matrix in Example 21-6 as just described. Place Prime forms along the left-hand side, Retrograde forms along the right-hand side, Inversion forms across the top, and Retrograde–Inversion forms across the bottom.

Composers' approaches to the 12-tone method have ranged from strict to casual. Schoenberg himself was fond of segmentation, using segments of the row, such as trichords (three-note segments), tetrachords (four-note segments), or hexachords (six-note segments) in a manner similar to the fragmentation of the themes and subjects in earlier music.

## FINDING THE ROW

A question most often asked by students is how does one find the prime series? There is no standard answer and some compositions reveal their rows more readily than others. In the opening movement of Schoenberg's Fourth String Quartet, you may wonder if the prime series first unfolds linearly in the first violin or vertically throughout the ensemble. Actually, the series unfolds both ways. In our analysis, we can use traditional musical sensibilities to detect the prime series.

# EXAMPLE 21-7 Schoenberg: Fourth String Quartet, op. 37 (first movement) 🔊

The texture is clearly homophonic, with a melodic element in the first violin forming a phrase coming to an end in measure 6. Since this phrase forms an **aggregate** (a chromatic total), we can assume we have found a row form. The lower strings of m. 1 contain nine pitches that, together with the first three Violin I notes, produce an aggregate. Likewise, in succeeding measures, each Violin I trichord is accompanied in the lower strings by the remaining three trichords of the row. We hear the row both horizontally and vertically. This series and its retrograde, inversion, and retrograde inversion are shown below:

## EXAMPLE 21-8

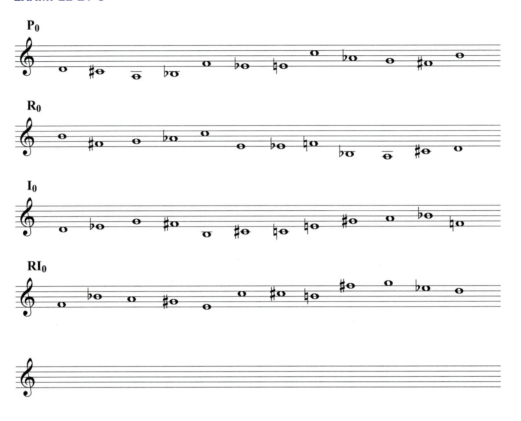

Since the trichord orientation permeates the opening of this composition both melodically and harmonically, a trichord analysis should be revealing. The beginning and ending trichords of the row are identical 0 1 5, meaning that the work is saturated with this sound since the retrograde and inversion and all their transpositions begin and end with 0 1 5.

## EXAMPLE 21-9

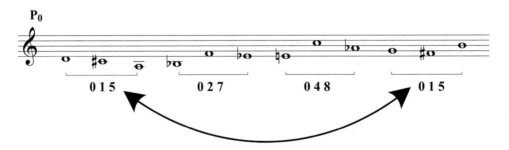

SERIAL ATONALITY 329

It may have occurred to you that a row can itself have a pronounced effect on the melodic and harmonic character of music based on it. For that reason, composers have not been casual in choosing their rows. In the foregoing Schoenberg example, we looked at the properties of contiguous sets, or sets that equally divide the row such as four trichords or three tetrachords. Such sets are known as **discrete sets.** However, composers may exploit the sounds in **non-discrete** or overlapping sets as well.

Such is the case in *Quaderno Musicale di Annalibera* by Luigi Dallapiccola. In the series illustrrated below, Dallapiccola exploits triadic sonorities in two **non-discrete** and two 026 **discrete** trichords.

### EXAMPLE 21-10 Dallapiccola: 12-tone row used in *Quaderno Musicale di Annalibera*

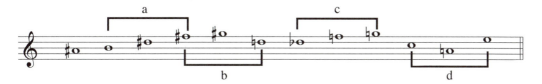

*Note*: With a major triad, two implied ninth chords, and a minor triad (bracketed) obtainable from adjacent row members, you'd expect this row to produce music that sounds different from Schoenberg's Quartet. And you'd be correct.

### EXAMPLE 21-11 Dallapiccola: *Quaderno Musicale di Annalibera* (Simbolo)

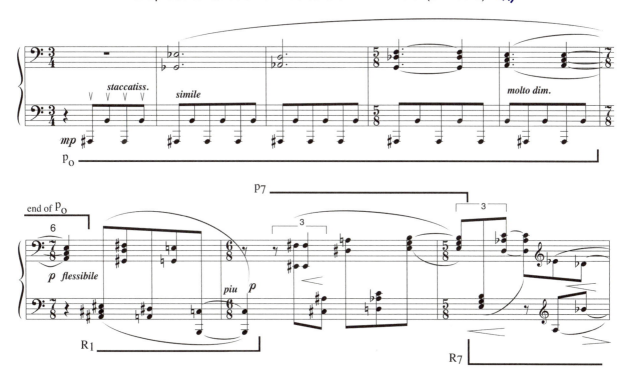

*Notes*:

1. The row is deployed in such a way that triads and seventh chords predominate.
2. The row members are voiced in such a way that the BACH motive—B (=B♭) A C H (=B)*—or its transposition, retrograde, or inversion is heard melodically at the top of the texture (hence the subtitle "symbol"). For example, the highest notes in mm. 2–5 are E♭–D–F–E: a transposition of B♭–A–C–B.
3. The row members are consistently segmented (2+2+2+3+3 or the reverse), lending harmonic and rhythmic uniformity.

How does one determine whether a piece is a 12-tone work? Following these steps should help:

1. In the opening measures and at phrase beginnings and important texture changes, examine the individual lines for evidence of a twelve-tone row.
2. Examine prominent harmonic structures for random pitch duplication that might suggest the work may not be serial.
3. If one passage fails to reveal insights, turn your attention to other passages.
4. If segmentation is employed extensively, you may find melodic lines and harmonic figures of less than twelve pitches. The work may even appear to be set-based. Discovering the row can be especially challenging in such works.
5. For all possible rows that you discover, construct the other three forms—R, I, and RI—and look for these.

### FOR PRACTICE

Complete a matrix for the row shown in Example 21-10.

---

*The German use of the letter B to symbolize B♭ and H to symbolize B♮ has its origins in medieval times when the symbols b and h stood for "soft B" (B♭) and "hard B" (B) respectively.

## EXAMPLE 21-12

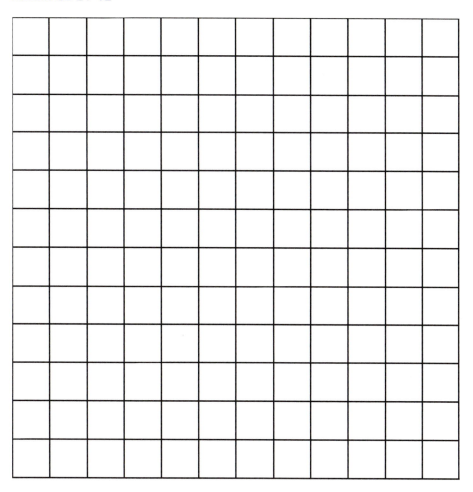

## HEXACHORDAL SYMMETRY

The hexachordal division in the row used in the first movement of Schoenberg's Fourth String Quartet (see Examples 21–7, 21–8, and 21–9) demonstrates a unique property. Known as **hexachordal symmetry**, the first and second hexachords produce the identical prime form, 0 1 4 5 6 8. This adds further harmonic unity to the "palindrome" effect of the 0 1 5 trichord that is heard at the beginning and ending of every row form.

## EXAMPLE 21-13

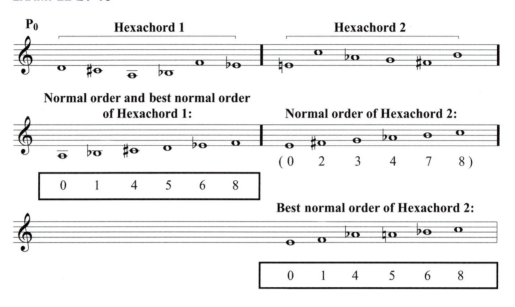

Another type of row symmetry exists in the **derived set** or **derived row,** in which all discrete trichords or tetrachords of a series produce the same prime form. In Anton Webern's *Concerto for Nine Instruments Op. 24*, his highly motivic style generated a trichord derived set of 0 1 5 as you can see and hear from the very beginning:

## EXAMPLE 21-14  Webern: *Concerto for Nine Instruments*, op. 24

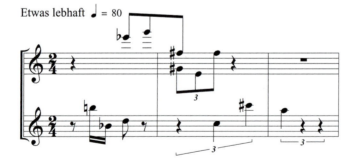

An examination of the row demonstrates Webern's segmentation of the series into four discrete trichords of 0 1 5, coinciding with his highly motivic writing in rhythmic groupings of three:

## EXAMPLE 21-15

Like a mountain road, the music of the twentieth century has followed a tortuous path, plunging forward into new musical terrain and then turning back into styles and techniques of the past. For example, Schoenberg's *Klavierstücke*, op. 11, no. , a work still modern-sounding in its relentless dissonance and renunciation of harmonic tradition, was composed nearly twenty years before Ravel's triadic and tonal Violin Sonata.

The century's musical pluralism has rendered the terms "contemporary" and "modern" musically meaningless. Moreover, their chronological significance is only relative, because what is contemporary today will become less so tomorrow. Virtually all musical styles and techniques are open for exploration today, making familiarity with them all the more important for today's musician.

## SUMMARY OF TERMINOLOGY

- serialism
- twelve-tone row
- row forms
- the matrix
- indexing
- aggregate
- segmentation
- discrete/non-discrete sets
- hexachordal symmetry
- derived set

# APPENDIX A

# Intervals, Modes and Keys

## OCTAVE DESIGNATION

The most common way of distinguishing pitches in various octaves is shown in Example A1–1, starting with the lowest C on the piano keyboard. All pitches in each successive octave are indicated with the numeric suffix "1" through "8."

### KEY CONCEPTS
- octave designations
- intervals
- mode
- key signature

**EXAMPLE A-1**

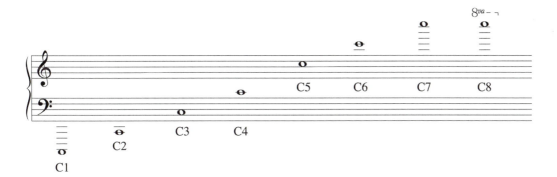

# APPENDIX A: SCALES AND INTERVALS

## INTERVALS

One way of spelling and recognizing intervals is to compare them to the intervals of the major scale, measured above or below the tonic:

### EXAMPLE A-2

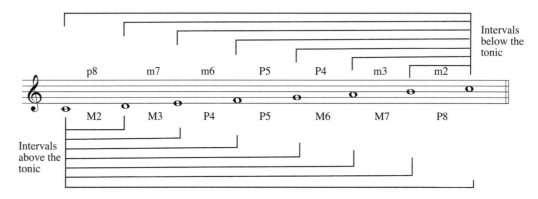

## Determining Interval Quality

Interval quality changes through a hierarchy of half steps:

*Major and Minor Intervals*

- A **major** interval *made smaller by a half step* becomes **minor.**
- A **major** interval *made larger by a half step* becomes **augmented.**
- A **minor** interval *made smaller by a half step* becomes **diminished.**
- A **minor** interval made larger by a half step becomes **major.**

*Perfect Intervals*

- A **perfect** interval made *smaller by a half step* becomes **diminished.**
- A **perfect** interval *made larger by a half step* becomes **augmented**

On the right is a complete list of interval names and semitone suffixes:

| Interval Name: | Number of ½ Steps | Interval Class |
|---|---|---|
| Perfect Unison | Zero | IC0 |
| Minor 2nd | One (1) | IC1 |
| Major 2nd | Two (2) | IC2 |
| Minor 3rd | Three (3) | IC3 |
| Major 3rd | Four (4) | IC4 |
| Perfect 4th | Five (5) | IC5 |
| Augmented 4th / Diminished 5th | Six (6) / Six (6) | IC6 / IC6 |
| Perfect 5th | Seven (7) | IC5 |
| Minor 6th | Eight (8) | IC4 |
| Major 6th | Nine (9) | IC3 |
| Minor 7th | Ten (10) | IC2 |
| Major 7th | Eleven (11) | IC1 |
| Perfect Octave | Twelve (12) | IC0 |

APPENDIX A: SCALES AND INTERVALS    337

## MEDIEVAL CHURCH MODES

The **church modes** were an attempt to classify the pitch basis of the early chants of the Roman Catholic liturgy (*c.* 5th–12th centuries). Each mode is a unique arrangement of whole and half steps, which occur between *the same pitches but at different points* in each mode.

### EXAMPLE A-3

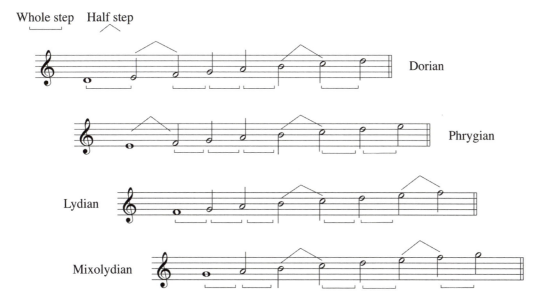

## KEY SIGNATURES

### Notation

Full key signatures of seven sharps or seven flats are notated in the following ways in treble, bass, alto, and tenor clefs.

### EXAMPLE A-4A

### EXAMPLE A-4B

*Note:* **Axis** slants downward to right for all clefs but tenor

*Note:* **Axis** slants upward to right for all clefs.

APPENDIX A: SCALES AND INTERVALS

## THE ORDER OF THE CIRCLE OF FIFTHS

Below is a chart of key names, major and minor, ordered by ascending and descending fifth root movement:

### EXAMPLE A-5

| Major key: | Relative minor key: | Key signature: |
|---|---|---|
| C | a | |
| G | e | 1 sharp |
| D | b | 2 sharps |
| A | f# | 3 sharps |
| E | c# | 4 sharps |
| B | g# | 5 sharps |
| F# | d# | 6 sharps |
| C# | a# | 7 sharps |
| Cb | ab | 7 flats |
| Gb | eb | 6 flats |
| Db | bb | 5 flats |
| Ab | f | 4 flats |
| Eb | c | 3 flats |
| Bb | g | 2 flats |
| F | d | 1 flat |

(Enharmonic Equivalents: B/Cb, F#/Gb, C#/Db paired with their relative minors g#/ab, d#/eb, a#/bb)

# APPENDIX B

# Selected Rhythm Topics

## RHYTHM AND METER

**Simple Meter Signature**: Any signature with an upper number of 2, 3, or 4. The beat divides into two parts.

**Upper Number** = The number of note values expressed by the lower number that are contained within a measure.

**Lower Number** = The note value that represents the beat.

### KEY CONCEPTS

- simple and compound meter
- rhythm and meter in conflict
- notating rhythm
- simple and compound meter

**EXAMPLE B-1A** Simple Duple Meter

Division of beat into two parts

**2** Signifies two beats in a measure.

**4** Signifies that the quarter note = the beat.

### EXAMPLE B-1B Simple Triple Meter

Division of beat
into two parts

3 Signifies three beats in a measure.

8 Signifies that the eighth note = the beat.

**Compound Meter Signature:** Any meter signature with an upper number that is a multiple of three—for example, 6, 9, and 12. The beat divides into three parts.

**Upper Number** = The number of note values expressed by the lower number that are contained within a measure.

**Lower Number** = The note value that represents *the three-part division* of the beat (*Three of this note value = one beat.*)

### EXAMPLE B-2A Compound Duple Meter

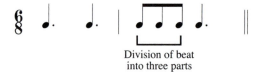
Division of beat
into three parts

6 Signifies six eighth note equivalents in a measure.

8 Signifies that the eighth note = one-third beat.

### EXAMPLE B-2B Compound Triple Meter

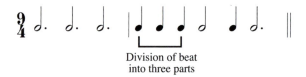
Division of beat
into three parts

9 Signifies nine quarter note equivalents in a measure.

4 Signifies that the quarter note = one-third beat.

*Note*: In compound meters, the note value that receives the beat will always be a dotted note, because only dotted values are equal to three of the next smaller value.

APPENDIX B: SELECTED RHYTHM TOPICS    341

## Rhythm and Meter in Conflict

Conflict between rhythm and meter creates musical interest.

**Borrowed divisions**: A note value that normally divides into two parts (simple) is divided into three parts (compound), and vice versa.

**EXAMPLE B-3A** Three-part division of beat (quarter note) where two-part division is the norm

**EXAMPLE B-3B** Four-part division of beat (dotted quarter note) where three-part division is the norm

b Four-part division of beat (dotted quarter note) where three-part division is the norm.

**EXAMPLE B-3C** Three-part division of half note where two-part division—into two quarter notes—is the norm

*Notes*:

1. An Arabic numeral is added to indicate the number of notes in the borrowed division.
2. When note values are not connected by a beam, a bracket can be used with the numeral for clarity.
3. The note *value* used for the borrowed division is that used for the normal division.

---

**Syncopation**: A normally unaccented part of a beat or measure is accented. A common means of accentuation is duration. A longer duration (an **agogic accent**) on the second or fourth beat of a 4/4 meter creates a syncopation.

### EXAMPLE B-4

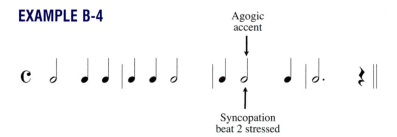

Syncopation can also occur *within* a beat. Since the first part of any beat (the downbeat) is stronger than any other part, a longer duration that begins anywhere but the downbeat can create syncopation.

### EXAMPLE B-5

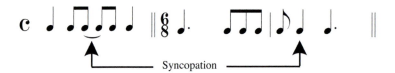

**Hemiola**: A syncopation involving the rhythmic ratio 3:2. It most often occurs when three equal-value notes are played in the time of two equal-value notes.

### EXAMPLE B-6A  Compound Duple Meter

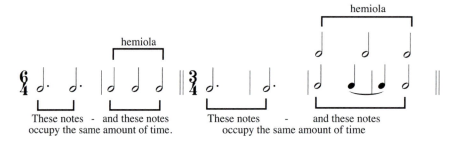

### EXAMPLE B-6B  Mozart: Symphony K. 550 (third movement)

*Note*: the juxtaposition of *two three-beat groupings* in the bass and *three two-beat groupings* in the melody.

# APPENDIX B: SELECTED RHYTHM TOPICS

## NOTATING RHYTHM

### Dots and Ties

A dot may follow any type of note, as long as it does not create a value too long for the measure *and* it does not obscure the beat for too long a period. Otherwise, the dotted value should be replaced by a tied value.

### EXAMPLE B-7

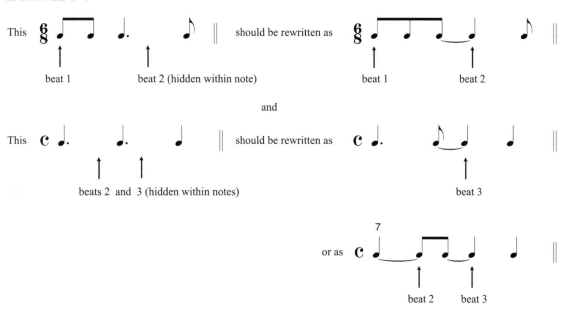

Double-dotted values are rare in actual practice.

### EXAMPLE B-8

unless the rhythm is repeated extensively.

In compound meters, double-dotted notes are not used.

## Beams

Beams should not cause confusion about where the beats occur in the measure.

### EXAMPLE B-9

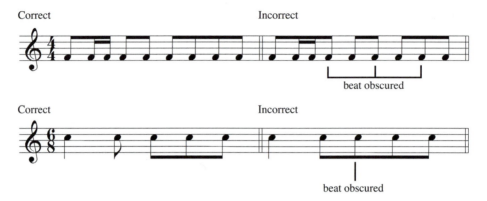

In 4/4, beams usually do not span the second and third beats.

### EXAMPLE B-10

All notes within a beat that *can* be beamed *should* be beamed.

### EXAMPLE B-11

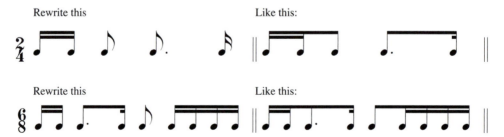

**General Guideline**
Except where a commonly used single note value is available, it is always acceptable to notate music so that an imaginary bar line can be placed just before each and every beat.

## Rests

Rests are never tied. As with note values, rests should not cause confusion about where the beat is.

### EXAMPLE B-12

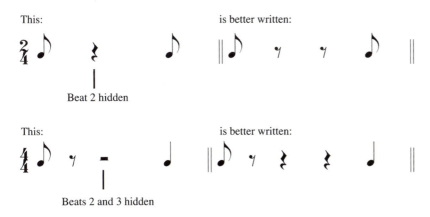

In simple meters, two rest values are preferred to dotted rests, except for values smaller than a quarter rest. However, in compound meters, dotted rests are common because they represent the beat or a multiple of it.

### EXAMPLE B-13

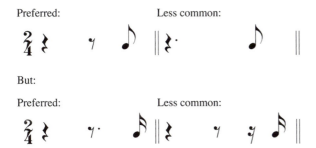

Two quarter rests are preferrred to a half rest in 3/4.

Whole rests may be used to fill an empty measure regardless of the meter signature. The rest is placed *in the center* of the measure.

## SUMMARY OF TERMINOLOGY

- agogic accent
- borrowed division
- compound meter
- hemiola
- simple meter
- syncopation

APPENDIX C

# Basic Harmonic Structures

## TRIADS

The four most common types of triad contain only major and minor thirds. A fifth—perfect, augmented, or diminished—is formed by the root and top note in this stack.

**KEY CONCEPTS**
- triads
- inverted triads
- seventh chords
- inverted seventh chords

### EXAMPLE C-1

| Triad Type | Symbol | Example on the Root **G** |
|---|---|---|
| Major Triad | M | M3　P5 |
| Minor Triad | m | m3　P5 |
| Augmented Triad | + | M3　+5 |
| Diminished Triad | ° | m3　°5 |

Major and minor triads are more stable sounding than augmented or diminished triads. This is due to the **perfect fifth** (a perfect consonance) that is part of the construction of the major and minor triad. While the perfect fifth provides *harmonic stability*, the third provides the *harmonic color*, giving the chords their respective **major** or **minor** sound.

## Triad Inversion

**Chord inversion** places a chord member other than the root in the lowest position. Triads can appear three ways.

### EXAMPLE C-2

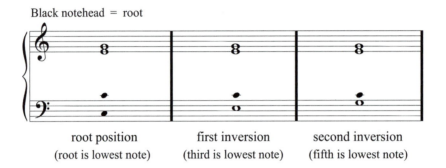

root position | first inversion | second inversion
(root is lowest note) | (third is lowest note) | (fifth is lowest note)

## Seventh Chords

A **seventh chord** is formed by stacking an additional third above the fifth in a triad, which is the same as adding a seventh above the chord root.

### EXAMPLE C-3

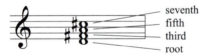

A seventh can be added above any triad type. The seventh—measured above the root—can be major, minor, or diminished (augmented sevenths are enharmonic duplications of the root). Seventh chords are classified according to the triad type and the quality of the seventh.

### EXAMPLE C-4

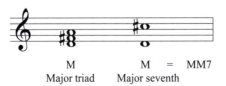

M     M = MM7
Major triad    Major seventh

The five common seventh chord types built on the *same* root:

## EXAMPLE C-5

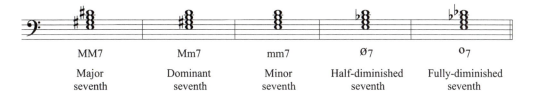

## Seventh Chord Inversion

As with triads, the sole determinant of inversion is the chord member that is in the bass.

## EXAMPLE C-6

# APPENDIX D

# Part-Writing Guidelines

## A. MELODIC PRINCIPLES

1. **Range:** Each voice should remain within its range.

2. **Interval structure:** Each line should be basically conjunct (the bass may be less so), with large leaps less common and leaps larger than a third usually approached and left by step.

3. **Nondiatonic intervals:** Avoid these.

4. **Leading tone and chromatic tones:** Resolve these, especially when in an outer voice.

## B. VOICING

1. **Spacing:** Allow no more than an octave between the soprano and alto or between the alto and tenor.

2. **Doubling:**
   - *General Guide:* The bass may be doubled unless it is the leading tone or another tendency tone (a chromatic pitch or a chord seventh, for example).
   - *Root Position and Second Inversion:* The bass is the *preferred* doubling in root position and second inversion major and minor triads.
   - *First Inversion:* Doubling in first inversion triads is often determined by melodic.
   
   Considerations, but in general the soprano is the preferred doubling.

## C. CHORD CONNECTION

1. **Outer voices**: Move the outer voices in contrary or oblique motion as often as possible.

2. **Consecutive perfect consonances**: Avoid moving perfect fifths, perfect octaves, or perfect unisons to another such interval in the same two voices on successive beats.

3. **Voice crossing and overlap**: Avoid this.

4. **Common tones**: Retain common tones between two chords in the same voice. When common tones are not present between two chords, move the upper voices contrary to the bass if possible.

5. **First inversion**: Use first inversion to improve the melodic character of the bass. Try to leave the doubled tone in contrary motion.

6. **Second inversion**: Restrict second inversion to only the cadential I, the passing V or I, the pedal IV or I, and arpeggiated I, IV or V.

7. **Nonchord tones**: Adding nonchord tones to the texture should not affect the basic voice leading.

## D. FINAL WORD

When a part-writing problem seems insurmountable, one of the following options may still be available:

- Change the structure or inversion of the chord.
- Use optional doubling.
- Change the harmony.
- Change the melody.

# Glossary

**Accent**: Emphasis placed on a particular note through metric placement, dynamic level, articulation, duration, or register.

**Accidental**: A sign placed before a note to indicate a temporary raising or lowering of its pitch or a cancellation of a previous accidental.

**Agogic accent**: Emphasis placed on a particular note by virtue of its longer duration than the surrounding notes.

**Altered chord**: A harmony that contains pitches not diatonic in the key in which it appears.

**Altered dominant**: A dominant or dominant seventh chord with a raised or lowered fifth.

**Altered predominants**: Chromatic harmonies, including the Neapolitan sixth chord and augmented sixth chords, that progress to the dominant with a heightened tendency to resolve owing to the altered tone.

**Alto**: 1) A female voice type with an approximate range from G3 to D4. 2) The term normally used to refer to the second highest musical line in a multi-voiced composition.

**Answer**: In a fugal exposition, the imitation of the subject at the level of the dominant.

**Antecedent**: In a period, the first of the phrases, ending without a sense of completion and requiring a consequent phrase to bring about a resolution.

**Anticipation**: An embellishing tone usually found at cadences, in which one voice, usually the soprano, resolves to its cadence pitch ahead of the other voices.

**Appoggiatura**: An embellishing tone approached by leap and resolved to a metrically weaker pitch by step, usually in the opposite direction of the leap.

**Appoggiatura chord**: A nineteenth-century harmony in which several of the chord members resemble appoggiaturas in that they are approached by leap and resolved by step. The true chord can be found at the point of their resolution.

**Arpeggiated six-four chord**: A second-inversion triad, most often a tonic or dominant, that results when the chord is outlined by the lowest voice of the texture.

**Arpeggio, arpeggiation**: The melodic outlining of a chord in a single voice.

**Asymmetric**: In melody, a period or phrase group in which the phrases are of unequal length. A binary form in which the second part is longer or shorter than the first part.

**Atonality**: The term given to music that contains neither traditional tonal references nor a pronounced sense that one pitch possesses greater stability than all the others and thus constitutes the tonal center.

**Augmentation**: A contrapuntal device in which a melodic/rhythmic figure appears in longer note values than its original form.

**Augmented sixth chord**: A group of altered predominant chords commonly found in eighteenth- and nineteenth-century music, characterized by an augmented sixth interval formed by the bass (a half step above the dominant) and the raised fourth scale degree (a half step below the dominant). Specific types are the Italian, French, and German sixth chords.

**Augmented triad**: A three-note chord built of major thirds in which the highest member is an augmented fifth above the root.

**Authentic cadence**: The harmonic formula V–I (or V–i in minor keys) that creates a conclusive point of punctuation and repose at the end of a musical thought.

**Bass**: 1) A male voice type with an approximate range from E2 to C4; 2) The term normally used to refer to the lowest voice of a multiple-voice texture.

**Bimodality**: The use of two modes simultaneously in a composition or a portion thereof. Typically, one voice or musical line is in one mode while another is in a different mode.

**Binary**: Any musical form that divides into two basic parts, usually designated A B. The form was extremely popular during the Baroque era, used almost exclusively in the instrumental suites of that period.

**Borrowed division**: The use of a simple division of the beat in a compound meter, or the reverse—a compound division of the beat in a simple meter.

**Borrowed harmonies**: The altered chords that result from the process of modal borrowing (see "Modal borrowing"). The chords most often used in this way are the ii°, ii$^{ø7}$, iv, vii°7, and ♭VI—all diatonic in a minor key but borrowed for use in the parallel major key.

**Bridge**: 1) In a fugal exposition, a short passage linking the end of the answer with the next entry of the subject, often serving to modulate from the dominant back to the tonic. 2) In popular music, a short section, usually in a different tonality, that separates the initial statement of the main melody and its return.

**Cadence**: A point of melodic and/or harmonic repose, often created through a slowing or pause in motion and serving as a punctuation between phrases.

**Cadential elision**: A process in which the end of one phrase and the beginning of the next phrase coincide, thereby avoiding a cadential separation between the two.

**Cadential extension**: The lengthening of a musical phrase upon repetition through a restatement or expansion of its cadence.

**Cadential process**: Music that either prepares for or extends a cadence.

**Cadential six-four chord**: A metrically strong second-inversion tonic triad preceding the dominant at a cadence, and in fact best analyzed as a dominant with nonchord tones a fourth and sixth above the bass.

**Chain suspension**: A series of suspension figures in which the resolution of one suspension becomes the preparation for the next.

**Change of mode**: In a musical composition, the shift from a major key to its parallel minor or the reverse.

**Changing tone**: A two-note embellishment involving the pitches a step above and below a more important tone and its repetition.

**Chorale**: A hymn tune that originated in the Lutheran Church during the sixteenth century, comprising several stanzas of verse sung to the same music.

**Chord**: A single musical sound comprising three or more different pitches (not counting octave duplications).

**Chordal mutation**: A gradual and subtle chord change, in which one member of the harmony changes at a time, often generating unusual harmonic successions in the process.

**Chromatic**: A term referring to music, intervals, or pitches not confined to the pitch material of a given scale or mode.

**Chromatic modulation**: A change of tonal center involving no common chords, usually signaled by a diatonic pitch moving to a chromatically altered pitch in one or more voices.

**Chromatic pivot**: The pivotal chord in a chromatic modulation. It usually serves a recognizable function in both keys. However, its function in at least one of the keys is chromatic, and in this way it differs from a common chord, which functions diatonically in *both* keys.

**Chromatic-third relationship**: Two chords with roots a third apart, in which one chord contains a chromatic alteration of one or both common tones. The term also refers to two tonalities in which the tonics are in a chromatic-third relationship.

**Church modes**: A set of scales that formed the basis of much medieval and Renaissance music, pre-dating and eventually evolving into our major and minor scales.

**Closely related keys**: The five tonalities that differ from a given tonality by no more than one flat or sharp—thus the relative major or minor, the dominant and its relative key, and the subdominant and its relative key.

**Coda**: An extension of the ending of a composition, which helps to create a convincing close by prolonging and reaffirming the tonic.

**Common chord**: In a modulation, a chord diatonic in both the old and new keys that serves as the pivotal point in the modulation.

**Common chord modulation**: Also called "pivot-chord modulation," a change of tonality aided by a chord diatonic in both keys that acts as a pivot between the two.

**Common practice period**: The period in musical history, roughly 1650–1900, in which composers used functional tonality as the harmonic basis of their music.

**Common tones**: The pitches shared between two chords in any harmonic relationship.

**Compound interval**: Any interval exceeding the octave in size.

**Compound meter**: A meter in which the primary division of the beat is into three parts.

**Conjunct**: Melodic motion involving stepwise intervals.

**Consecutive perfect consonances**: A succession of perfect fifths, perfect octaves, or perfect unisons between the same two voices, considered objectionable practice in strict part writing.

**Consequent**: The final phrase of a period, which, due to its more conclusive cadence, provides a greater sense of completion than the preceding (antecedent) phrase(s).

**Consonance**: Two or more pitches that, when sounded together, produce a sense of stability and repose.

**Continuo**: The name given to the figured bass line in baroque-era compositions or the group of instruments that plays the figured bass (usually a keyboard instrument and a melodic bass instrument, such as the viola da gamba).

**Contrary motion**: The movement by two voices from one tone to the next in the opposite direction.

**Contrasting period**: Phrases in antecedent-consequent relationship that are composed of different material and differ in general character.

**Counterexposition**: In a fugue, a group of subject–answer entries in the tonic, usually appearing immediately after the exposition or separated from the expostion by a brief episode.

**Countermotive**: A distinctive counterpoint that appears more or less consistently against the principal motive in an invention.

**Counterpoint**: Music consisting of two or more melodic lines heard simultaneously but displaying a certain degree of independence (of contour and rhythm).

**Countersubject**: A counterpoint that is employed frequently against the subject or answer in a fugue, providing a contrasting idea and additional material for development.

**Deceptive cadence**: A two-chord formula punctuating a musical thought, in which the dominant moves to any chord but the tonic. The chord most often substituted for the expected tonic is the submediant.

**Development**: A section of a musical work where a musical idea is worked out and its potential realized through various compositional devices such as imitation, inversion, rhythmic variation, and so on.

**Developmental process**: The musical process involved in working out a musical idea. It usually involves rapid tonal changes, abrupt shifts in tempo, dynamics, texture, and unstable harmonies with infrequent resolutions.

**Diatonic**: A term referring to music or intervals confined to the pitch material of a given scale or mode.

**Diatonic-third relationship**: Two chords whose roots lie a third apart and which contain two common tones, as in I–vi, I–iii, i–VI, and so on.

**Diminished seventh chord**: The chord formed by the addition of a diminished seventh above the root of a diminished triad. It most often occurs on the leading tone of a minor key, as a vii°7.

**Diminished triad**: A three-note chord formed when a minor third is stacked above a minor third, the highest note forming a diminished fifth against the root.

**Diminution**: The restatement of a melodic/rhythmic figure in shorter note values.

**Disjunct**: Melodic motion involving intervals larger than a whole step.

**Dissonance**: The effect of two or more pitches sounding together that produce a sense of instability and desire for resolution.

**Dominant**: The functional name given to the fifth degree of a scale and to the triad formed on this pitch.

**Dominant-major ninth chord**: The harmony formed when a third is placed above the seventh of a major-key dominant seventh chord, forming a major ninth above the chord root.

**Dominant-minor ninth chord**: The harmony formed when a third is placed above the seventh of a minor-key dominant seventh chord, forming a minor ninth above the chord root.

**Dominant seventh chord**: The seventh-chord type formed on the fifth scale degree, consisting of a major triad with a minor seventh above its root. Because this type of seventh chord appears diatonically only on the dominant, it is simply called the dominant seventh chord.

**Dorian**: One of six church modes that pre-dated and led to the major and minor scales, viewable today as a natural minor scale with a raised sixth degree.

**Double period**: Four phrases in which the final phrase ends more conclusively than the preceding three. The phrases may be similar (called a parallel double period) or dissimilar (called a contrasting double period).

**Doubling**: In four-part writing, reinforcing one of the members of a triad by including it in two of the voices.

**Doubly augmented fourth chord**: A German sixth chord with the mediant respelled enharmonically as a supertonic to reflect its upward resolution to the third of a major tonic six-four chord.

**Eleventh chord**: A chord formed by the addition of a third above the ninth in a ninth chord.

**Embellishing diminished seventh chord**: A fully diminished seventh chord that functions not as a leading tone chord but as an auxiliary chord, usually to the tonic or dominant. The seventh of this chord is a common tone with the root of the embellished chord.

**Embellishing tone**: A pitch that serves as a connection between or decoration of the more important pitches of a melodic line.

**Enharmonic**: A term referring to different spellings of the same pitch or interval.

**Enharmonic change of mode**: A shift to the parallel major or minor key accompanied by an enharmonic respelling of that key, as in G♭ major to F♯ minor.

**Enharmonic diminished seventh chord**: A diminished seventh chord used enharmonically, usually in a modulation, so that a chord member other than its root functions as the new root.

**Enharmonic equivalence**: Two pitches, intervals, or chords that sound the same but are spelled differently.

**Enharmonic German sixth chord**: See **doubly augmented fourth chord.**

**Enharmonic pivot**: A chord which, at the point of a modulation, is diatonic in the old key and, respelled enharmonically, diatonic in the new key.

**Entry group**: In a fugue, two or more statements of the subject in immediate or near-immediate succession, in a manner similar to the exposition but appearing at later points in the fugue.

**Episode**: In a fugue, a short passage in free counterpoint that separates those sections containing complete statements of the subject. The material of an episode may be derived from the subject or countersubject or may use unrelated material, but by definition, an episode does *not* contain a complete statement of the subject.

**Escape tone**: An embellishing tone approached by step and left by leap.

**Exposition**: The first section of a fugue, in which each voice enters in turn with a statement of the subject or its answer.

**Extended tonicization**: A common procedure in jazz, wherein a secondary predominant is added before a secondary dominant to create a secondary ii–V motion to a tonicized chord.

**Fifth relation**: Two chords whose roots are related to each other by the interval of a fifth, as C and G.

**Figured bass**: A notational method in general use for keyboard instruments during the seventeenth and eighteenth centuries. Numbers beneath the pitches of the bass line indicate the intervals to be added above the line, and thus indicate the harmonies as well.

**Final**: The central tone of a mode, usually the tone upon which melodies in the mode end.

**Form**: The shape of a musical work as created by cadences, the similarity and contrast of the musical elements, and the interaction of the musical processes.

**Fragmentation**: A technique wherein small portions of a melodic idea are heard in isolation and used in sequences, imitation, or other developmental ways.

**French sixth chord**: An augmented sixth chord consisting of the half step above the dominant (in the bass), the half step below the dominant (in an upper voice), the tonic, and the second scale degree.

**Fugue**: A contrapuntal composition for a fixed number of voices (usually two to five) in which a subject, stated by all voices in turn at the beginning, recurs at various points in a variety of tonalities and contrapuntal textures.

**Functional tonality**: A term describing the system by which the chords of a major or minor key are related to each other and to the tonic.

**Fundamental**: The lowest (and usually the loudest) tone in a harmonic series, produced by a string or air column, vibrating in its entire length.

**Gamut**: G on the bottom line of the bass clef, the lowest note in Guido's hexachord system. Generally refers to the entire range of a pitch system.

**German sixth chord**: An augmented sixth chord consisting of the half step above the dominant (in the bass), the half step below the dominant (in an upper voice), the tonic, and the third scale degree.

**Grand staff**: The combined treble and bass clef staves on which keyboard music is notated.

**Ground bass**: Short, repeated bass line, usually four to eight measures long, that form the basis of many Baroque-era works.

**Half cadence**: Most commonly, a harmonic cadence ending on the dominant triad.

**Half-diminished seventh chord**: The chord formed by the addition of a minor seventh above the root of a diminished triad. This chord appears diatonically on the leading tone of a major key and the supertonic of a minor key.

**Half step**: The smallest interval normally used in Western music and the smallest interval on the piano.

**Harmonic minor**: The natural minor scale with the seventh degree raised by one half step. It is the form most often the harmonic basis of music in minor keys.

**Harmonic rhythm**: The rate of chord change, or the series of durational patterns formed by the chord changes in a musical work.

**Harmonics**: Frequencies above a given fundamental that form whole-number ratios with it, coloring the basic sound.

**Harmonic sequence**: A harmonic pattern repeated at a different pitch level.

**Harmonic series**: In a complex waveform, the spectrum of frequencies that are whole-number multiples of the fundamental. This series of frequency components is responsible for a sound's timbre, or tone quality.

**Harmony**: The effect produced by the simultaneous sounding of several discrete pitches.

**Hemiola**: A particular type of 3:2 rhythmic ratio involving successive or simultaneous divisions of the quantity six in two ways—as two groups of three units and as three groups of two units.

**Hexachord**: 1) Any six adjacent notes of different pitch (excluding octave duplications). 2) A collection of six pitches, usually comprising a segment of a twelve-tone row. 3) The basis of Guido's organization of the pitch gamut of his day into overlapping six-note groups.

**Homophony**: A texture in which individual voices having neither melodic nor rhythmic independence.

**Hypermeasure**: Measures that exhibit a regular pattern of accentuation in the same way that the beats within a measure do, creating a higher-level metric organization.

**Hypermeter**: A large level of metric structure created by a regular pattern of accented and unaccented measures. Many folk songs exhibit a hypermetric structure that mirrors their meter. For example, in 4/4, measures that group into fours with the first and third measures of each group accented.

**Imitation**: The restatement in close succession of a melodic figure by a different voice.

**Imperfect consonance**: Traditionally, thirds and sixths, which were considered less pure and simple than octaves, unisons and fifths but more pleasing to the ear than seconds and sevenths.

**Implied harmony**: The chords suggested by a single melodic line or by a combination of lines in which all members of the harmony are not heard. The chords are aurally inferred either from the intervals generated by the lines or from the chords outlined in one of the lines.

**Implied polymeter**: Music in two different meters sounding simultaneously but notated in a single meter signature.

**Incomplete neighbor**: The name preferred today for an unaccented appoggiatura.

**Index number**: A subscript placed after the letters P, R, I, or RI to indicate the transposition level of a row form. P and I forms are indexed according to their first pitch while R and RI forms are indexed according to their last pitch. In this way, a P form and its corresponding retrograde have the same index number, as do an I form and its corresponding retrograde (RI).

**Interval**: The musical distance between two pitches.

**Interval class**: The smallest possible distance between two pitch classes. This means any interval comprising one to six half steps along with its inversion, its compound forms (those larger than an octave), and enharmonic spellings, symbolized by a number from 1 to 6 to indicate the number of half steps spanned.

**Invention**: The name given to two sets of short keyboard studies by J. S. Bach, in two and three voices respectively. In these studies, a short idea (motive) is developed in a continuous imitative counterpoint featuring various contrapuntal devices.

**Inversion**: 1) Octave transposition of one of the pitches of an interval so that the lower pitch becomes the higher and vice versa. 2) Any position of a triad or seventh chord in which the root is not the lowest tone.

**Invertible counterpoint**: Counterpoint constructed in such a way that the lower part may become the higher part and vice versa through transposition of one or both lines.

**Italian sixth chord**: An augmented sixth chord containing the half step above the dominant (in the bass), the half step below the dominant (in an upper voice), and the tonic.

**Key signature**: An inventory of the flats or sharps used consistently in a composition or in a section of a composition, grouped together and placed immediately after the clef sign at the beginning of each staff.

**Lead sheet**: In popular music and jazz, the representation of the music through a melody along with chord symbols placed above it to guide musicians in their melodic and harmonic interpretation.

**Leading tone**: The functional name given to the major or minor scale degree one half step below the tonic, or to the triad formed on this pitch.

**Linear chromaticism**: Chromatic harmonies formed as the byproducts of chromatic melodic motion.

**Lydian**: One of six church modes that pre-dated and led to the major and minor scales, viewable today as a major scale with a raised fourth degree.

**Major**: The mode based on the major scale and its seven diatonic chords.

**Major ninth chord**: A five-member sonority extending a major triad with the addition of a major seventh and major ninth above the root (symbolized MMM9).

**Major seventh chord**: The chord formed by the addition of a major seventh above the root of a major triad. It most often is found on the subdominant in a major key (IV$^7$) and on the submediant and mediant (VI$^7$ and III$^7$) in a minor key.

**Major triad**: A three-note chord consisting of two intervals above its roo—a major third and a perfect fifth—and appearing as the tonic, dominant, and subdominant of a major-key work.

**Measure**: One complete cycle of the accentual pattern in a given meter.

**Mediant**: The functional name given to the third degree of a major or minor scale, or to the triad formed on this pitch.

**Melodic inversion**: Turning a melodic figure "upside down" so that its contour and interval structure are a mirror of the original form, with upward steps and leaps becoming downward steps and leaps of the same size, and vice versa.

**Melodic minor**: The natural minor scale with the sixth and seventh degrees raised by one half step in ascent. In descending passages, the sixth and seventh degrees usually are those of the natural minor scale. It is the form most often the basis for minor-key melodies.

**Melodic tonality**: The tendency of a melody to define its tonal center by emphasizing one certain pitch in various ways.

**Meter**: A regularly recurring pattern of strong and weak pulses that forms the background on which the many rhythms of a piece of music are imposed.

**Metric shift**: A type of syncopation involving the temporary but extended displacement of the primary accent of a measure.

**Minor**: The mode based on the minor scale and its diatonic chords.

**Minor ninth chord**: A five-member chord extending a minor triad with the addition of a minor seventh and major ninth above the root (symbolized mmM9).

**Minor seventh chord**: The chord formed by the addition of a minor seventh above the root of a minor triad. It is most often found on the supertonic of a major key and the subdominant of a minor key.

**Minor triad**: A three-note chord consisting of two intervals above its root—a minor third and a perfect fifth—and appearing as the tonic and subdominant in a minor-key work.

**Mixolydian**: One of six church modes that pre-dated and led to the major and minor scales, viewable today as a major scale with a lowered seventh degree.

**Modal borrowing**: A process involving the brief and occasional use of a harmony called a "borrowed harmony" from the parallel major or minor mode.

**Modal cadence**: A harmonic pattern containing an inflection characteristic of one of the church modes.

**Mode**: See **church modes**.

**Mode mixture**: A general procedure wherein the harmonic resources of the parallel major and minor modes are combined. It includes modal borrowing and change of mode.

**Modulation**: The process of changing tonal centers.

**Motive**: A short melodic/rhythmic idea that serves as the basis for an invention or, through its frequent occurrence, lends unity to any composition.

**Motivic analysis**: Analysis that seeks to understand how all elements of a musical composition relate to each other by identifying motivic similarities among sections, subsections, phrases, and so on.

**Musical process**: The collective functioning of the musical elements to create a sense that a passage is serving one of several purposes—stating a theme, developing an idea, changing tonality, mood, or character, prolonging a cadence, and so on.

**Natural minor**: A seven-tone scale with the interval pattern of whole step, half step, whole step, whole step, half step, whole step, whole step, identical to the Aeolian mode.

**Neapolitan sixth chord**: A major triad with the lowered supertonic as its root, most often serving a predominant harmonic function in minor keys.

**Neighbor tone**: An embellishing tone occurring stepwise between a more important pitch and its repetition.

**Nonchord tone**: The term used to describe embellishing tones when they occur in a harmonic context and are not members of the prevailing harmony.

**Nondominant seventh chord**: Any seventh chord that functions neither as a V (dominant) nor as a viio (leading tone chord).

**Normal order**: The arrangement of the pitches of a set from lowest to highest, so that the first and last pitch span the smallest possible interval.

**Oblique motion**: The movement by one voice from one tone to a different tone while a second voice remains on the same tone.

**Octatonic scale**: Literally, a scale of eight tones. The name has been appropriated for a scale used by Debussy and others that consists of eight alternating whole and half steps.

**Octave**: A term referring to the interval spanned by twelve half steps, from a given pitch to the next higher or lower pitch of the same latter name. The frequency ratio between two such pitches is 2:1.

**Order number**: A number indicating the positions (from one to twelve) occupied by the notes of a twelve-tone row.

**Ottava sign**: A symbol (*8va*) that, placed above a pitch, directs that it be performed an octave higher than written.

**Overtone**: Any of the harmonics occurring above a fundamental frequency.

**Pandiatonicism**: The use of pitch material from a given scale or mode, with few or no extraneous pitches and lacking the usual functional harmonic and melodic relationships.

**Parallel major–minor**: A major and minor scale or key sharing the same tonic.

**Parallel motion**: The movement by two voices from one tone to the next in the same direction and by the same number of steps or half steps.

**Parallel perfect consonances**: The movement of two voices from one perfect consonance to another of the same type. Considered objectionable practice in strict four-part writing. (Also called "consecutive perfect consonances.")

**Parallel period**: Phrases in antecedent-consequent relationship, the last beginning with the same or similar material as the first but ending more conclusively.

**Part writing**: Composing or arranging for multiple voices so that each voice forms a melodic line that fits together with the other voices to produce a harmonic structure.

**Passing six-four chord**: A second-inversion triad, usually a dominant or tonic, in which the motion of the individual voices through the doubled chord tone (the fifth) resembles a passing tone. The resulting chord becomes, in effect, a passing chord.

**Passing tone**: An embellishing tone occurring stepwise between two more important tones of different pitch.

**Pedal point**: A pitch that is sustained or repeated while the other voices of the texture change pitch, creating dissonances against it.

**Pedal six-four chord**: A second-inversion triad, usually a subdominant or tonic, in which the bass line remains stationary prior to and following the chord itself, resembling a pedal point.

**Pedal tone**: On a wind instrument, the fundamental tone of the harmonic series produced by the instrument vibrating in its whole aspect. Usually not part of the normal playing range, pedal tones are those that are overblown to produce the notes in the normal playing range.

**Pentachord**: Any consecutive five pitches.

**Pentatonic scale**: An ascending or descending pitch collection that consists of five tones to the octave, most often containing no half steps and no more than two whole steps in succession.

**Perfect authentic cadence**: A V–I harmonic pattern in which the tonic appears in the highest voice on the final chord *and* the two chords are in root position.

**Perfect consonance**: The designation given by early theorists to intervals having the simplest frequency ratio, specifically, the perfect fourth, perfect fifth, perfect unison, and perfect octave.

**Period**: Two phrases, sometimes three, that are perceived as a unit because the final phrase ends more conclusively than the preceding phrase(s), providing a greater sense of completion.

**Permutation**: Any reordering of the pitches of a set or twelve-tone row.

**Phrase**: A melodic unit, typically four to eight measures long, which expresses a more-or-less complete musical thought.

**Phrase extension**: A means of expanding a phrase upon repetition by adding material to its beginning, middle, or end.

**Phrase group**: Two or more phrases that, although not forming a period, are nevertheless related and convey a sense that they belong together.

**Phrygian**: One of six church modes that pre-dated and led to the major and minor scales, viewable today as a minor scale with a lowered second degree.

**Phrygian cadence**: A type of half cadence, found only in minor, comprising the chords iv$^6$–V.

**Picardy Third**: The major tonic triad that often ends a minor-key movement in the Baroque era.

**Pitch**: The sensation of highness or lowness attributed to a musical tone, the result of a periodic waveform's frequency.

**Pitch class**: A term used in set theory to denote a single pitch along with all of its octave duplications and enharmonic spellings.

**Pitch class interval**: The interval formed by two pitch classes.

**Pitch class set**: A collection of pitch class intervals in any order.

**Plagal cadence**: A conclusive cadence involving two-chord formula IV–I—or iv—in minor keys).

**Planing**: Two or more voices moving together in parallel motion, generating intervals or harmonies of the same general or specific type.

**Polychord**: Two or more harmonic structures sounding simultaneously but perceivable as discrete chords.

**Polyphony**: A texture consisting of lines that are melodically and rhythmically independent.

**Polytonality**: Music suggesting the simultaneous presence of more than one tonal center.

**Post-cadential**: Referring to extensions that occur after a cadence has been completed and thus prolong the effect of its final chord.

**Pre-cadential**: Referring to extensions that occur in the approach to a cadence, often prolonging the effect of its first chord.

**Predominant**: Chords that normally proceed directly to the dominant—the subdominant and the supertonic. According to a more recent view, one of only three harmonic functions, the other two being tonic and dominant.

**Preparatory process**: The collective functioning of the musical elements in a way that sets the style or mood of the music to come.

**Prime**: In twelve-tone music, the original form of the twelve-tone row.

**Prime form**: The expression of the best normal order for a set and its inversion. Prime form assigns the first (lowest) pitch the number "0" and the remaining pitches numbers that correspond to their distance in half steps above the lowest pitch.

**Progression**: The strongest type of harmonic motion, in which each chord moves to the next closest chord to the tonic, as measured in descending-fifth root movements. Harmonic progression generates a satisfying feeling of forward momentum in music.

**Proportional**: A term referring to the rhythmic aspect of our notation system, in which durational values are not absolute but are fixed only in relationship to one (i.e. a half note is half as long as a whole note, and so on).

**Quartal**: A chord built of superposed fourths.

**Quintal**: A chord built of superposed fifths.

**Ragtime**: A highly syncopated style of piano music, mainly African-American in origin, in vogue in the United States at the turn of the twentieth century and one of the forerunners of jazz.

**Range**: The distance spanned by the highest and lowest pitches of a melodic line.

**Real**: Referring either to sequences or imitation that constitute exact intervallic repetitions of a preceding idea.

**Realize, realization**: The term describing what a performer does when he or she plays a figured bass line, filling out the chords and adding embellishments as the style requires.

**Recapitulation**: Generally, any restatement of originally heard material near the end of a musical work. More specifically, the return of the exposition material in a sonata-form movement following the development section.

**Relative major–minor**: A major and minor scale pair sharing the same key signature but not the same tonic.

**Repetition**: A type of harmonic motion in which a chord is repeated or moves to another chord of the same class (i.e. pre-dominant to predominant).

**Resolution**: The motion from a tone or chord to another tone or chord of greater stability.

**Retardation**: An upward-resolving suspension.

**Retrograde**: A row transformation involving the reversal of the pitch order.

**Retrograde inversion**: In twelve-tone music, the statement of the melodically inverted row in retrograde.

**Retrogression**: A harmonic motion in which each chord moves to a new chord more distant from the tonic as measured in ascending-fifth root movements, such as a supertonic to a submediant.

**Rhythm**: A term referring generally to the temporal aspects of music—the duration of its sounds and silences.

**Root position**: Any arrangement of the tones of a chord in which the root appears as the lowest pitch.

**Root**: In a triad or seventh chord, the note above which the others can be arranged as a stack of thirds.

**Rounded binary**: A two-part form in which the second part is "rounded off" by a (usually abbreviated) restatement of initial material, symbolized A|BA'.

**Row form**: In twelve-tone works, one of the four basic aspects of a twelve-tone row—prime, retrograde, inversion, or retrograde inversion.

**Scale**: An inventory of the pitches that form the basis of a musical composition, arranged in ascending or descending order.

**Secondary dominant, secondary function**: Chords that momentarily serve as dominants with respect to a temporary tonic.

**Secondary leading tone**: In a secondary dominant or leading tone chord, the note that serves momentarily as the leading tone to the root of the tonicized chord.

**Second relation**: Two chords whose roots are a second apart.

**Segmentation**: A technique in which a twelve-tone row is divided consistently into fragments—usually trichords, tetrachords, or hexachords—that are treated similarly to the motives in a theme.

**Sensitive tones**: The least stable tones in a scale or key, each usually separated by a half step from a member of the tonic triad and displaying pronounced inclination to resolve to that pitch. (Also called "tendency tones.")

**Sequence**: A melodic or harmonic pattern repeated in close succession at a pitch level other than the original.

**Set**: A collection of pitch classes that serves as the basis for an atonal work.

**Set type**: A way of describing the interval content of a pitch-class set. The pitch classes are placed in ascending order in the closest possible position, the lowest (first) pitch is assigned the number "0," and the other pitches are assigned numbers indicating the number of half steps between them and the first pitch.

**Seventh chord**: A four-note chord formed when a seventh above the chord root is added to a triad.

**Similar motion**: The movement by two voices from one tone to the next in the same direction but by a different interval.

**Simple interval**: An interval spanning an octave or less.

**Simple meter**: A meter in which the primary division of the beat is into two parts.

**Single entry**: In a fugue, an isolated statement of the subject, as opposed to statements occurring in groups.

**Six-four chord**: A second-inversion triad.

**Solmization**: The act of singing melodic lines using a system of syllables developed by Guido where each syllable corresponds to a scale degree (do, re, mi, fa, sol, la, ti).

**Song form**: A term that describes the ABA (ternary) form applied to a song.

**Soprano**: 1) A voice type with an approximate range from C4 to G5. 2) The term normally used to refer to the highest musical line in a multi-voiced vocal or choral composition.

**Spacing**: The manner in which the notes of a chord are distributed among the various voices of the texture.

**Staff**: A set of five horizontal lines, on and between which the musical notes are written. In conjunction with a clef sign, it indicates the pitches of the notes appearing on it.

**Step progression**: The stepwise connection of important (usually nonadjacent) pitches in a melody that contribute to its sense of overall direction.

**Stretto**: A feature often found in the later parts of a fugue involving overlapping statements of the subject in two or more voices.

**Strophic**: A formal structure in which all verses of a song are sung to the same music.

**Subdominant**: The functional name given to the fourth degree of a major or minor scale, or to the triad formed on this pitch.

**Subject**: A melodic idea that serves as the basis for a fugue, presented initially in each voice in turn and subsequently restated at various points in a variety of textures and tonalities.

**Submediant**: The functional name given to the sixth degree of a major or minor scale, or to the triad formed on this pitch.

**Subtonic**: The functional name given to the lowered seventh degree of a minor scale, or to the triad formed on this pitch.

**Supertonic**: The functional name given to the second degree of a major or minor scale, or to the triad formed on this pitch.

**Suspension**: The dissonance created when one voice in a texture of two or more voices is delayed in its downward stepwise motion from one tone to the next.

**Symmetric**: Periods in which the antecedent and consequent phrases are roughly of equal length. Forms characterized by correspondence on both sides of their midpoint, such as and ABA in which both A sections are the same length.

**Syncopation**: The shift in accentuation to a normally unaccented part of a beat or measure.

**Syntax**: The way harmonies are strung together to form harmonic patterns.

**Tempo**: The speed of the beat.

**Tendency tone**: See **Sensitive tones**.

**Tenor**: 1) A male voice type with an approximate range from C3 to G4. 2) The term normally used to refer to the third highest musical line in a multi-voiced composition, below the alto and above the bass.

**Ternary**: Any musical form dividing into three basic parts.

**Tertian**: Referring to chords constructed of thirds.

**Tetrachord**: A four-note segment of a scale or mode.

**Text setting**: In song, the fashioning of a melody to suit the words.

**Texture**: The density and complexity of the musical fabric of a work, determined by the number of lines, their degree of independence, the complexity of the harmonies, the instrumentation, the degree of rhythmic animation, and other factors.

**Thematic process**: The collective functioning of the musical elements to create passages that are mainly melodic, with strongly contoured and identifiable phrasing, clear cadences, and stable harmonies.

**Third relation**: Two chords whose roots are related by the interval of a third.

**Thirteenth chord**: A chord formed by the addition of the thirteen above an eleventh or ninth chord.

**Tie**: A curved line connecting two adjacent notes of the same pitch, binding them into a single sound equal to their combined durations.

**Timbre**: A term referring to the quality of a musical tone (tone color), which is determined in part by its overtone content.

**Tonal**: A term used to describe music in which a particular pitch is endowed with a feeling greater importance and finality than the other pitches.

**Tonal accent**: Emphasis on a particular pitch by its placement in a register different from the pitches that surround it.

**Tonal sequence**: A sequence in which the quality of certain intervals is changed, usually to remain diatonic in the key of the original statement.

**Tonic**: The first and most stable pitch of a given major or minor scale and the pitch for which the scale is named.

**Tonicize, tonicization**: A process whereby a chord other than the tonic is caused to sound temporarily like a tonic by being preceded and supported by its own dominant (or dominant seventh chord) or leading tone chord.

**Tonicizing chord group**: A group of chords (most commonly ii–V) that function most clearly with respect to a secondary tonic and thus enhance its momentary status as a tonic.

**Tonicizing tritone**: The interval comprising the two sensitive tones (fa and ti) in any secondary dominant seventh chord or secondary leading-tone triad. It is their strong tendency to resolve that creates the tonicizing effect.

**Transitional process**: Passages that signal a change in musical condition—i.e. from subdued to agitated, from soft to loud, from fast to slow, from one tonality to another, and so on.

**Transposition**: The process of rewriting a scale, or a passage based on a scale, at a different pitch level, in a different key.

**Triad**: A three-note chord in which two of the notes can be arranged as a third and fifth above the lowest note (the root).

**Triadic extension**: Any triad above which additional thirds have been stacked.

**Trichord**: A three-note segment of a scale, mode, or twelve-tone row.

**Tritone**: A musical interval comprising three whole steps that splits the octave precisely in half. It is normally spelled as a diminished fifth or augmented fourth.

**Twelve-tone method**: A method of composing in which a twelve-tone row and its various transformations serves as a basis for the composition.

**Voice**: The generic term for any musical line.

**Voice crossing**: A motion between two voices in which the lower voice moves above the upper voice momentarily, or conversely, the upper voice moves below the lower voice. Considered objectionable practice in strict four-voice writing.

**Voice leading**: The process of leading each voice in a multi-voiced texture to its next tone in such a way that pleasing melodic lines and chord voicings result.

**Voice overlap**: An exceptional part-writing practice in which a voice is moved *above* the preceding pitch of a higher voice or *below* the preceding pitch of a lower voice.

**Voicing**: The manner in which a chord is spaced and doubled.

**Whole step**: An interval comprising two half steps.

**Whole-tone scale**: A six-note scale made up entirely of whole tones.

# Credits

## CREDIT LINES FOR *THEORY ESSENTIALS FOR TODAY'S MUSICIAN*

Example 1-1: "When I Need You" by Albert Hammond (music) and Carol Bayer Sager (words) © 1976 (renewed) Albert Hammond Enterprises, R & M Music, Inc., Begonia Melodies, Inc. and Leonard Cohen Stranger Music, Inc. All rights for Begonia Melodies, Inc. and Leonard Cohen Stranger Music, Inc. administered by Warner-Tamerlane Publishing Corp. All rights reserved.

Example 1-18b: "Autumn Leaves" by Johnny Mercer (English lyrics), Jacques Prevert (French lyrics), and Joseph Kosma (music), © 1947, 1950 (renewed) Enoch et Cie. Sole selling agent for U.S. and Canada: Morley Music Co. by agreement with Enoch et Cie. All rights reserved. Reprinted with permission of Hal Leonard Corporation.

Example 2-11: "Maria" from *West Side Story*, by Leonard Bernstein and Stephen Sondheim © 1956, 1957, 1958, 1959 by Amberson Holdings LLC and Stephen Sondheim. Copyright renewed. Leonard Bernstein Music Publishing Company LLC, publisher. Boosey & Hawkes, agents for rental. International copyright secured. Reprinted by permission of Boosey & Hawkes, Inc.

Example 4-3: "Can't Help Falling in Love" by George David Weiss, Hugo Peretti and Luigi Creatore. © 1961, renewed 1989 Gladys Music (ASCAP). All rights in the U.S. administered by Imagem Sounds. International copyright secured. All rights reserved. Reprinted with permission of Hal Leonard Corporation.

Example 8-9b: "Tonight" from *West Side Story*, by Leonard Bernstein and Stephen Sondheim © 1956, 1957, 1958, 1959 by Amberson Holdings LLC and Stephen Sondheim. Copyright renewed. Leonard Bernstein Music Publishing Company LLC, publisher. Boosey & Hawkes, agents for rental. International copyright secured. Reprinted by permission of Boosey & Hawkes, Inc.

Example 11-4: "Winter Wonderland" by Dick Smith (words) and Felix Bernard (music). © 1934 (renewed) WB Music Corp. All rights reserved. Used by permission of Alfred Music Publishing.

Example 18-6b: "Slaughter on Tenth Avenue" by Richard Rodgers. © 1936 by Williamson Music, a division of Rodgers & Hammerstein: an Imagem company. Copyright renewed. International copyright secured. All rights reserved. Reprinted with permission of Hal Leonard Corporation.

Example 19-11: "Boating" No. 125, Vol V from *Mikrokosmos* by Bela Bartók. © 1940 by Hawkes & Son (London) Ltd. Reprinted by permission of Boosey & Hawkes, Inc.

## CREDIT LINES FOR *WORKBOOK TO ACCOMPANY THEORY ESSENTIALS FOR TODAY'S MUSICIAN*

*From Chapter 20, 20-6*:
Anton Webern, "5 Sätze für Streichquartett op. 5" © 1922, 1949 by Universal Edition A.G., Wien/PH 358

*From Chapter 20, 20-7*:
"The Drums of Moria," from *Time Out of Mind: Six Tales for Middle Earth* by Daniel McCarthy. © 2006. Used by permission of C. Alan Publications.

*From Chapter 21, 21-4*:
"Klavierstücke" op. 33a by Arnold Schoenberg. Used by permission of Belmont Music Publishers.

# Index

## A

accidentals: in figured-bass notation 7; in modulations 156–157
Aeolian mode 278, 337
aggregate 327
agogic agogic 30, 341
altered chords: altered dominants 151–154; altered pre-dominants 137; *see also* secondary dominants
alto voice: defined 31; range 31
answer (fugal), 218: real and tonal 219
antecedent phrase *see under* phrase
anticipation 40
appoggiatura 38
arpeggiated six-four chord 74
atonality 301
augmentation 210
augmented sixth chords: as clue chord 156; defined 144; constructing 146–147; and modulation 165–168; and voice leading 148–150; *see also* French sixth, German sixth, Italian sixth
augmented triad: and whole-tone scale 284; doubling in 48; introduced 347; in twentieth-century music 277
authentic cadence 22: *see also under* cadences

## B

Bach inventions; form in 209; implied harmony in 215–217; invertible counterpoint in 214; motives in 209; tonality in 215

bass voice: defined 31; doubling of 48; and inversion 63–64; and lead-sheet notation 4; range 31; soprano-bass counterpoint 33; and spacing 47; and suspensions 60–61
best normal order 308
bimodality 295
binary form 242
borrowed harmonies 125: voice leading in 127
bridge *see* link *under* fugue

## C

cadences: authentic 22; deceptive 24; defined 19; elided 203; extended 204–205; half 23; and harmonic rhythm 28; imperfect authentic 22; modal 279–280; in modulations 157; perfect authentic 22; and phrasing 197; Phrygian half 23; plagal 23; summary of 26; variants 25
cadential elision *see* cadences, elided
cadential extension *see* cadences, extended
cadential process 234
cadential six-four chord 70
chain suspension 86
change of mode: defined 121; enharmonic 123; keys related through 123; *vs.* modal borrowing 125
chorale: defined 54
chord mutation 186–188
chords: connecting 50, 58; short rule of chord connection 58; voicing 47–49; *see also* harmonic structure; inversion; lead-sheet notation; part writing
chromatic alteration *see* chromatic pitches; accidentals
chromatic harmony *see* altered chords; mode mixture; modulation; linear chromaticism
chromatic intervals and modulation 112
chromatic modulation *see under* modulation
chromatic passing tone 36
chromatic pitches: as tendency tones 32; in modulations 155; resolution of 32; *see also* accidentals
chromatic pivot 160
chromatic-third relationship: common chromatic-third relationships 130; defined 129; and mode mixture 131; and tonicization 131; voice leading in 133; *see also* third relationship
church modes: introduced 337; major and minor modes compared 278; in twentieth-century music 277–280
circle of fifths: introduced 14; and functional tonality 15–16; and keys 338
closely related keys 110: common chords in 110–111
"clue chords" 156
coda 225, 240: in fugue 225; in sonata form 261
codetta 255

common-chord modulation *see under* modulation
common practice period 18
common-tone diminished seventh chord, *see* embellishing diminished seventh chord
complement 303
composing: counterpoint 33–35
compound meter 340
consecutive (parallel) perfect consonances 35, 50
consequent phrase *see under* phrase
consonances: and counterpoint 33
continuo 5
contrary motion: and chord connection 52; and counterpoint 32; defined 32; *see also under* motion
contrasting period 199
counterexposition *see under* fugue
countermotive 209
counterpoint: and the Bach inventions 209; composing 33; defined 31; devices of 210; invertible 214; melodic principles 31–32; and motion types 32; note-against-note 33; and rhythmic independence 36
countersubject *see* under fugue

### D

deceptive cadence: described 24; part writing of 56–57
deceptive resolution 102
delayed resolution 82
derived set *see under* twelve-tone method
developmental process 233
development: in fugue 223; in sonata form 255
diatonic triads 9, 11
diatonic seventh chords 12
diatonic-third relationship *see* third relationship
diminished seventh chord: introduced 12; embellishing *see* embellishing diminished seventh chord; enharmonic 168–172; enharmonic jugglng 172; and octatonic scale 287
diminished third: in Neapolitan 139
diminished triad: doubling in 48; introduced 347; and octatonic scale 287; and tonicization 98
diminution 210

dissonances: and counterpoint 217; and embellishing tones 36
dominant eleventh chord *see* eleventh chord
dominant-functioning seventh chords 77–83: dominant seventh 77–82; leading-tone seventh 82–83
dominant-major ninth chord *see under* ninth chord
dominant-minor ninth chord *see under* ninth chord
dominant 9
dominant prolongation 256
dominant seventh chord 349
Dorian mode 278, 337
double neighbor 39
double passing tone 43
double period 200
doubling (voices): alternative doubling 49; guidelines for 48; in first inversion 64; and secondary function 100; in second inversion 69; and seventh chords 84; short rule of 48; in suspensions 60, 67; in triads 48
doubly augmented fourth chord *see* enharmonic German sixth chord

### E

eleventh chords 182–183
elided resolution (of secondary leading tone), 103
embellishing tones: chromatic 36; and counterpoint 36; defined 36; multiple 43; step-leap combinations 38; step-repetition combinations 40; step-step combinations 36; enharmonic change of mode 123
enharmonic diminished seventh chord 168–172
enharmonic equivalence 302
enharmonic German sixth chord *see under* German sixth chord
enharmonic modulation *see under* modulation
enharmonic pivot 166
enharmonic spelling: of chords *see under* diminished seventh chord; and whole-tone scale 284; *see also under* German sixth chord
entry group 223
episode: in fugue 223; in rondo 263
escape tone 38
exposition: in fugue 222; in sonata form 250

extension, cadential: postcadential 205; precadential 205

### F

figured-bass notation 5–8
first inversion: and bass 63–64; defined 348; and harmonic weight 65; and Neapolitan chords 137; and part writing 64; and suspensions 66–68
form *see* musical form
fragmentation 210, 215
French sixth chord 145
fugue: answer, real and tonal 219; basics of 218; bridge 221, 225; coda 225; counterexposition 225; countersubject 223; defined 218; entries and episodes 223; exposition 222; link 221, 225; stretto 223; subject 218
fully diminished seventh chord *see* diminished seventh chord
functional tonality 13–16: and circle of fifths 14; defined 14; and ground bass 16; and progression 16

### G

German sixth chord 145: enharmonic 147, 166–168
ground bass patterns 16

### H

half cadence: defined 23
half-diminished seventh chord 12 tonization with 98–99
harmonic rhythm 26–28
harmonic rhythm and meter 28
harmonic sequence *see under* sequence
harmony: implied 215–217
hemiola 342
hexachordal symmetry 331
homophonic *vs.* polyphonic 207–208

### I

imitation 208, 210
imperfect authentic cadence 22
implied harmony *see under* harmony
implied polymeter 300
incomplete neighbor 38
incomplete seventh chords 85–87
index numbers 304, 326
interval class 303
interval class vector 311

intervals: determining 336; listing of 336; in major scale 336
invention *see* Bach inventions
inversion: and bass line 63–64; and chord connection 65; defined 348; and diatonic chords 348; and figured bass notation 5–8; and harmonic weight 65; lead-sheet notation of 5; part writing of 63–76; of seventh chords 349; in suspensions 67–68
inversional symmetry 310
invertible counterpoint 214
Ionian mode 278, 337: *see also under* church modes
Italian sixth chord 145

## K

keys: closely related 110; and diatonic chords 9–11
key signatures 337

## L

leading tone: and altered predominants 138, 144; defined 9; and part writing 32, 57–58, 78, 81; secondary 95; unresolved 81
leading-tone seventh chord 82: tritones in 83
leading-tone triad 9
lead sheet 3
lead-sheet symbols 3–5: expanded symbols 4; symbol overview 4
linear chromaticism 186–188: and harmonic sequence 188
Lydian mode 278, 337: *see also under* church modes

## M

major-minor seventh chord: nonfunctional Mm7, 274; structure of 349; *see also* dominant seventh chord
major ninth chord *see under* ninth chord
major-scale intervals 336
major scale and Ionian mode 278
major seventh chord 349
major triad 347
matrix *see under* twelve tone method
mediant 9
melodic form *see* phrase, phrases
melodic inversion 210
melodic principles 46, 351
melody: repetition in 193–195

meter, meter signatures: classification of 339–340: and harmonic rhythm 28: overview 339–340: compound 340: simple 339
metric shift 30
minor eleventh chord *see* eleventh chord
minor ninth chord *see under* ninth chord
minor seventh chord 13
minor triad 347
Mixolydian mode 278, 337: *see also under* church modes
modal borrowing: common borrowed harmonies 125; defined 125; voice leading 127; *vs.* change of mode 125
modal cadence 279–280
mode mixture: and chromatic-third relationship 131; defined 121; keys related through 123; and voice leading 127; *see also* change of mode and modal borrowing
modes *see* church modes
modified sequence 194
modulation: in Bach's inventions 215; chromatic 112–116, 158, 160–165; clues to 155–158; common-chord 107–111; defined 107; enharmonic modulation 169–172; and enharmonic diminished seventh chord 168; and German sixth chords 165–168; and secondary function (tonicization), 116; signals for 155
modulo 12, 303
motion: between voices 32; contrary 32; oblique 32; parallel 32; similar 32
motive 193
motivic analysis 231
multiple common chords 109
musical form 231: and cadences 232; melodic form *see* phrases; and motivic analysis 231–232; and musical process 233–236 *see also* cadential process, developmental process, preparatory process, thematic process, transitional process; sectional *vs.* continuous 242; and similarity and contrast 232; statement-contrast 242; statement-contrast-restatement 244; statement-restatement 236; symmetric *vs.* asymmetric 243
musical sentence *see* sentence

## N

Natural minor scale and Aeolian mode 278
Neapolitan chord 137–142
Neapolitan and augmented sixth chords compared 151
neighboring six-four chord *see* pedal six-four chord
neighbor tones 37
ninth chord: dominant-major ninth chord 176; dominant minor ninth chord 176; inversion of 178; major ninth chord 180; minor ninth chord 180; secondary function 179
nonchord tones: defined 36; and part-writing 352; and seventh chords 79; and ninth chords 176; *see also* embellishing tones
nondominant seventh chords 84–85
nonharmonic tone *see* nonchord tone
nonfunctional Mm7 chord 275
normal order 306
notation, rhythmic 343
note-against-note counterpoint *see under* counterpoint

## O

oblique motion *see under* motion
octatonic scale *see under* scale
octave: designation in pitch notation 335; equivalence 302; and intervals 336
ordered pitch-class interval 302
ordered pitch-class set 304
order number 322
ostinato 298

## P

Pandiatonicism 295–296
parallel perfect consonances 50
parallel double period 200–201
parallel motion *see under* motion
parallel period 199
part writing: and augmented sixth chords 148; doubling 48, 351; chain suspensions 86–87; and chord connection 50, 352; first inversion 63–66; and melodic line 50; melodic principles in 46, 351; nondominant seventh chords 84–88; root-position triads 54–59; and secondary function 100; second-inversion triads 69–76; seventh chords 12, 77–89;

short rule of chord connection 58;
  suspensions 59–62; voicing chords
  47, 351; voice-leading guidelines
  75, 351
part–writing summary 351–352
passing six-four chord 71
passing tones: and altered dominants
  151–153; and altered predominants 141, 145; and
  counterpoint 36–37; defined 36;
  multiple 43; and seventh chords 79
pedal six-four chord 74
pentatonic scale *see under* scale
perfect authentic cadence 22
period: contrasting 199; defined 199;
  double 200; parallel 199
phrase, phrases: and cadences 197;
  antecedent 198; consequent 198;
  defined 194–195; length of 195;
  phrase group 200; phrase
  relationships summarized 198
Phrygian half cadence 23
Phrygian mode 278, 280, 337
Picardy third 80
pitch class 302
pitch-class interval 302
pitch class set 304
pivot chord 107
plagal cadence 23
planing 274–276
polychord 291–293
polymeter, implied 300
polyphony *see* counterpoint
polytonality 293–294
postcadential extensions *see under*
  extension, cadential
precadential extensions *see under*
  extension, cadential
pre-dominants: and circle of fifths 16;
  defined 16; and modulation 111;
  preparatory process 233
primary triads 10
prime *see* row forms *under* twelve-
  tone method
prime form 309
progression 16

## Q

quartal harmonies 282–283, 290–291
quintal harmonies 282–283, 290–291

## R

ranges, voice 31
real answer *see under* fugue
real sequence *see under* sequence
recapitulation 256

refrain 263
repetition: in functional harmony 16;
  in phrasing 198
resolution: of suspension 42
retardation 40
retransition: in sonata form 256
retrograde *see* row forms *under*
  twelve-tone method
retrograde inversion *see* row forms
  *under* twelve-tone method
retrogression 16
rhythm: notation of 339–346; roman
  numeral symbols 10, 12
rondo 263: analysis of Beethoven
  Piano Sonata Op. 13 (III),
  264–270; cadential process in 269;
  episode in 263; refrain in 263;
  retransition in 265; thematic
  process in 264
root-position triads: chord connection
  guidelines 58; in fifth relationship
  54; in second relationship 56; in
  third relationship 55
rounded binary form 244–246: *vs.*
  ternary form 247–248
row forms 321
rule of chromatics 112

## S

scalar motion: bass patterns 16; and
  transitional process 234
scales: and modes 278; octatonic 286;
  pentatonic 281; whole tone 284
secondary dominants: and harmonic
  sequence 104; and part writing
  100: and tonicization 94–95
secondary dominant seventh chord
  96
secondary dominant ninth chord
  179
secondary function: and altered
  dominants 153; and chromatic lines
  103; defined 93; and harmonic
  sequence 104; and part writing
  100
secondary leading tone 95
secondary leading-tone seventh chord
  98
secondary leading-tone triad 98
second inversion: and altered
  dominants 153; arpeggiated six-
  four chord 74; cadential six-four
  chord 70; defined 348; and part
  writing 69–76; passing six-four
  chord 71; pedal six-four chord 74;
  six-four chords 56–58

segmentation 330
sensitive tones: defined 32; and part
  writing 32, 48; and secondary
  function 100–102; and seventh
  chords 77–79
sentence 198
sequence: in Bach's inventions 210,
  214; defined 194; in fugues 225;
  harmonic 188–190; modified 194;
  real 194; tonal 194; and
  transitional process 234
serialism 319
set *see* pitch class set
set class 312
set names 305
set type 308
seventh chords: and chain suspensions
  86–87, 89; construction and
  classification of 348; defined 42;
  dominant-functioning 77–83;
  figured bass notation of 7;
  frequency of occurrence 84;
  incomplete 84–86; inversion of 12,
  349; lead-sheet notation of 4;
  nondominant 84–88; and part
  writing 77–88; types 349
seventh, delayed resolution 82
seventh, unresolved 81
short rule of the seventh 77
similar motion *see under* motion
simple meter 339
six-four chord *see* second inversion;
  arpeggiated six-four chord;
  cadential six-four chord; passing
  six-four chord; pedal six-four chord
sonata form: analysis of *Eine Kleine
  Nachtmusik* 250–262; cadential
  process in 254; description
  250–262; developmental process in
  255; history of 249; primary
  thematic area 250; recapitulation
  256; retransition 256; thematic
  process in 250, 253; transitional
  process in 251
soprano-bass counterpoint 33–35,
  208
soprano voice: doubling of 48; range
  31
spacing 47
statement and contrast *see under*
  musical form
statement-contrast-restatement *see
  under* musical form
statement-restatement *see under*
  musical form
stretto *see under* fugue

subdominant 9
subject (fugue) *see under* fugue
submediant 9
subtonic 11
superset 316
supertonic 9
suspension: bass suspension 41; chain suspension 86–87; defined 40; and part writing 59–62; and seventh chords 86–87, 89
syncopation: defined 341; and harmonic rhythm 29
syntax: defined 273; and nonfunctional major-minor seventh chords 275; and planing 274; in twentieth-century music 273

**T**

tendency tone *see* sensitive tone
tenor voice range 31
ternary form 246: *vs.* rounded binary form 247
thematic process 233
third inversion 84, 349
third relationship: chromatic 129; diatonic 129; defined 129; and part writing 55
thirteenth chords 184–186
tonal accent *see under* accent
tonal answer *see under* fugue
tonal border 108
tonal sequence *see under* sequence
tonic: defined 9; and functional tonality 13–16; and harmonic motion 16
tonicization: defined 93, 94; *vs.* modulation 116
tonicizing tritone 96
transition 251
transitional process 234: *see also under* sonata form and rondo form
triads: diatonic in major keys 9; diatonic in minor keys 10; doubling in 48; inversion of 348
triad types 347
tritone 83: augmented fourth or diminished fifth 336; *see also* tonicizing tritone
twelve-tone method: analysis 326–333; basic tenets 319–322; derived set 332; matrix 324–326; row forms 321; twelve tone row 320
twentieth-century music: atonality 301; octatonic scales in 286; pentatonic scales in 281; quartal/quintal harmonies in 282; serial procedures in 319; syntax in 273–275; whole-tone scales in 284
Two-Part Inventions *see* Bach Inventions
two-voice counterpoint 31–35, 209–218

**U**

unordered pitch-class interval 302
unordered pitch-class set 304
unordered set analysis 305
unresolved leading tone 81
unresolved seventh 81

**V**

Voice: defined 45; ranges 31; types 31
voice crossing 51
voice exchange 214
voice leading: defined 31; melodic principles 46; *see also* part writing
voice leading guidelines 89
voice leading summary 89, 351–352
voice overlap 51
voicing chords 47

**W**

white-key intervals *see under* interval
whole-tone scale *see under* scale

**Z**

Z relationship 312

# Track Listing

The following examples can be found on the companion website for this volume
www.routledge.com/cw/turekessentials

| Exercise No. | Track Title |
|---|---|

## Chapter 1

| | |
|---|---|
| 1-3 | Albert Hammond and Carol Bayer Sager: "When I Need You" |
| 1-5 | G. F. Handel: "Hallelujah" (from *The Messiah*) |
| 1-9 | "Amazing Grace" (folk hymn) |
| 1-11 | "Amazing Grace" (folk hymn) |
| 1-18A | W. A. Mozart: Rondo K. 494 |
| 1-18B | Joseph Kosma and Johnny Mercer: "Autumn Leaves" |
| 1-22 | G. F. Handel: *Concerto Grosso* op. 6, No. 12 (second movement) |

## Chapter 2

| | |
|---|---|
| 2-2 | Mozart: Piano Sonata, K. 332 (first movement) |
| 2-3B | "Scarborough Fair" (English folk song |
| 2-4 | Schubert: "Standchen" |
| 2-8A | Beethoven: Piano Sonata op. 26 (first movement) |
| 2-8B | Mendelssohn: Kinderstuck, op. 72, No. 1 |
| 2-10A | Brahms: Waltz op. 39, no. 15 |
| 2-11 | Stephen Sondheim and Leonard Bernstein: "Maria" (from *West Side Story*) |
| 2-13 | Beethoven: Piano Sonata op. 22 (second movement) |
| 2-14 | Schumann: "Volksliedchen" (No. 9 from *Album for the Young*, op. 68) |
| 2-16 | J. S. Bach "Herz und Mund und Tat und Leben" (Chorale from Cantata 147) |

# TRACK LISTING

| Exercise No. | Track Title |
|---|---|
| 2-17 | Chopin: Nocturne op. 37, no. 1 |
| 2-18 | Chopin: Etude op. 10 no. 3 |

## Chapter 3

| | |
|---|---|
| 3-10 | Rossini: *Petite Messe Solonelle* ("Kyrie") |
| 3-12 | Mendelssohn: *Overture to The Hebrides*, op. 26 |
| 3-13A | Mozart: Piano Sonata K. 279 (first movement) |
| 3-13B | Mozart: Piano Sonata K. 283 (first movement) |
| 3-14 | Rodgers and Hammerstein: "Some Enchanted Evening" (from *South Pacific*, act 1, no. 9) |
| 3-18 | Beethoven: Piano Sonata op. 27, no. 2 (second movement) |
| 3-20 | Mozart: Piano Sonata K. 331 (first movement) |
| 3-21 | Tchaikovsky: "Arabian Dance" (from *The Nutcracker*) |

## Chapter 4

| | |
|---|---|
| 4-1 | Stephen Sondheim and Leonard Bernstein: "Somewhere" (from *West Side Story*) |
| 4-3 | George Weiss, Hugo Peretti, and Luigi Creatore: "Can't Help Falling in Love" |
| 4-11 | John Fawcett and Hans George Naegeli: "Blest be the Tie" |
| 4-21 | J. S. Bach: "Ermuntre dich, mein schwacher Geist" |

## Chapter 5

| | |
|---|---|
| 5-2 | J. S. Bach: "Schmücke dich, o liebe Seele" |
| 5-3 | J. S. Bach: "Wo soll ich fliehen hin" |
| 5-10 | J. S. Bach: "Schaut, ihr Sünder" |
| 5-13 | Beethoven: Symphony no. 9 (fourth movement) |
| 5-15 | J. S. Bach: "Valet will dir geben" |
| 5-17 | George Elvey: "Come, Ye Thankful People Come" |
| 5-20 | "Michael, Row the Boat Ashore" (spiritual) |

## Chapter 6

| | |
|---|---|
| 6-6 | Beethoven: Piano Sonata op. 10, no. 1 (third movement) |
| 6-9 | J. S. Bach: "Das neugeborne Kindelein" |
| 6-10 | (Points 1, 2, and 5) Martin Corrigan: "Cockles and Mussels" |
| 6-11 | (Points 1, 2, 4, and 6) J. S. Bach: "O Ewigkeit, du Donnerwort" |
| 6-13 | Purcell: *Ode for St. Cecilia's Day* |
| 6-15 | Mozart: Rondo, K. 494 |
| 6-17A | Delange, Mills, and Ellington: "Solitude" |

| Exercise No. | Track Title |
|---|---|

## Chapter 7

| | |
|---|---|
| 7-7 | Beethoven: Symphony no. 1, op. 21 (first movement) |
| 7-9 | Mozart: Piano Sonata K. 284 (third movement) |
| 7-10 | Schumann: Kinderszenen no. 6 ("An Important Event") |
| 7-13 | Beethoven: String Quartet op. 18, no. 1 (third movement) |
| 7-15 | Schubert: Impromptu op. 142, no. 3 |
| 7-18 | Friedrich Kuhlau: Sonatina op. 55, no. 5 (first movement) |
| 7-19A | J. S. Bach: Prelude no. 11 from *The Well-Tempered Clavier*, Book I |
| 7-19B | Handel: *Concerto Grosso* op. 6, no. 1 (Allegro) |

## Chapter 8

| | |
|---|---|
| 8-1 | J. S. Bach: "Wach auf, mein Herz" |
| 8-2 | Mozart: Symphony no. 40 in G minor, K. 550 (third movement) |
| 8-3 | Anonymous: Minuet (from the *Notebook for Anna Magdalena Bach*) |
| 8-8 | Chopin: Mazurka op. 56, no. 1 |
| 8-9A | Schubert: "Kennst du das Land" |
| 8-9B | Stephen Sondheim and Leonard Bernstein: "Tonight" (from *West Side Story*, act 1, no. 7) |
| 8-10 | Brahms: "Erinnerung," op. 63, no. 2 |
| 8-11 | Mozart: Piano Sonata K. 310 (first movement) |
| 8-12A | Brahms: Variations on a Theme of Robert Schumann, op. 9 |
| 8-12B | Schubert: Symphony no. 8 (first movement) |
| 8-13 | J. S. Bach: "Helft mir Gott's Güte preisen" |

## Chapter 9

| | |
|---|---|
| 9-1 | Mozart: Piano Sonata K. 332 (second movement) |
| 9-3 | Beethoven: Piano Sonata op. 26 (second movement) |
| 9-6A | Brahms: "Die Mainacht" |
| 9-6B | Gilbert O'Sullivan: "Alone Again (Naturally)" |
| 9-8 | Leslie Bricusse and John Williams: "Can You Read My Mind?" (from the movie *Superman*) |
| 9-9 | Brahms: Symphony no. 3, op. 90 (second movement) |
| 9-11 | Schubert: "Kennst du das Land" |
| 9-14 | Beethoven: Piano Sonata op. 14, no. 1 (third movement) |
| 9-15 | Haydn: Piano Sonata H. XVI:34 (first movement) |
| 9-17 | Dvorak: New World Symphony, op. 95 (Largo) |

| Exercise No. | Track Title |
|---|---|

## Chapter 10

| | |
|---|---|
| 10-3 | Beethoven: Piano Sonata op. 27, no. 2 (first movement) |
| 10-5B | Verdi: "Stride la vampa!" from *Il Trovatore* (act 2, scene 1) |
| 10-7 | Mozart: Piano Sonata K. 280 (second movement) |
| 10-8 | Gounod: "Marcha Funebre de un Volatin" |
| 10-9 | Chopin: Valse, op. 64, no. 2 |
| 10-10 | J. S. Bach: *The Well-Tempered Clavier*, Book I, BWV 844 (Prelude no. 1) |
| 10-11 | Beethoven: Thirty-Two Variations on an Original Theme in C Minor, WoO.80 |
| 10-16 | Joplin: "The Sycamore" |
| 10-20A | Schubert: Sonatina for Piano and Violin, op. posth. 137, no. 2 |
| 10-20B | Mozart: String Quartet K. 421 (third movement) |
| 10-20C | Chopin: Etude op. 10, no. 3 |
| 10-21 | Schumann: "Am leuchtenden Sommermorgen" (no. 12 from *Dichterliebe*, op. 48) |
| 10-23A | Beethoven: Sonata op. 28 (third movement) |
| 10-23B | Chopin: Nocturne op. 27, no. 1 |
| 10-25A | Beethoven: Bagatelle no. 8, op. 119 |
| 10-25B | Wolf: "Gebet" (No. 28 from *Mörike Songs*) |

## Chapter 11

| | |
|---|---|
| 11-1 | Brahms: "Wie Melodien zieht es mir," op. 105, no. 1 |
| 11-3 | Brahms: Quintet no. 1, op. 88 |
| 11-4 | Smith and Bernard: "Walking in a Winter Wonderland" |
| 11-5 | Beethoven: Sonata for Violin and Piano op. 24 (second movement) |
| 11-6 | Liszt: Consolation no. 2 |
| 11-7 | Schubert: "Sehnsucht" |
| 11-12 | Tchaikovsky: Onegin's Aria from *Eugene Onegin* |
| 11-14 | Chopin: Fantasy in F Minor, op. 49 |
| 11-16 | Brahms: Ballade op. 10, no. 4 |
| 11-17 | Beethoven: Piano Sonata op. 13 (first movement) |
| 11-18 | [no caption] |
| 11-20 | Beethoven: Symphony no. 5, op. 67 (second movement) |

## Chapter 12

| | |
|---|---|
| 12-4 | Chopin: Etude op. 10, no. 3 |
| 12-5 | Tchaikovsky: Lenski's Aria from *Eugene Onegin* (act 2, scene 2) |
| 12-7 | Puccini: "Che gelida manina" from *La Boheme* (act one) |
| 12-10A | Burt Bacharach and Hal David: "What the World Needs Now" |

| Exercise No. | Track Title |
|---|---|
| 12-13 | Wagner: "Wahn! Wahn!" (*Die Meistersinger von Nürnberg*) (act 3, scene 1) |
| 12-15 | Hart and Webber: "All I ask of you" (from *Phantom of the Opera*) |
| 12-20 | Chopin: Nocturne op. 32, No. 1 |
| 12-21A | Chopin: Mazurka op. posth. 68, no. 4, Analysis by Roman Numeral |
| 12-22 | Chopin: Prelude op. 28, no. 4 |
| 12-23 | Chopin: Mazurka op. 17, no. 4 |
| 12-25 | Chopin: Nocturne op. 48, no. 2 |
| 12-26 | Saint-Saëns: Trio in E Minor, op. 92 (third movement) |

## Chapter 13

| | |
|---|---|
| 13-1A | Chopin: Prelude op. 28, no. 20 |
| 13-3A | Mozart: *Eine kleine Nachtmusik*, K. 525 |
| 13-3B | Chopin: Prelude op. 28, no. 20 |
| 13-4 | Mozart: *Eine kleine Nachtmusik*, K. 525 (continued) |
| 13-5 | J. S. Bach: "Herz und Mund und Tat und Leben" (Chorale from Cantata 147) |
| 13-6 | Mozart: Piano Sonata, K. 283 (first movement) |
| 13-8 | Nikolai Rimsky-Korsakov: Scheherazade (third movement) |
| 13-10A | Beethoven: Piano Sonata op. 26 (first movement) |
| 13.10B | Chopin: Fantaisie-Impromptu op. 66 |
| 13-11 | Mozart: Piano Sonata, K. 309 (first movement) |
| 13-12A | Mozart: "Durch Zärlichkeit und Schmeicheln" (no. 8 from *Die Entführung aus dem Serail*) |
| 13-12B | Haydn: Piano Sonata, H. XVI: 34 (first movement) |

## Chapter 14

| | |
|---|---|
| 14-3 | J. S. Bach: Two-Part Invention no. 1 in C major., BWV 772 |
| 14-4 | J. S. Bach Invention no. 6 in E major, BWV 777 |
| 14-10D | J. S. Bach: Fugue No. 16 (*Well-Tempered Clavier* Book I, BWV 861) |
| 14-11 | J. S. Bach: Fugue no. 16 (*Well-Tempered Clavier*, Book II, BWV 885) |
| 14-12 | J. S. Bach: Fugue no. 12 (*Well-Tempered Clavier*, Book II, BWV 881) |
| 14-13 | J. S. Bach: Fugue no. 12 (*Well-Tempered Clavier*, Book II, BWV 881) |
| 14-14 | J. S. Bach: Fugue no. 16 (*Well-Tempered Clavier*, Book I, BWV 861) |

## Chapter 15

| | |
|---|---|
| **15-1** and **15-2** | Brahms: Waltz op. 29, no. 3 |
| **15-3** and **15-4** | Kuhlau: Sonatina op. 20, no. 1 (first movement) Thematic Process |
| 15-5 | Kuhlau: Sonatina op. 20, no. 1 (first movement) Cadential Process |
| 15-6A | Mozart: Piano Sonata, K. 332 (first movement) |

| Exercise No. | Track Title |
|---|---|
| 15-6B | [no caption] |
| 15-6C | [no caption] |
| 15-7 | Chopin: Prelude op. 28, no. 7 |
| 15-8 | Clementi: Sonatina op. 36, no. 1 (Vivace) |
| 15-9 | Beethoven: Piano Sonata op. 13 (second movement) |
| 15-11 | J. S. Bach: French Suite no. 5 (Gavotte) |
| 15-12 | Beethoven: Sonata op. 14, no. 2 (second movement) |
| 15-13 | Schumann: Kinderszenen no. 6 ("Wichtige Begebenheit") |

## Chapter 16

| | |
|---|---|
| 16-2 | Mozart: *Eine kleine Nachtmusik* (primary thematic/tonal area) |
| 16-3 | Mozart: *Eine kleine Nachtmusik* (transition) |
| 16-4 | Mozart: *Eine kleine Nachtmusik* (secondary thematic/tonal area) |
| 16-5 | Mozart: *Eine kleine Nachtmusik* (codetta) |
| 16-6 | Mozart: *Eine kleine Nachtmusik* (development) |
| 16-7 | Mozart: *Eine kleine Nachtmusik* (recapitulation) |
| 16-8 | Mozart: *Eine kleine Nachtmusik* (recapitulation continued) |
| 16-9 | Mozart: *Eine kleine Nachtmusik* (coda) |

## Chapter 17

17-1, 17-2, 17-3, 17-4, 17-5, 17-6 Beethoven: Piano Sonata op. 13, (second movement)

## Chapter 18

| | |
|---|---|
| 18-6B | Richard Rodgers: "Slaughter on Tenth Avenue" |
| 18-6C | Prokofiev: Classical Symphony op. 25 (third movement) |
| 18-7 | Debussy: "*Minstrels*" (Preludes, Bk. I, no. 12), mm. 37–43 |
| 18-9A | Carlos Chavez: Ten Preludes (no. 1) |
| 18-9B | Ralph Turek: "Carnival Days" (from *Songs for Kids*) |
| 18-10A | Debussy: "*Hommage a Rameau*" (Images, Book I) |
| 18-10B | Debussy: "*Les collines d'Anacapri*" (Preludes, BK. I, no. 5) |
| 18-13 | Debussy: "*Voiles*" (Preludes, Bk. I, no. 2) |
| 18-15 | Debussy: *Pour le piano* (Sarabande), mm. 23–28 |
| 18-16 | Hindemith: Ludus Tonalis (Fugue No. 5) |
| 18-20 | Debussy: "*Voiles*" (Preludes, Bk. I, no. 2) |
| 18-21B | Debussy: "*Soirée dans Grenade*" (Estampes, no. 2) |

| Exercise No. | Track Title |
|---|---|

## Chapter 19

| | |
|---|---|
| 19-1A | Hindemith: "Un cygnet," from *Six Chansons* (1939) |
| 19-1C | Bartók: *Fourteen Bagatelles* op. 6, no. 11 (1908) |
| 19-4A | William Schuman: *Three Score Set* (second movement) (1943) |
| 19-4B | Vincent Persichetti: *Harmonium* op 50, no. 3 (1959) |
| 19-5 | Honegger: Symphony no. 5, first movement (1950) |
| 19-6A | Ravel: "Blues" (Sonate pour Violon et Piano, 1897, second movement) |
| 19-6B | Stravinsky: *The Rite of Spring*, "The Sacrifice" (1913) |
| 19-7A | Bartók: "Major and minor" no. 59 (from *Mikrokosmos* vol. II) |
| 19-8 | Dello Joio: Piano Sonata no. 3 (first movement) (1949) Variation IV |
| 19-9 | Stravinsky: *The Rite of Spring* (introduction) not on original list |
| 19-10 | Stravinsky: *The Rite of Spring* ("Spring Rounds") |
| 19-11 | Bartók: "Boating" (from *Mikrokosmos* vol. V (1939)) |

## Chapter 20

| | |
|---|---|
| 20-7 | Schoenberg: Klavierstücke, op. 11, no. 1 |
| 20-12 | Schoenberg: "*Nacht*" from *Pierrot Lunaire* |
| 20-17 | Daniel McCarthy: Visions and Apparitions (second movement) |
| 20-19 | David S. Bernstein: Three Silhouettes for Guitar (second movement) |
| 20-20 | Daniel McCarthy, An American Girl (second movement) |

## Chapter 21

| | |
|---|---|
| 21-1A | Schoenberg: *Fünf Klavierstücke*, op. 23, no. 4, mm. 1–3) |
| 21-1B | Schoenberg: *Fünf Klavierstücke*, op. 23, no. 4, mm. 24–26) |
| 21-4A | Ralph Turek: Three by Twelve (first movement) |
| 21-4B | Ralph Turek: Three by Twelve (second movement) |
| 21-7 | Schoenberg: Fourth String Quartet, op. 37 (first movement) |
| 21-11 | Dallapiccola: *Quaderno Musicale di Annalibera* (Simbolo) |

# Taylor & Francis eBooks

## Helping you to choose the right eBooks for your Library

Add Routledge titles to your library's digital collection today. Taylor and Francis ebooks contains over 50,000 titles in the Humanities, Social Sciences, Behavioural Sciences, Built Environment and Law.

**Choose from a range of subject packages or create your own!**

**Benefits for you**
- Free MARC records
- COUNTER-compliant usage statistics
- Flexible purchase and pricing options
- All titles DRM-free.

**Benefits for your user**
- Off-site, anytime access via Athens or referring URL
- Print or copy pages or chapters
- Full content search
- Bookmark, highlight and annotate text
- Access to thousands of pages of quality research at the click of a button.

**REQUEST YOUR FREE INSTITUTIONAL TRIAL TODAY**

**Free Trials Available**
We offer free trials to qualifying academic, corporate and government customers.

## eCollections – Choose from over 30 subject eCollections, including:

| | |
|---|---|
| Archaeology | Language Learning |
| Architecture | Law |
| Asian Studies | Literature |
| Business & Management | Media & Communication |
| Classical Studies | Middle East Studies |
| Construction | Music |
| Creative & Media Arts | Philosophy |
| Criminology & Criminal Justice | Planning |
| Economics | Politics |
| Education | Psychology & Mental Health |
| Energy | Religion |
| Engineering | Security |
| English Language & Linguistics | Social Work |
| Environment & Sustainability | Sociology |
| Geography | Sport |
| Health Studies | Theatre & Performance |
| History | Tourism, Hospitality & Events |

For more information, pricing enquiries or to order a free trial, please contact your local sales team:
**www.tandfebooks.com/page/sales**

 Routledge Taylor & Francis Group | The home of Routledge books

**www.tandfebooks.com**